Leadership Guide
for
Elementary School
Improvement

Procedures
for
Assessment and Change

Carl D. Glickman
The Ohio State University,
Marion

James P. Esposito
The University of Virginia,
Charlottesville

Allyn and Bacon, Inc.

Boston   London   Sydney

Library of Congress Cataloging in Publication Data

Glickman, Carl D
    Leadership guide for elementary school improvement.

    Includes bibliographical references and index.
    1. Elementary schools—Evaluation—Handbooks, manuals, etc. 2. Leadership—Handbooks, manuals, etc. I. Esposito, James P., joint author.
II. Title.
LB2822.5.G55   372.1'2   78-21499
ISBN 0-205-06443-4

Printed in the United States of America.

To
Sara, Joan, Jennifer, Rachel,
Matthew, and Tony

Contents

Section Three

Implementing the Curriculum Dimension

Section Four

Implementing the Student Management Dimension

Section Five

Implementing the Supervisory Dimension

Section Six

Implementing the Resource Management Dimension

Section Seven

Assessment

Section Eight

Schools within Schools

Section Nine

Important Internal Considerations about the Changing School

Section Ten

Important External Considerations about the Changing School

Appendixes

Indexes

Preface

This book is written for current or prospective educational leaders who are contemplating, or in the midst of, change. We have attempted to address ourselves directly to those leaders who are searching for ways to better meet the needs of children. Our writing is on a personal and practical level; educational jargon is avoided.

Much of the content comes from our own experiences in schools. The difficulties of working within a complex organization and with even more complex individuals have left their impression on us. We hope to share our experiences with you; tell about our mistakes and our triumphs, what we have learned, and what kind of advice and knowledge might be helpful to persons, like you, who are committed to the best possible education for children. We have not detailed all that needs to be said; we do not claim to have even come close. Instead, we suggest that you make use of the reference materials we have listed throughout the book in order to more closely examine the ideas we have presented.

We would like to acknowledge all the children and adults who have become an inextricable part of our lives. They are too numerous to mention by name, yet too important not to have them know that we remember them. In particular, we would like to acknowledge the students and staffs of the various school systems in Mathews, Virginia; Portland and Unity, Maine; Massena and Potsdam, New York; and Tallahassee, Florida. Special mention must be made of the Hilltop and Chandler Elementary Schools in the Somersworth, New Hampshire school district. The professional staff at these schools has created a unique place for children and has shared with us many of the experiences we write about in this book.

We would also like to thank the following people for their invaluable assistance: Hiram Howard for his editorial guidance and continuous reinforcement from the beginning of this project; Joanne Dauksewicz, our production editor, for her suggestions and improvement of the manuscript; Marie Guarino and David Abbey, graduate assistants at the University of Virginia, for their help in the proofreading of the manuscript and indexing; and Helen Ayres, our typist.

We would like to extend special thanks to William H. Seawell, Chairman of the Department of Educational Administration and Supervision, University of Virginia, for his continuous support and guidance.

Section One

Beginning

1

Introduction

After a typical school day, the principal makes his way home. He opens the door, kicks off his shoes, pulls a beer out of the refrigerator, and flops into an easy chair. Putting his feet up on a stool, loosening his tie, and taking a few sips of his drink, he begins to think about the day.

His mind wanders back to the steady stream of misbehaving students sent to him, the phone call from an upset parent, the argument with the custodian, and, to top off the day, the refusal of two teachers to take an extra recess duty. "If this series of events was unusual," he thinks to himself, "I could forget it. But it's not. It's one brushfire after another." Feeling despondent, some other thoughts cross into his consciousness, "What am I really accomplishing? What is our school really doing for children? What can I do to alter our school so that I could come home feeling a sense of satisfaction?"

Hundreds of books and articles have been written which focus on changing public schools. Thousands more have been written about philosophy, curriculum, administration, supervision, student management, and resource management. If you are a principal, ask yourself (or ask an administrator if you are not) how much these books have really helped the school administrator to change daily operation. We believe this book is unique because it focuses on theory *only* as it applies to practice. We take a holistic view of the change process and so will explain not only new educational directions and procedures for implementation, but also the mundane happenings that often get in the way of change. Synergistic theory is based upon the assumption that the whole is greater than the sum of its parts. As one aspect of a particular system is altered there must be a concurrent alteration in other parts of that system if it is to function effectively. We believe that change efforts in many public schools have attempted to make these system aspects change without consideration of other schooling dimensions. The administrator concerned with institutionalizing meaningful, effective, and lasting change cannot view any one aspect of schooling in isolation from others.

Our conceptualization of this book stemmed not only from our own experience but also from Silberman's concern, which he labels the "mindlessness" of public schools. He defines mindlessness as "the failure or refusal (of school personnel) to think seriously about educational purpose (and), the reluctance to question established practice."[1] This failure, refusal, and reluctance has contributed to the institutionalization of change for the sake of change and is reflected in the inconsistencies that exist between purpose and practice. Little thought is given to whether or not a new curriculum package, advocated or mandated by the central office, is in fact facilitative of the local school staff's goals and objectives for children. Change efforts are focused in too many directions and, as Blumberg has stated, "Change without direction, except for the anarchist, is senseless."[2]

If the problems of school were due to ignorance or stupidity of educators, there would be no hope. However, we believe, as does Silberman, that administrators and teachers are intelligent and caring people. For these reasons, problems can be solved by "infusing schools with thought about purpose and about the ways in which techniques, content and organization fulfill or alter that purpose."[3] Alternatives must be explored. Educators must become aware of them, lest they administer and teach in the same way they were taught. This lack of alternative awareness keeps them "spinning their wheels," and facing the same kinds of problems they have always faced.

We will present information related to alternative school models which involve or emanate from three distinct educational philosophies. Our position is not to advocate any particular model but to present behaviors and practices that would be consistent with each. We believe that consistency of behavior and practice with philosophy, goals, and objectives will make schools effective in achieving what is desired for children. Ideally there should be different alternative models in the same school to meet the needs of all children and staff, yet this is not a realistic way to begin. A school needs one effective program before it goes on to include others. We will show how different models can evolve within schools.

Our basic premise is somewhat contrary to the opinions of numerous educational critics. *We believe that schools have the inherent power to achieve their goals and objectives.* What has been lacking is the channeling of this power in a consistent direction. When power or energy is expended in opposing directions, goals and objectives will not be attained. In other words, the effectiveness of schools is related to the degree to which *all* of the dimensions of schooling are consistent with purpose. Total consistency may be ideal,

and seemingly unrealistic. However, we believe that school personnel should continually strive to become as consistent as they can be.

What we are attempting to depict in the following chart are three
distinct, alternative models of schooling. Each of the three models is
based upon a different generic educational philosophy which defines
a school's basic goals and objectives. In other words, school goals and
objectives evolving from the essentialist philosophy would have
different priority and value when compared with the goals and
objectives evolving from the experimentalist and existentialist
philosophies. The dimensions of schooling, that is, the actual *practice*
of education, should logically and consistently flow from the goal and
objective statements which evolve from each philosophical position.

For example, consistency with the essentialist philosophy goals
and objectives (Alternative Model One) would be represented in the
curriculum dimension by a curriculum model that has predictable
outputs and directive methods and materials. Teacher and administrative strategies and the student management dimension, which includes the way in which children are viewed in psychological terms
by educators, would have practices that are behaviorist in orientation.
The supervisory dimension, which includes staff supervision and staff
development, would have practices which are respectively criterion
referenced and administratively determined. The resource management dimension, which includes fiscal and environmental management, would be characterized by behaviors that are respectively
centralized and of low arousal.

The Alternative Two and Three models would also be characterized by educational practice across the four dimensions of schooling which would evolve from the experimentalist (Alternative Two)
and existentialist (Alternative Three) educational philosophies.

At this point, we don't expect that most readers will have a full
understanding of this illustration. If this were so, there would be no
reason to read on, and naturally we wish for you to continue! In
subsequent chapters we will discuss the educational practices within
each schooling dimension that are consistent with each of the three
educational philosophies.

The main thrust of institutional change is directed toward getting
a staff working together in a purposeful manner. But successful
change does not end here. There is much more that a leader has to
contend with. The last third of this book is addressed to those every
day extraneous concerns that, if not dealt with properly, can throw the
smooth operation of a school into disarray. We are talking about the
whole gamet of immediate concerns from the psychological climate of
the school to ways of dismissing a cantankerous custodian.

Chapter 2 deals with some considerations which should be

DIMENSIONS OF SCHOOLING	ALTERNATIVE ONE Essentialism	ALTERNATIVE TWO Experimentalism	ALTERNATIVE THREE Existentialism
	Goals & Objectives	Goals & Objectives	Goals & Objectives
Curriculum			
A. Curriculum Models	Predictable	Predictable/ Unpredictable	Unpredictable
B. Methods and Materials	Directive	Directive/Nondirective	Nondirective
Student Management			
A. Psychological view of child			
B. Teacher strategies	Behaviorist	Interactionalist	Humanist
C. Administrator strategies			
Supervision			
A. Staff Supervision	Criterion Referenced	Clinical	Individualistic
B. Staff Development	Administrative Determination	Shared Determination	Individual Determination
Resource Management			
A. Fiscal	Centralized	Shared	Individualized
B. Environmental	Causing Low Arousal	Causing Low Arousal High Arousal	Causing High Arousal

Figure 1.1. *Alternative Models of Schooling*

addressed before the administration engages in any strategies to assess and facilitate change in the school. Section Two focuses on the importance of school philosophy, and Chapter 3 presents some procedures for developing one. Chapter 4 discusses the development of goals and objectives reflective of philosophy. Section Three is concerned with the curriculum dimension of schooling. Chapter 5 deals with alternative curriculum models while chapter 6 discusses alternative methods and materials. The student management dimension is discussed in Section Four. Chapter 7 presents alternative psychological views of children, and chapters 8 and 9 deal with alternative management strategies and methods for teachers and administrators. Section Five is concerned with the supervisory dimension. Chapters 10 and 11 focus on alternative strategies for supervising staff and staff development. The resource management dimension is the target of Section Six. Chapter 12 deals with fiscal management and chapter 13 with environmental management. Section Seven focuses on assessment. Chapter 14 presents techniques for assessing the previously discussed four dimensions of schooling. A strategy for analyzing the data generated by the assessment instruments is presented in chapter 15. Chapters 16 and 17, which are included in Section Eight, provide a rationale for and a description of a school model that encompasses all three alternatives. Section Nine has three chapters which focus on important internal considerations for the administrator of the changing school: chapter 18, entitled "Climate for Change"; chapter 19, "Staffing: Group Solutions for Individual Problems"; and chapter 20, "Extra Help" (i.e., volunteers, student teachers, and peer tutors). Section Ten, "Important External Considerations," has three chapters which focus on dealing with power groups (chapter 21), meeting with parents (chapter 22), and awareness of the all important hidden group (chapter 23).

NOTES

1.   Charles E. Silberman, *Crisis in the Classroom: The Remaking of American Education* (New York: Random House, 1971), p. 11.

2.   Arthur Blumberg, *Supervisors and Teachers: A Private Cold War* (Berkeley, California: McCutchan Publishing Co., 1974), p. 2.

3.   Silberman, *Crisis in the Classroom*, p. 11.

2

Preconditions for Change

Do you really care?

This is a question which appears to be devious and trite. If you did not care, why would you get this far in the book? However, our experience in schools makes us ask the question. Please introspect for a little while, look at yourself and your motives for being in education. Almost every professional educator gives lip service to the belief that schools are for children. Surprisingly enough, what people do in schools often contradicts what they profess to believe. The studies done by Silberman and Jencks give support to the observation that most schools are organized and run for the convenience of adults.[1,2] If change is to occur, it implies a certain amount of personal risk and dedication to the idea that schools must keep up with the needs of our children in a changing society.

We so often get caught up in the day to day, common work tasks that we have little time to assess who we are, what we are doing, and what our motives are. Take some time now and answer these questions with integrity.

> Why did you go into education?
> Why are you in education now?
> Why do you plan to remain in education?

Other than setting perspective, the first two questions are not very important. The answer to the third puts the finger on whether or not you have the motivation or desire to begin or to continue to make your school a better place for children. If you answered the question by citing your personel needs, such as

> working hours
> tenure—job security

> long vacations
> salary—retirement plan
> status—advancement

then we congratulate you for being honest. You see education for its external worth to you. As a result, you are not ready to be involved in the educational change process, as your motivation is with the external conditions of work (conditions outside yourself). However, this does not imply that you will be an obstacle to change, it simply means that you will not be an initiator.

If you answered the question by reasons such as

> I want to improve myself as an educator and person;
> I enjoy being with children and people;
> I want to get to know myself better;
> I want to try out more ideas;

then you are the person we are primarily addressing. You see education for its internal worth to you as a person. You are concerned with your own self-actualization and your relationship with other people. As a result, you are concerned with wanting to do things that are people-oriented.

Of course, you may have motives that are both internal and external. The follow-up question, then, is what are your priorities? If the motives cannot be separated in your mind then you are probably a cautious person who is willing to improve. You need to go slowly, checking back now and then to make sure that you are comfortable with the external work conditions.

The great majority of people really do want to improve themselves. They desire to act in accordance with what they believe is in the best interest of children. Usually, when external conditions have become a priority, it is the result of accumulated, negative experiences. Teachers have been thwarted time after time in experimenting or trying out creative approaches . After a while it becomes much easier to draw back, say, "to hell with it," and go along with secure, standard practices. Then, satisfaction can only come from those external work conditions.

The positive feeling of wanting to be better is like an ember that may lie smoldering under a heap of ashes (negative experiences) for years and years. However, if someone can remove those ashes, let in the oxygen before the ember dies out, then the fire of vitality and creativity can be relit. In little Unity Grammar School in Maine, two teachers with over sixty years of experience between them, and nearing retirement, followed the secure and accepted practices of the past. Suddenly, with a new administration and program for staff development, they were encouraged to try, to fail, to experiment. They were given planning time to read, to visit others, to question who they were and what they were doing. Within four months time, they became the initiators of change. Their classrooms became their "living" rooms. One of those teachers went to the principal and, fighting back tears, explained that she had finally reached a problem child in ways she could never have reached the child before. The ember always smoldered underneath, yet now it was alight and blazing.

If you are willing to look at other ways of doing things and would like to get going, what are the preconditions you must consider as far as physical environment, materials, and people are concerned? From this point on, we are going to assume that since you are still with us, you are open and eager to get started. As a result, the focus will not be on responding to the negative reasons people might give for not exploring new directions, but rather on the positive ways to help you, the inquisitive, eager learner.

In itself, the physical environment is never an obstacle to trying different approaches. Such factors as the age of a building, the conditions of maintenance, the location of walls, corridors, and closets have nothing to do with the quality of the educational interaction within the building. In fact, through our direct experience, we found it was more often the older school buildings (some built as early as 1890) without ample facilities that had the most excitement going on. People often take a more creative approach to education when they need to rearrange classrooms or buildings in ways for which they were not designed. On the other hand, a new building that is designed for great flexibility may be easier to adapt to new ideas for meeting the needs of children. However, there is no research to show that a new physical plant is by itself a catalyst for greater individualization. In many modern, open-space schools, the environment at first glance is most impressive. One's senses are immediately hit by the bright, clean, temperature controlled, lushly carpeted, and wide open areas of the school. After the initial reaction, however, a closer look at the instruction and the degree of student involvement makes one conclude that what is going on is really no different from what goes on in more traditionally built schools. In such cases, only the surface appearance is different. (We recently conducted a statewide study that focused on determining the relationship between the psychological climate or atmosphere and the structure of the facility. We asked the question, "Do schools which are built (structurally) based upon the open school concept have more open psychological climates than traditionally built schools?" We found no difference in the psychological climate as related to building structure.)[3]

Materials needed to begin have to be looked at in two ways. First, commercial materials can hold the same degree of importance as the physical plant. The fact that a school has all kinds of commercial programs, laboratory kits, and audio-visual software is nice, but not important if they are not used for dealing directly with the child. A school or classroom that has little of such materials is not necessarily at a disadvantage in beginning something new. In fact, when we take a look at the process of implementing change, the school that has little, will probably move along in a slower, more gradual way by acquiring and field testing materials suited to the new directions. Schools that already have a wealth of "things," might cause the staff to be tempted to jump in and use everything during the first euphoric stage of experimentation. Those educators with a wealth of commercially made objects will need to pick and choose. Educators with limited commercial materials will need to create, borrow, steal, and ask their students to bring in discarded items. We make no pretension that one type of material is better than another. What fits a student's need is what should be used, regardless of where it came from. Therefore, in regard to materials, a classroom or school does not need a great abundance to begin. However, as a program develops, more materials will be necessary. A more in-depth analysis of the type of materials and realities of use will be explored in chapter 6, entitled "Methods and Materials."

The physical environment and materials are not preconditions for changing your classroom or your school. The optimum physical environment and an abundance of materials may be of help, but the lack of such elements are not a hindrance. The only time that physical conditions become a hindrance is when they are used by some people to prevent other people from experimenting. For example, a teacher has a small, self-contained room in the standard 1950s "egg crate" structured school. He wants to attempt some activities that require more free space. He proposes to utilize the hallway and a closet. The principal or other teachers say no, that the hallways and closets were not meant for such use. It is not the physical environment that obstructs this change, it is a "people" decision. The same holds true for a modern school plant. A teacher wishes to bring in old furniture for the students to use. People object, it will mar the appearance of the school. Again, it is not the physical plant or even the materials that are not conducive to change. Physical elements can be manipulated in any way (within legal limits), as long as the people who hold the power of operating the school sanction it. It is a sad but true statement that the vast majority of people that hold the power of operating a school, predominantly principals, are more concerned about preserving the physical elements of a school than adjusting it to human needs. We never cease to be amazed when we enter a school for the first time. The principal usually greets us warmly and proceeds to take us on a tour of "his" building. He is proud (as well he should be) of the bright cafeteria, the sparkling gymnasium, the new media center and wall to wall carpets. Yet, how they are used and what kids do in these environments never appears to be as important as the physical surroundings and equipment. Most persons who have attempted change in a school have had to overcome such obstacles as not being able to bring in furniture, put down a rug, hang art work from the ceiling, use the halls, put student work on walls, build an art area, rearrange desks, etc. Going back to the first question in this chapter, "Do you really care?" those who choose education for its external work conditions and who have power continually frustrate those who are in education for its internal worth.

The single most important factor as a precondition to changing yourself as a person, changing your classroom, and changing your school is that of human support. Without it, do not even begin. Unless there is someone else who will encourage, sympathize, and move along with you, you are doomed to fail. In attempting change, a person needs to interact with someone else. He or she needs to share the excitement, the disappointment, the frustration, and the mental work of doing something different. The human person cannot stand alone in the day-in-and-day-out grind of trying to survive in an environment where everybody else is either indifferent or consciously putting up barriers. However, the human organism in attempting improvement has a tremendous resilience to obstacles if only one other person cares. Even when the entire power structure of a school is nonsupportive, two people can improve their own instruction of children. There may not be much hope for the rest of the school, but the constant mutual reinforcement and camaraderie of sharing a meaningful personal experience will result in more growth and educational value for the two people involved and their students. We all need the psychological support from at least one other person.

The importance of support in bringing about not only classroom, but school change, hits the leader square between the eyes. There are many "how to" books for teachers to use in their classroom, but school reform must be a process that involves the active support of the status leader. It is our opinion that an optimum environment for children is not solely the result of being in a particular classroom that is positive, responsive, and individualized. If the rest of the school is not consistent, then other adult treatment of the student, either in other classrooms, hallways, and lunchrooms, will negate the overall positive climate. There is research which indicates that the organizational climate in a school is positively related to the attitude and achievement levels of students. Such studies done by Reilly, Smith, and Panushka seem to indicate that the more positive and open the staff is towards each other, the more positive and open the students will be.[4,5,6] Organizational climate is really another word for the amount of interpersonal support that teachers and administrators give to each other. We discuss the climate for change more fully in chapter 19. The leader, i.e., the principal, sets the climate in the school.

The principal is the model for the staff. The way that he or she relates to the staff influences the ways in which teachers will relate to their students. If the principal encourages involvement, creative problem solving, and parity in decision making, then the teachers will be more comfortable and more likely to use related techniques in the classroom. It is hypocritical to expect teachers to allow their students to be active participants in their classrooms if teachers are not able to be active participants in their school. The organizational model must be consistent throughout.

For most principals, the problem of power and parity is a disturbing one. The community, school board authorities, and central office will probably always hold the principal responsible for his school. When one is being held responsible, one does not like to take the sole blame for a joint decision. This is the area where parity is misunderstood. Parity does not mean that everyone in your school has equal say on every matter. You would not expect students to have an equal say about everything that happens in the classroom, some immediate and organizational decisions might have to be the major responsibilities of the teacher. On the other hand, some decisions regarding interests and use of time might be the major responsibility of the student. In the same way, some decisions that are closer to the administrative realm (such as schedules, requests for additional monies, etc.) might be decided with greater weight given to the principal. Other matters that are closer to the teacher such as curriculum, the hiring of aids, classroom supplies, etc. might have greater teacher weight. Full parity is achieved when each category of decision making is decided upon and given varying weight to administrator and teacher, and the total weight or influence across all categories balances evenly.

A parity chart might be negotiated between the different groups with the following example of percentages possibly resulting.

	Budget	Curriculum	Evaluation	Discipline	Total
Administration	20%	15%	40%	25%	100%
Teachers	30%	35%	10%	25%	100%

*We thank Dr. Ed Pino, former Superintendent of Schools, Cherry Creek, Colorado, for introducing this chart to us.

Of course the categories and the percentages need to be defined and negotiated by the people involved. Consensus is desirable and true parity is achieved when the total percentages are equal. If a school decides to include parents and students in decisions, then a chart needs to be settled upon by all four groups.

If you are willing to involve your staff in the decision-making process; if you are willing to remove the external physical obstacles for teacher improvement; if you have at least two teachers who can support each other and who are willing to support you; and if you really care about children; then all the preconditions are met. The role of the leader in educational innovation is crucial. The most successful innovations in schools can almost always be traced to a strong leader. In those projects that started well but nose-dived, it usually was the result of the leader resigning and not being replaced by someone as strong. No management system involving people will ever be able to run itself. The human element of support and commitment is vital.

NOTES

1.   Charles E. Silberman, *Crisis in the Classroom* (New York: Random House, 1971), p. 8.

2.   Christopher Jencks et al., *Inequality: A Reassessment of the Effect of Family and Schooling in America* (New York: Harper & Row, 1973).

3.   James P. Esposito, "The Relationship Between School Structure and Psychological Climate" (University of Virginia, 1977).

4.   J. Reilly, "Organizational Climate and Pupil Achievement" (Ph.D. diss., Michigan State University, 1973).

5.   A. Smith, "The Relationship of School Organization Climate and Student Morale in Selected Schools" (Ph.D. diss., University of Miami, 1973).

6.   W. Panushka, "Elementary School Climate and Its Relationship to Pupil Achievements" (Ph.D. diss., University of Minnesota, 1970).

Section Two

Setting a Direction

3

Your Philosophy and Direction

After assessing your personal readiness to begin moving your school in innovative directions, there is an obvious but often overlooked first step. In what direction do you move? Why select one innovation over another? A change in school practices needs a framework and rationale. It is our contention from here on in this book that effective change in schooling comes about only where there is staff agreement with the purpose of such change. Only then can all of the dimensions of schooling contribute in a consistent manner to the purposes of change. In other words, to begin the change process, the administration and faculty must consider an appropriate educational philosophy. We'll bet we know what you are thinking now! Our experience has taught us that many administrators usually react to any outside force urging them to develop a school philosophy in more negative than positive ways. The same can be said of teachers. "We've got too much to do to be able to survive tomorrow without sitting around philosophizing about what education should be or seriously discussing what our goals and objectives are for kids." This reaction is understandable.

Discussion of philosophy is usually viewed as a frivolous pursuit by those in the schools. One perhaps remembers the philosophy course taken as an undergraduate student. At that time the questions, what is real? what is knowledge? what is truth? may have held some interest for the college student who was trying to forge his own identity in the real world. Yet even at that young period, philosophy also meant rambling discourse on shades of meanings and interpretations that seemed of little purpose. Most of us who have come up in the ranks of professional "doers" in education (teachers and administrators) have held in reserve a slight contempt for persons who were professional "thinkers" (college professors and writers). Somehow the gap between thinking and doing, theorizing and practicing, and philosophizing and applying has not been well bridged. How many college professors could actually leave the confines of academia, go into a school, and put into practice their well-thought-out ideas? How many educational leaders could leave the bustle of children and staff to participate in a panel discussion on the universal ramifications and consequences of school practices. This is a sad state of affairs. This separation of philosophy from practice must be halted and the two brought back together if a school is to have purpose, commitment, and effectiveness in educating children. Consider the following quote from Kilpatrick:

> Whatever competing values are at stake, philosophizing is essential if choice is to be wise. It is essential, moreover, in the degree that the values at stake are significant for the lives of people. And certainly this is the case as regards educational method, where human beings are formed—their character, their personality, the quality of their living.[1]

A philosophy of education is a guide to practice, a base from which all that goes on within each educational setting should emanate. Each dimension of the schooling enterprise—goals and objectives for students and teachers, curriculum methods and materials, student management and evaluation, allocation of resources and building use, staff supervision and staff development—should be consistent with that philosophy. Kilpatrick illustrates quite clearly that differences in educational philosophy are certainly reflected in educational practice. He speaks about two historical figures whom we all know well and how schools based on their philosophy might be different. "Napoleon," he says, "had no faith in the thinking of people and no wish for it, asserting that they must be told from childhood on what to think. Jefferson, by contrast, believed exactly in the thinking of the people...."[2] He goes on to discuss the differences in a Napoleonic school and a Jeffersonian school and points out several of the dimensions of schooling which would be different. Some of those differences include the schoolhouse structure itself, the nature of curriculum activities and instructional materials, and the ways in which students are managed and evaluated.[3] In short, a philosophy of education does in fact determine the details of school practice. It appears logical that if a philosophy is a guide to practice, then schools with similar philosophies would have similar goals and objectives and implement similar (although not identical) procedures, practices, and methods. The outputs that the school is seeking to accomplish might also be similar.

Now let's get practical again. In our experience as teachers, supervisors, and administrators and through our work with schools and school systems in a number of states, we have perceived some things related to school philosophy which cause us some concern. As we have moved from school to school and examined each school's statement of educational philosophy (every school has one somewhere!) we have found much similarity. Yet, we have found a great deal of difference across each of the dimensions of schooling. For example, recently we visited two starkly different high schools, the first in an urban school in a large metropolitan area. The building was constructed in the late thirties and was traditional in design. No significant modification in the structure of the building itself had taken place since its construction. The majority of students (ninety-five percent as reflected in school data) were from lower socio-economic levels and minority ethnic backgrounds, they ranked well below national norms in standardized tests, did not aspire to higher levels of education, and generally speaking (from our assessments) had rather negative attitudes toward school. The second was a suburban school (a nine-mile trip from the first school described) which was built in the early seventies. The building was contemporary in design. The majority of students (eighty-five percent) were from upper-middle and higher socio-economic levels, had a white ethnic background, ranked above national norms on standardized tests, aspired to higher levels of education, and generally speaking (from our assessments) held more positive attitudes toward school. Both faculties as well as administrators informally verbalized the purposes of schooling to be rather different. However, upon examination of each school's formal, written philosophy it was quite apparent that they were almost identical while at the same time actual school practices were significantly different. The ways that students were managed and evaluated, the curriculum methods and materials used, and the supervision of staff were in no way alike. In at least one of the schools there obviously was a great deal of incongruence between their intentions, as reflected in their philosophy, and their actions.

Let us now examine some differing philosophies that have application to educational philosophy. After this examination let's scrap your school's existing philosophy (for the moment, anyway) and decide what philosophy is most applicable to your staff and your students. The brief summaries of three educational philosophies which follow are by no means meant to be definitive or exhaustive. The administrator should consider becoming familiar with some of the suggested readings which follow this chapter.

CONTEMPORARY PHILOSOPHIES

It is widely acknowledged that many philosophies exist. Some, such as idealism, realism, and neo-thomism date back to ancient times. Others such as pragmatism and behaviorism have been developed within the last century. More recent has been the emergence of progressivism, reconstructionism, and existentialism. One must note that philosophies are numerous, that they overlap in areas, and that many have historical roots in each other. To unravel the major philosophical trends of education, one must decipher how philosophies differ from each other and then build overriding conceptual categories. Each conceptual category or "superphilosophy" is made by grouping various philosophies that have central agreement on the type and scope of education. In other words, there may be disagreement on the specific nature of knowledge, truth, and reality yet they hang together as a general educational philosophy because they have in common an agreement of the purpose and treatment of education.

With educational application in mind, we feel comfortable in making simplifications and classifications of divergent philosophies. We understand that this might set the teeth of a true classical scholar grinding. If so, then so be it. There are three major educational *super* philosophies that have direct relevance to schools. These categories have been labeled according to Johnson, Collins, Dupuis, and Johansen as *essentialism, progressivism,* and *existentialism*.[4] We would like to substitute the more general term *experimentalism* as described by Van Cleve Morris for progressivism.[5]

Essentialism

Essentialism as a philosophy is derived from idealism and realism. Idealism, which dates back to Plato, espouses a belief in absolutes. The world that we live in is merely a reflection of reality. Reality, truth, and standards of morality exist beyond our common ways of knowing. Only by training the mind do we glimpse the ultimates. Yet training the mind is not sufficient in itself. It only brings the mind nearer to grasping reality. Divine revelation, insight, and faith are the necessary elements for a final knowledge of what exists. Therefore, idealism places a stress on truth and reality existing outside of man. It is absolute and never changing. Realism, developed at the onset of the industrial age, places a similar stress on truth and reality being outside of man. Yet, instead of man and the outer environment being separated from each other, realism espouses that man is part and parcel of that environment. The world is a preordained, mechanistic reality. All of existence operates according to scientific, cause and effect relations. It is as if existence is a clock that always runs according to mechanical principles governing levers, gauges, and gears. Man has no existence apart from this clock. He is a part of that predetermined machine. Knowledge is the learning of how that machine works. Truths are the scientific laws of regulation. Morality (belief in good or bad) has no existence. Nothing exists outside of the principles of nature. The purpose of education is to condition the mind to think in a natural, logical way. The mind should be trained to become consciously aware of the predeterminism of the world.

Essentialism was created by William L. Bagley in 1938. He encompassed the educational philosophies of idealism and realism into one. He took the ideas of knowledge being eternal and outside of man (idealism—absolutes, realism—natural laws) to form pedagogy. Essentialists stress that there is a body of timeless knowledge, both historical and contemporary, that is of value to the living. The task of education is to preserve these truths by having those most knowledgeable of them become teachers. Teachers then must use the mechanistic principles of realism to tailor that knowledge in a systematic way for their students. As students digest these parcels of information and exercise their minds, they move closer to understanding reality.

Experimentalism

As western society became more industrialized, optimism and confidence in man's ability to control nature emerged. The philosophy of pragmatism by Charles S. Pierce and William James placed emphasis on what man can do to nature rather that what nature does to man. John Dewey, circa 1920, further expanded on the writings of James by putting the individual squarely in the context of society. Man can both reform and be reformed by society. Dewey's philosophy is, of course, the well-known school of progressive thought. Reconstructionism is a further offshoot of both pragmatism and progressivism. Richard Pratt cites the pamphlet, *Dare the Schools Build a New Social Order*, written by George S. Counts in 1932 as a guiding document for the then radical emphasis of schools and students being the reformers of society.[6]

Experimentalism emerges from the philosophies of pragmatism, progressivism, and reconstructionism. They hold in common a historical break from the more traditional philosophies of realism and idealism. The essentialist idea that knowledge, truth, and morality existed as absolute and outside of man was rejected. The emerging faith in the scientific method; the fact that man could create his own laws, principles, and machines; and that such man-made inventions would work for him demanded an accompanying philosophy. Experimentalism provided that philosophy.

Reality was what worked. If man could form a hypothesis, test it and find it to work, then it was regarded as tentatively true. Upon repeated experimentation with the same results, it became real. Yet experimentalists never would claim an absolute truth. Man's environment was believed to be constantly changing so that what one can do and prove today, may not be provable tomorrow. A new situation and a different approach may alter yesterday's reality. The experimentalists point to the historical evidence of Newton's law of gravity as a past truth that has given way to Einstein's theory of relativity, and believe that in time a new theory will replace Einstein's.

Morality is also viewed in regard to what works for man and his society. Morality is that behavior which promotes one's working with the group to achieve greater ends. To be wise is to understand how the environment (of things and people) affects oneself and how one might in terms affect it. Whether action is moral or not is determined by the degree of advancement or progress that has been achieved by the group. The use of trial and error in a laboratory-like setting is the key to evaluating the outcome of action. Therefore, the experimentalists do not view knowledge as absolute or external to man's capabilities. Rather, knowledge is a result of the interaction between scientific man and his environment.

The educational application of experimentalist thinking is well documented in the writing of Dewey. Students need to learn what are the "truths" of the time but not rest content with that parcel of knowledge. Schools are laboratories for them to test the old hypotheses and to try new ones. The school is an environment for social change. The student learns how to work democratically with others to achieve collective ends that will help everyone. Teachers are not solely conveyors of age old wisdom, they are both the conveyors of the rudimentary knowledge of the time and the scientific guides of trial-and-error, exploratory learning.

Existentialism

Existentialism as a school of thought is derived out of the rejection of the other philosophies encompassed in essentialism and experimentalism. As such, it is a large category for many diverse philosophers. What they have in common is a scorn for rational, empirical, and systematic thinking as the way of knowing reality. If you remember, the essentialists believe in rational thinking to help elevate the mind to uncover the absolutes of the universe. Experimentalists believe in rational, scientific thinking to explore and frame the relevant knowledge of the times. However, the Existentialists believe that this same rational thinking restricts man from discovering existence, and therefore keeps man ignorant.

This philosophy has roots in the writings of Soren Kierkegaard in the mid-nineteenth century. It has become popularized in drama and literature by such exponents as Albert Camus and Jean Paul Sartre. The current popular cults of transcendental thinking, meditation, and introspection, (knowing oneself) have a kinship with the existentialists. The basic tenent of the philosophy is that the individual is the source of all reality. There is no existence in the world other than the meaning that the individual puts on his own experiences. There is no absolute knowledge, no mechanical working of the universe, and no systematic thinking. Rather to believe in such inventions is merely man's narrow and incorrect way of interpreting his own experience.

Outside of the individual exists only chaos. The only reality that exists is one's own existence. It is by looking within oneself that one can discern the truth of outside disorder. Man is paramount. His dignity and worth is of most importance. He is the source and dispenser of all truth. It is with this realization that one acquires a profound respect for all human beings and their individual uniqueness. Human relations become very important. They affirm individual worth and protect the individual's right to discover his own truth. Morality is the process of both knowing oneself and allowing others the freedom to do likewise. Faith, intuition, mysticism, imagery, and transcendental experiences are all acceptable ways of discovery. Man is a totally free individual. He is not shaped by others, he is not restricted by the flux of the times. He holds within him the capacity to form his own destiny.

The application of this philosophy to education is the full commitment to individual development. The child needs a facilitating environment which will enable him to explore his own physical and mental capabilities. He must learn for himself. The teacher does not dispense information and shies away from intrusive guiding of a child's discovery. The student is "on his own," the teacher helps when needed, protects the rights of others, and encounters the child as a person of full importance.

WHERE ARE YOU?

Now that you have examined three differing philosophies of education, and teachers and administrators have become familiar with the reference material listed after chapter 3, you have before you a major task—the development of your own school philosophy. English and Kaufman have stated that most philosophical statements of education written by school people are "muddled attempts to define the nature and purpose of schooling and the type of educational program desired by the schools' patrons or the Board."[7] Although we agree with English and Kaufman's perception, we also believe that there are reasons why attempts to develop a school philosophy have not been successful. Based on our experience, we believe that the major variable associated with poorly written philosophical statements about what education should seek to attain is that it is a low priority to administrators and teachers. Too often the task is perceived as perfunctory. The development of an educational philosophy has not been perceived as being important. When teachers and administrators are assigned the task, it becomes a matter of being more concerned with the completion of the task, rather than the development of a sound philosophy. Administrators who do not take the process seriously and who fail to communicate this to their teachers will wind up in the final analysis with, as Kaufman and English have stated, muddled philosophies which no one can translate into action, let alone determine congruence and consistency across each of the dimensions of schooling. It is possible that more time and effort will be expended in the process of establishing an educational philosophy than any other task. We will briefly present four approaches for the administrator to consider. We will move from the simplest approaches that can be used with a relatively unsophisticated staff to more abstract approaches that might stimulate the thinking of an intellectual group of educators. The purpose will be the same, to reach agreement on what is the overriding purpose of education in your school. No one approach is advocated as the best, and ways to arrive at a school philosophy are not limited to the four presented. There are a number of other paper and pencil assessments that, when analyzed appropriately, may also facilitate understanding of one's educational philosophy. *The Minnesota Teacher Attitude Inventory,* published by The Psychological Corporation, and Burton and Brown's *Teacher Belief Inventory* are tools that the administrator may make use of to facilitate his own, as well as others', philosophical position.

Approach Number One: Ranking Description

The easiest approach is to flip back to the section in this chapter on philosophies of education. Have each staff member read the descriptions and rank order the three from the most strongly believed in to the most objectionable. Small groups can then be formed to come up with a group priority. Finally each group could have a representative to form a school group to come up with a staff priority.

Approach Number Two: Assessing Practice
Reflecting Philosophy

The second approach would be to flip ahead in this book to chapter 14, "Assessing the Four Dimensions." Have each staff member fill out each assessment according to *what currently goes on in the school*. After tabulating the scores (as shown in chapter 15), the staff can readily see what philosophy their practices indicate. Discussion can then center on whether such a practicing philosophy is indicative of what they really believe about education. If it is not, then they can return to approach number one and rank descriptions of philosophies to come up with a new conceptual framework.

Approach Number Three: Ranking
Educational Assumptions

Jersin has developed a test which identifies an individual's or group's educational philosophy.[8] The administrator may want to consider this test as a procedure which might facilitate educational philosophy building. We reprint it in its entirety in Appendix A to show how specific educational assumptions can be scored to indicate a philosophy.

Approach Number Four: Ranking
Philosophical Assumptions

A more sophisticated approach in developing a meaningful school philosophy might be identifying some basic beliefs or philosophical assumptions related to a more global philosophy of life. (A philosophy of education does not exist in a vacuum but evolves or emanates from this more general philosophy.) Marler has developed a "Philosophical Concepts—Assumptions Checklist" which may be found in Appendix B.[9] The administrator may wish to use this as a tool to gather some basic information during this initial phase.

REACHING A SCHOOL PHILOSOPHY

The administrator who is serious about establishing a meaningful philosophy will involve all of those directly connected with the process of schooling. This list would definitely include all staff, administrators, and supervisors and might reach out to include older students, parents, and Board of Education members. Realistically, the place to begin is with the principal and immediate staff; they should be first in identifying their own philosophy. The administrator could use any of the four approaches for philosophy building.

Initially, a series of three meetings could be set up. The first one would be of an explanatory nature. The principal could explain the philosophies; hand out ranking, checklist, or assessment forms; and discuss the purposes of a philosophy. The second meeting would be for individuals to bring their completed forms and for small groups to come up with a group philosophy. The third meeting would be to develop a staff philsophy through discussions involving representatives from each group. Philosophical positions would be expressed and all parties made more aware of each other's perceptions. If school personnel are ambitious and have the necessary resources to implement schools within schools (this is discussed and presented in chapters 16 and 17), major differences in philosophical assumptions as they relate to educational activities could be accommodated in different programs. However, this is not readily the case in most schools and strong opposing beliefs among staff members does present a major problem for the school administrator. It is fallacious to assume that many persons can easily agree on one educational philosophy. This is where the administrator's job becomes difficult. However, we also believe that this is why principals get paid more than teachers. They must make those decisions which are difficult to make. Theoretically we believe that the school staff should come to a consensus as to the philosophical position which they embrace or call their own. Practically we also know this may never happen. The administrator should be actively engaged in facilitating consensus. When the situation becomes such that it is apparent that consensus will never occur, the administrator (principal) must make the final decision as to which educational philosophy should serve as the base from which all school change will evolve.

We have included a list of reference material which the school administrator may want to consider before attempting to take his staff, students, and community through the process of building an educational philosophy. The first section of reference material presents general material about the different philosophies, the second presents references related to approaches for developing a school philosophy.

NOTES

1.   William H. Kilpatrick, *Philosophy of Education* (New York: Macmillan Co., 1951), p. 283.

2.   Ibid., p. 283.

3.   Ibid., p. 11.

4.   James A. Johnson et al., *Foundations of American Education* (Boston: Allyn and Bacon, 1973).

5.   Van Cleve Morris, *Philosophy and the American School* (Boston: Houghton Mifflin Co., 1961), pp. 355–82.

6.   Richard Pratte, *Contemporary Theories in Education* (Scranton: T. Y. Crowell, 1971), p. 207.

7.   Fenwick W. English and Roger A. Kaufman, *Needs Assessment: A Focus for Curriculum Development* (Washington, D.C.: Association for Supervision and Curriculum Development, 1975), p. 21.

8.   Patricia D. Jersin, "What is Your EP? A Test which Identifies Your Educational Philosophy," *Clearing House* 46 (January 1972): 274–78.

9.   Charles Dennis Marler, *Philosophy and Schooling* (Boston: Allyn and Bacon, 1975), pp. 319–22, 369–84.

SUGGESTIONS FOR FURTHER READING

General Knowledge

Butler, J., Donald. *Four Philosophies and Their Practice in Education and Religion.* New York: Harper & Row, 1968.

Hanson, Kenneth. *Philosophy for American Education.* Englewood Cliffs, N.J.: Prentice-Hall, Inc., 1960.

Johnson, J. A.; Collins, H. W.; Dupuis, V. L.; and Johansen, J. H. *Foundations of American Education.* Boston: Allyn and Bacon, Inc., 1973.

Kilpatrick, William H. *Philosophy of Education.* New York: Macmillan Co., 1963.

Marshall, John P. *The Teacher and His Philosophy.* Lincoln, Nebraska: Professional Educators Publications, Inc., 1973.

Morris, Van Cleve. *Philosophy and the American School.* Boston: Houghton Mifflin Co., 1961.

Peters, Richard S., ed. *The Concept of Education.* London: Humanities Press, 1967.

Pratte, Richard. *Contemporary Theories of Education.* Scranton: T. Y. Crowell, 1971.

School Philosophy Development

Afton, A. "Writing a School Philosophy." *Pennsylvania School Journal* 116 (January 1968); 252–53.

Brameld, Theodore. *Philosophies of Education in Cultural Perspective.* New York: Holt, Rinehart and Winston, Inc., 1955.

Hug, W. E. "Are You Philosophically Consistent?" *Science Education* 54 (April 1970): 185–87.

Lincoln, J. R., and Wood, W. "Dare We Evaluate Our Philosophy and Objectives?" *School and Community* 57 (October 1970): 8–9.

Marler, Charles D. *Philosophy and Schooling,* pp. 352–367. Boston: Allyn and Bacon, Inc., 1975.

Morris, Van Cleve. *Philosophy and the American School.* Boston: Houghton Mifflin Co., 1961.

4

Goals and Objectives

Discussing goals and objectives with a school administrator can be likened to constantly reading about newspaper accounts of rising inflation. We know that it effects us directly but we could care less about being informed of all the economic details. To most of us it is simply boring. Setting goals and objectives probably ranks, along with formulating a philosophy, as one of the least exciting endeavors for school practitioners. They want to "get on with it." They want to know what to do in the school and in the classroom. Well, we will soon enough present the "doing" part of it. Yet, setting goals and objectives which emanate from a philosophy is the basis for what you are going to do! Without an operational plan, the doing is meaningless. With this in mind, we can explore how to make goals and objectives consistent with philosophy and meaningful for judging what practices of change to engage in.

An educational philosophy provides a school with a consensus of beliefs about children and the nature of their growth within the world. Goals and objectives are clear statements, emanating from a philosophy as to what the school intends to accomplish. It is only when we have clear statements of what the school is seeking to achieve in terms of student outcomes that we begin to move out of the conceptual, abstract world into the concrete world of action. By stating what student outcomes will be, we step into the accountable arena. Accountability is an issue debated ad nauseam between the public and the schools about the use of money. We don't wish to become entangled in that argument because it is our belief that meaningful accountability is more importantly an internal school matter. School personnel need to know and state what they hope their students will accomplish before they can be accountable to themselves as to the success or failure of their enterprise. Without goals and objectives, individual teachers and an entire staff can pay lip service to a philosophy and justify any amount of bumbling around as their subjective way of responding to that philosophy. Goals and objectives take the license "to do anything," away from individuals.

WHAT ARE GOALS AND OBJECTIVES?

Goals are general statements of intent that emanate directly from a philosophy. Objectives are specific, operational, and evaluative statements that tell all listeners or readers what the student outcomes will be and how those outcomes will be evaluated. For example, this is a common goal which is found in most school handbooks: "The Development of a Good Citizen for a Democratic Society." Obviously, we have an inkling that democracy and a child's learning to function within it is the general sense of this school goal and it could very well be congruent with an overarching philosophy. However, this goal is not sufficient in itself for a school to develop consistent practices to assure its success. After all, what is good citizenship within a democratic society? One teacher might allow children complete freedom of choice as her concept of good citizenship in a democracy. Another teacher might spend endless hours lecturing and testing children on the workings of the various levels of government according to her concept of good citizenship in a democracy. The goal tells us all that citizenship and democracy are important but we are still left without answers as to what students will know or do as a result of this emphasis. Objectives must be clear and concise so that all staff members can act in a coherent, consistent manner. Examples of clear objectives emerging from this goal follow.

Goal: The Development of a Good Citizen for a Democratic Society.

Objectives:

1. Students will express their opinions freely in daily classroom meetings.
2. Students will explain views that are contrary to their own.
3. Students will exercise decision-making power by formulating school and classroom rules by majority vote.
4. Students will hold mock political elections.
5. Students will write letters to government officials to register satisfaction and dissatisfaction with a current issue.

We are not of the opinion that objectives have to be written within a uniform, technical way. For those who wish such precision, Mager's book entitled *Preparing Instructional Objectives* will provide the necessary guidelines.[1] Also, objectives can be continually broken down into smaller parts. Some schools, based on their essentialist philosophical view, will welcome such specificity; other schools, based on an existentialist philosophy, will see such detail as restrictive to their overall aims. For our purposes in this beginning section, a listing of goals with clarifying objectives is sufficient enough for a later examination of consistency.

GOALS AND OBJECTIVES AS REFLECTIVE OF PHILOSOPHY

Again, trying not to be overly critical, most schools have goals that do not reflect a philosophical purpose. For example, here is a listing of typical goal statements taken from a typical elementary school.

We at   School, believe each child should:

- attain optimum proficiency in the basic skills of listening, observing, speaking, reading, writing, and mathematics
- gain skill in logical and critical thinking
- acquire spontaneity and creativity
- understand his or her self and the relationship each has to other people
- acquire habits and attitudes which will permit him or her to become a responsible and contributing member of society
- gain the necessary skills to learn independently
- display pride in good workmanship
- understand the functioning of the human body and practice sound habits of personal health
- understand the need to practice wise use of human, natural, and material resources
- adjust to changing situations
- develop his or her own capabilities, interests, and talents
- have knowledge of the emergence of the world's societies, particularly his or her own
- develop a problem-solving capacity regarding real world issues
- exercise free choice
- develop an appreciation for, and an enjoyment of literature, art, music, and other aesthetic experiences.

Each of these goals is admirable, but what is the purpose of this school? There is no clear direction and, furthermore, no objectives to clarify what the goals mean. Can a school really be all things to all children? A few extraordinary schools and staffs might come closer to pulling this off than others. But let's be frank. Almost every school claims that this is what they are doing; but if one looks at internal practices, staff commitment to full philosophical and methodological eclecticism is not readily apparent. If a school is to be effective, it needs a philosophy with corresponding goals and objectives that focus on desired and rated outcomes.

Even schools with a particular philosophy will eventually list most of the goals cited above. What will be different, however, is the ranking of those goals and the corresponding, explanatory objectives. A previous example of good citizenship in a democracy might be evident in all three philosophical positions. However, an existential school would rank this statement down on its list, an experimentalist school would rank it near the top of its list, and an essentialist school would rank it somewhere in the middle. Of course the interpretation of the goal would be quite different for each of the three schools. The essentialists would stress knowledge, the experimentalists, problem solving, and the existentialists, free choice. We will look at what the ranking of goals and objectives might look like for each of the three schools of thought. As examples we list five goals as well as objectives based upon the first goal statement. Please do not view these as exhaustive of all the goals which schools are seeking to accomplish. Rather, they are illustrative of the differences in philosophical positions. For the remainder of the book, we will refer to essentialist thought as Alternative One, experimentalist thought as Alternative Two, and existentialist thought as Alternative Three.

Essentialism—Alternative One

Goals:

1. The student should attain optimum proficiency in the basic skills of listening, observing, speaking, reading, writing, and mathematics.
2. The student should gain skill in logical and critical thinking.
3. The student should have knowledge of the emergence of the world's societies, particularly one's own.
4. The student should understand the need to practice wise use of human, natural, and material resources.

5. The student should acquire habits and attitudes which will permit him or her to become a responsible and contributing member of society.

Objectives for Goal One:

1. The student, in reading proficiency tests, will score at a minimum fifth-grade level before exiting from school.
2. The student, in mathematics proficiency tests, will score at a minimum fifth-grade level before exiting from school.
3. The student will be able to write an essay of three hundred words with ninety percent accuracy of spelling, grammar, and sentence structure by the sixth grade.

Experimentalism—Alternative Two

Goals:

1. The student should develop problem solving capacities of real world issues.
2. The student should acquire habits and attitudes which will permit him or her to become a responsible and contributing member of society.
3. The student should understand the need to practice wise use of human, natural, and material resources.
4. The student should adjust to changing situations.
5. The student should attain optimum proficiency in the basic skills of listening, observing, speaking, reading, writing, and mathematics.

Objectives for Goal One:

1. The student will be able to verbalize the major issues confronting society.
2. The student will be able to seek out the resources of others.
3. The student will use the scientific method of hypothesizing, collecting data, and evaluating societal problems.
4. The student will be able to generate alternative solutions to current problems.

Existentialism—Alternative Three

Goals:

1. The student should exercise free choice.
2. The student should understand himself and his own relationship to other people.
3. The student should develop his own capabilities, interests, and talents.
4. The student should acquire spontaneity and creativity.
5. The student should develop an appreciation for aesthetic experiences.

Objectives for Goal One:

1. The child will schedule himself.
2. The child will select his own learning materials.
3. The child will decide with whom to work.
4. The child will find his own physical space.
5. The child will develop his own guidelines for action.

PROCEDURES FOR WRITING GOALS AND OBJECTIVES

After a school has identified an educational philosophy, it is the educational leader's role to facilitate the writing of goals and objectives that will, in turn, be the springboard for the selection of those operational practices of curriculum, materials, and methods of management. After deciding upon a philosophy, it is relatively easy for a staff to take a list of typical goals (as shown on the previous pages) and rank them. Each individual can make his or her own ranking. Several groups can then make a collective ranking, and, finally, the members can make a school ranking. At this point, the staff can check their priorities against their philosophy and see if their goals are indeed reflective. A more direct approach, but perhaps more time consuming, would be for the principal to form a small group of three to four representative members to write their own goals, using the school philosophy as a guide. They would then need to report their findings to the entire staff for comment and possible revision before making the goals final.

The next step, writing objectives which reflect goals, will require the effort of all staff members. It is difficult for a staff to attempt to form objectives as an entire assembly. It is much easier to parcel out the different goals to small groups of two to four members and give them the responsibility for developing the corresponding objectives. These small groups usually meet on their own to complete the task. An "all staff" meeting can then be held to offer input on each group's objectives, to incorporate revisions, and lastly, to make changes. Voilà, the task is done. (It always appears so easy on paper, if only it would be so simple in actuality!)

EVALUATION OF GOALS AND
OBJECTIVES

If objectives clearly indicate what student outcomes will be, then evaluation is relatively straightforward. Using some of our preceding examples of possible objectives, these outcomes can easily be documented. Can students express opposing views? Can students read at a minimum fifth-grade level by the end of elementary school? Can students generate alternate solutions to current problems? Can students schedule themselves? Evaluation becomes a matter of documenting whether they can or cannot do what the school intended.

Evaluation should obviously reflect a school's goals. It is surprising how so many schools and state boards of education have goals that rank both cognitive and affective skills highly. Yet evaluation does not jive with such a ranking. Most of the funds that are used for evaluation go for cognitive instruments that measure academic achievement. Virtually no money goes toward affective measures of attitudes, perceptions, and the self-concepts of students. If a school ranks such affective goals as high in priority, then they should be expending money, finding evaluation devices, and committing energy to evaluate such outcomes. Whether goals and objectives are affective, cognitive, or otherwise, there is no room for ifs, buts, or maybes; the school is either effective or it is not. This is what we mean by accountability, being accountable to oneself to achieve what one believes is important.

The heart of this book begins in the next section. We discuss alternative approaches to each schooling dimension. It is our belief that there are certain practices within the school that are consistent with particular philosophical aims. By pulling all the dimensions of schooling—curriculum, methods and materials, management of students, staff supervision, and resource management—in line with a school's direction (philosophy, goals, and objectives), the school will be more likely to accomplish their intended outcomes for students. The sections on each dimension of schooling provide practices and approaches which correspond to the three alternative philosophies of schooling.

The reader might question how the school's dimensions of resource management and staff supervision have the same degree of influence on achieving student outcomes as compared with curriculum and student management. Our answer is that the ways in which administrators and staff work together within the macrosphere of the organization have great influence on what transpires within the microsphere of a classroom. The school is a total system and one dimension out of line can create the frustration, tension, and inconsistency that interferes with everything else.

NOTES

1.   Robert F. Mager, *Preparing Instructional Objectives*. (Palo Alto, Calif.: Fearon Publishing Co., 1962)

SUGGESTIONS FOR FURTHER READING

Goals and Objectives

English, Fenwick W., and Kaufman, Roger A. *Needs Assessment: A Focus for Curriculum Development*, pp. 24–48. Washington, D.C.: Association for Supervision and Curriculum Development, 1975.

Gorton, Richard A. *School Administration: Challenge and Opportunity for Leadership*, pp. 21–36. Dubuque, Iowa: Wm. C. Brown Co., 1976.

Mager, Robert F. *Preparing Instructional Objectives*. Palo Alto, Calif.: Fearon Publishing Co., 1962.

Marler, Charles D. *Philosophy and Schooling*, pp. 352–69. Boston: Allyn and Bacon, Inc., 1975.

Schmuck, Richard A., and Runkel, Philip J. *Handbook of Organization Development in Schools*, pp. 98–123. Eugene, Oregon: University of Oregon, Center for the Advanced Study of Educational Administration, National Press Books, 1972.

Section Three

Implementing the Curriculum Dimension

5

Alternative Curriculum Models

After going through the processes presented in the previous chapters, a school can determine the direction it will go to meet the individual needs of students. At this point, everyone must come face to face with the actual classroom practices to be used. Without a blueprint of philosophy and goals and objectives, a school is simply buffeted by the winds of traditional practices, current fads, or each staff member's whim. A study by Biber and Minuchin found that those staffs who were most consistent in practice with their school's philosophy, were most effective in reaching their objectives.[1] Again, this sounds like a most reasonable and obvious conclusion, yet we have been involved in numerous school self-studies where the opposite was inevitably true. Schools have well-written and comprehensive statements of their philosophy and goals and objectives, yet a visit to the ongoing operation shows a hodgepodge of practices. Teachers have no idea of the inconsistency of their practices. For example, during one of our visits to an elementary school, we spoke with teachers about their primary objectives. In this particular school "promoting a positive self-concept" was ranked as the number one goal. We visited a few classrooms and observed some teacher practices. One teacher had a tremendous facility in the use of sarcasm. Another had a student sitting in a corner with his back to the class (he had been interrupting other students as they were responding to the teacher's questions). Still another had a student sitting at a desk outside his classroom (he had forgotten to bring his book to class for the second day in a row). All three children were visibly upset.

Some of the reasons for this inconsistency might be as follows: (a) teachers do not know what their school philosophy is; (b) the school philosophy never gets beyond the blueprint stage to the definition of appropriate methods; or (c) teachers simply use the methods that they were taught in college or that their teachers used with them, without knowledge of other practices.

The scope of the following chapters is to go beyond the "blueprint" stage and to define methods consistent with certain philosophies. Effective teaching is not the exercising of techniques without the knowledge of what the implications will be. If teaching consisted of merely using methods without first thinking of their implications, then teachers would not be necessary—technicians would suffice. Education is a human endeavor and, as such, teachers must be given the responsibility to make knowledgeable decisions of how to best carry out, in their own interaction with students, the school philosophy.

Individualized instruction is simply a term meaning that the student is learning according to his own abilities. The term itself does not imply what the goals or practices of such an educational program should be. For example, both programmed instruction and free-choice activities are labeled as individualized instruction but each are related to a different goal. One predetermines everything the child will learn; the other is completely open-ended. To help simplify a vision of curriculum, let's look at it from two ends. One end states that the goal of education is to promote creative or unpredictable behavior. The other end states that the goal is to insure that students learn certain matters in a certain way and thus promotes predictable behavior. One may classify these opposite views in other ways. Religiously, the view of one is that the child is born inherently good; the other is that the child is born inherently impulsive and destructive. Psychologically, the child is an internal-reaching creature as opposed to the child as being passively conditioned by the environment. These views oversimplify the issue and before the reader aligns with one side, it is important to amplify the implications of each position with its corresponding curriculum. To do so, we will look at three positions on a "promoting behavior line," the two end points and the midpoint. We will call them Alternative Curriculums One, Two, and Three.

Diagram of Alternative Curriculums

Promoting Behavior	Alternative 1	Alternative 2	Alternative 3
	Predictable	Both predictable and unpredictable	Unpredictable

ALTERNATIVE ONE

In this realm, the goal of education is to prepare the student to fit into society. The school is to teach those skills, processes, and content matter that are essential for a person to manage and hopefully be successful in the outer world as it now exists. Emphasis is on the basics, with the atmosphere of the school being as close as possible to the atmosphere and conditions of society. Students compete with each other for status recognition and achievement. Rewards come in the form of grades, rank, and honors. The body of knowledge to be learned is already determined by experts (either the teacher, administration, or textbook publishers). The student has little say in what is to be learned since he or she is regarded as needing the wisdom of the experts before being wise enough to make his or her own decision. Knowledge of content with its corresponding use of repetition and memorization is stressed. Individualized instruction in such a school is a systematic approach to fitting a student into the linear progress of knowledge at his own level. All students will go through the same predetermined units but at their own rate.

The way in which most schools set up such a curriculum after going beyond the blueprint stage, is to list specific skills for each subject area that needs to be learned. A behavioral objective is then written for each skill. A pretest for the student is then designed to determine if he already possesses the skill. Following the pretest, a list of sequential activities for the student to progress through is provided. The culmination of the unit is a post-test to assess the level of mastery. Each skill with its objective, pretest, activities, and post-test is placed in a curriculum book, by subject and in sequence of difficulty. This curriculum comes to the student's hands in the form of different individual practices such as programmed books, learning packets of modules, and learning centers. They are used to predict or control the learning outcome. They direct the student through a predictable sequence, test the achievement, and then move the student to the next step. The activities may or may not be multisensory (reading, writing, filmstrip, film, lectures, tv, tape, concrete building materials, etc.), but they all converge, hopefully to accomplish one end—the achievement of the predetermined objective. Prime examples of such an approach to individualized instruction are the schools that primarily use learning packets, worksheets, programmed materials (textbooks, workbooks, and machines) or have bought into computerized systems.

ALTERNATIVE THREE

The goal of education is to enable the student to go beyond society as it now exists and to exercise free will. The function of the school is to provide a supportive environment for the student to explore and progress according to his own interests and abilities. The school stresses the process of how to go about learning for oneself, or in other words, resourcefulness. As a result, basic skills are only one of the many tools of learning.

The curriculum is determined by the student. The teacher needs to have knowledge of activities and skills which will enhance student-initiated projects. The staff's function in planning curriculum becomes one of listing activities that might extend the project of a child in such a way as to refine or learn new skills. Therefore, after the blueprint of the general philosophy and its goals and objectives are established, numerous alternative activities are written to extend possible projects. These are activities that could "spin off" from the initial activity. At the final stage, skills that would result from the activities are listed and used as a basis for evaluation. This curriculum then serves as a guide for the teacher in setting up the environment that would invite the student to initiate projects to be followed up with extending activities. The teacher, in conjunction with the student, can then add, revise, or change the environment to provide for unforeseen explorations.

The teacher in such a school has identified certain skills as generally necessary for learning, yet the curriculum is determined by the student, not the skills. The teacher can assist in teaching a skill that a student blocks out or misses. However, the point is that the term "individualized instruction," in this type of school, means that a minimum of control is used to determine a student's learning outcomes. The student may go in many directions, the resultant learning being unforeseeable. The teacher is concerned mainly with the processes of setting up a creative environment, assisting, counseling, interacting, and knowing when to leave the child alone. The type and sequence of learning is left largely to the curiosity and abilities of the student. Learning is rarely superimposed and the student is not channeled through a set of predetermined objectives.

The methods used in such a school are usually activity centers, spin-off units, probe pacs, and open-ended learning centers. The labels for schools that follow this educational process are commonly "activity-centered classrooms," "informal schools," and "free schools."

ALTERNATIVE TWO

The aim of education in this alternative is to promote the ability of students to adjust to present society as well as the ability to reformulate society for the future. The student is to become a social problem solver. The school places equal emphasis on both rudimentary and creative skills. Learning is thus a combination of superimposed content instruction as well as student-initiated discovery. In effect, this alternative is the supreme effort to make schools all things to all people. It is not so much a compromise between the extreme views of alternative one and three, but a belief that individuals need to be both externally and internally disciplined. Its weakness is that it is extremely difficult to implement. For a school to successfully practice this philosophy, teachers have to be "jacks of all trades." They must be experts and believers in all forms of instruction—lecturing, drilling, facilitating, intervening, and nonintervening. Unfortunately, it is a rare person who can do all equally well. Most "content" believers have a hard time tolerating students actively learning with the inevitable noise and confusion. Most "process believers" have an uncomfortable time in asserting themselves in a lecture or directing the use of mandated materials. Most school staffs would probably claim that, philosophically, they fit into this alternative. However, in practice, most schools tilt toward one or the other alternative.

A school based on this philosophical persuasion uses all of the methods of the other alternatives in individualizing instruction. Basic skills are learned through sequential, lockstep instruction. The programs are developed by experts and the students are slotted into the sequence. The use of lecture, programmed materials, learning packets, and learning centers are all used. Equal time is also given to fitting materials and activities to the child in a more spontaneous, personal way. The informality required to provide a supportive environment for discovery is sought through interest and activity centers, group discussions, personal conferences, and open-ended inquiry. The heavy stress on social interaction, cooperation, and problem solving can be most readily identified with the labels "progressive schools" and "open education."

AMPLIFICATION

Since our book is addressed to fitting all dimensions of schooling into a consistent whole, we cannot fully amplify all the details of each dimension. There are numerous books that do provide this amplification for us. We have listed a sampling of curriculum books that correspond to our three alternative models. It is up to the principal and staff to pursue those readings on curriculum that fit with their overall philosophy, goals, and objectives. We will expand on the consistency of curriculum practices with philosophy in the next chapter.

SUGGESTIONS FOR FURTHER READING

Alternative One

Eisele, James E. *Computer Assisted Planning of Curriculum and Instruction: How to Use Computer Based Resource Units to Individualize Instruction.* Englewood Cliffs, N.J.: Educational Technology Publishers, 1971.

Engelmann, Siegfried. *Preventing Failure in the Primary Grades.* New York: Simon and Schuster, 1969.

Esbensen, Thorwald. *Working with Individualized Instruction: The Duluth Experience.* Belmont, Calif.: Fearon Publishing Co., 1968.

Karlin, Muriel Schoenbran, and Berger, Regina. *Individualizing Instruction: A Complete Guide for Diagnosis, Planning, Teaching, and Evaluation.* West Nyack, N.Y.: Parker Publishing Co., 1974.

Lipham, James, and Furth, Marvin. *The Principal and Individually Guided Education.* Reading, Mass.: Addison-Wesley Publishing Co., 1976.

Stephens, Thomas. *Implementing Behavioral Approaches in Elementary and Secondary Schools.* Columbus, Ohio: Charles E. Merrill Publishing Co., 1975.

Alternative Two

Cook, Myra; Caldwell, Joseph; and Christiansen, Lina. *Dynamic Teaching in the Elementary School.* West Nyack, N.Y.: Parker Publishing Co., 1970.

Frazier, Alexander. *Adventuring, Mastering, Associating: New Strategies for Teaching Children.* Washington, D.C.: Association for Supervision and Curriculum Development, 1976.

Frazier, Alexander. *Teaching Children Today: An Informal Approach.* New York: Harper & Row, 1976.

Hollaway, Otto. *Problem Solving: Toward a More Humanizing Curriculum.* Philadelphia: Franklin Publishing Co., 1975.

Jarolimek, John, and Foster, Clifford. *Teaching and Learning in the Elementary School.* New York: Macmillan Publishing Co., 1976.

Rathbone, Charles H., ed. *Open Education: The Informal Classroom.* New York: Citation Press, 1971.

Alternative Three

Berman, Louise, and Roderick, Jessie A. *Curriculum: Teaching the What, How, and Why of Living.* Columbus, Ohio: Charles E. Merrill, 1977.

Hendricks, Gay, and Fadiman, James. *Transpersonal Education: A Curriculum for Feeling and Being.* Englewood Cliffs, N.J.: Prentice-Hall, Inc., 1976.

Mann, John. *Learning To Be: The Education of Human Potential.* New York: The Free Press, 1972.

Pinar, William, ed. *Heightened Consciousness, Cultural Revolution and Curriculum Theory.* Berkeley, Calif.: McCutchan Publishing, 1974.

Thatcher, David A. *Teaching, Loving and Self-Directed Learning.* Pacific Palisades, Calif.: Goodyear Publishing Co., Inc., 1973.

Weber, Lillian. *The English Infant School and Informal Education.* Englewood Cliffs, N.J.: Prentice-Hall, Inc., 1971.

All Models

Biber, Barbara, and Minuchin, Patricia. "The Impact of School Philosophy and Practice on Child Development." In *The Unstudied Curriculum: Its Impact on Children,* edited by N. Overly. Washington, D.C.: The Association for Supervision and Curriculum Development, 1970.

6

Methods and Materials

In this chapter we describe the methods and materials available for individualizing instruction. There are different forms of individualized instruction and they vary for each of the alternative school models. The only agreement is that students work at their own pace. In an Alternative One curriculum, students progress through a set, prescribed sequence. In an Alternative Three curriculum, students learn through the pursuit of their own interests. In an Alternative Two curriculum, there is a balance of both sequential and spontaneous learning.

The methods and materials that we are about to describe range from sequential and predictable to nonsequential and spontaneous learning. Our task would be easy if each method or material was used by only one alternative school model to the exclusion of others. As we explained in the preceding chapter, with most methods and materials this is not the case. Instead, it is the manner in which the materials are presented for student use that make the difference. In our description of each, we will define what the method looks like, how it should be used differently according to the alternative model, and how it is developed. We will also discuss any peculiar considerations. In describing differences in use, we will focus primarily on Alternative One (predictable curriculum) and Alternative Three (unpredictable curriculum). The reader can fill in the Alternative Two (predictable-unpredictable) curriculum by combining the other two.

At the end of this chapter, we will describe the methods, materials, and kind of student involvement an observer would see upon walking into each of the three alternative school classrooms. Finally, we will conclude with a resource list of books that amplify each approach.

We know that it is not strictly kosher to so glibly combine the terms "method" and "materials" as though they were the same. However, we feel justified in doing so because we are referring to method as the teaching approach that uses a certain kind of material. Is the extensive use of learning packets for student instruction a method or a material? It is both; the method is using learning packets and the materials are what goes into making each packet. So much for that.

DESCRIPTIONS OF METHODS AND MATERIALS

Learning Packets (or Learning Modules)

Definition. A self-directed, systematic, instructionally valid, motivating instructional lesson designed (usually for one child) for one lesson (usually thirty to sixty minutes) and related to one specific objective.[1]

Use. Packets correspond to a tightly sequenced hierarchy of skills that are determined to be essential for students to learn. They are usually worked on individually by children with specific steps to follow. In many cases, packets are used as the core of instruction but they can also be used to supplement other types of instruction.

How to. After determining the skills that are to be taught, one skill is taken at a time. The skill is rephrased into a behavioral objective. The packet then includes a pretest, instruction on various activities to do, and then a post-test.

In simplified form, a packet would look like this.

    I. Skill: The student is able to identify major cities in America.

   II. Objective: Given an unidentified map of America, the student will be able to mark out and label the ten major cities at a proficiency level of 100 percent.

 III. Pretest: Using an unidentified map, the student is asked to identify and label the ten major cities.

 IV. Activities (to be undertaken if pretest is unsuccessful)
    A. Read geography book.
    B. Look at filmstrip with record.
    C. Write down the ten major cities after doing activities A and B. Describe where they are located by longitude and latitude, and describe their major characteristics.
    D. Play geography map game.

V. Post-test: The post-test is the same as the pretest (If the objective is still not mastered, there are usually additional activities assigned or the student is recycled through the same packet.)

Discussion. Learning packets lend themselves to paper and pencil work, particularly in the pretesting and post-testing. The activities can be varied with the use of games, discussion, and observations. The packets can have all the information needed within their covers or they can direct the student to activities in the classroom (multi-resource packets). Students with poor reading ability have a difficult time, particularly with self-contained packets but also with following directions in multiresource packets. Young children, for the same reasons, do not do well with packets. Verbal or taped instructions can alleviate this problem somewhat. Since packets are put together in a directive way to accomplish a specific objective, they usually do not challenge the imagination of students. However, they do have real strength in assuring the mastery of skills at a set rate of proficiency.

Packets can be time consuming for an individual teacher to make. A teacher trying to individualize all of his or her coursework in this way, faces an overwhelming task. For this reason, schools committed to packet instruction either purchase commercial programs or work on packets as an entire team. For example, two intermediate teachers will work on science packets for all the intermediate students; two other intermediate teachers will do the arithmetic packets, and so on. Such programs take years to develop but when finished provide an orderly year-to-year sequence for students.

Activity Cards

Definition. An individual card giving specific directions as to the activity to be performed.

Use. Activity cards are used to provide a short, interesting pursuit of either a teacher-directed study or a student-initiated exploration. They are used as enrichment and time fillers in the predictable curriculum (Alternative One). They are used mostly as a teacher substitute for stimulating questions and suggesting activities that could incorporate the available classroom materials in the unpredictable curriculum (Alternative Three). In Alternative Two, they are used in both ways.

How to. Activity cards can be stretched and developed in many directions. A typical one would be the size of an index card—colorful

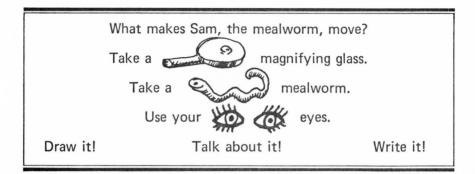

Figure 6.1. *An Example of a Typical
Activity Card*

and laminated. The card would be hung above the materials to be used.

Discussion.   Activity cards are an exciting way to individualize. They can be a supplement to or the core of instruction. For younger children, directions need to be of the picture or sign type. The cards do not need to rely on reading ability and often can be made by students for other students. Teacher-made cards can be made quickly and inexpensively.

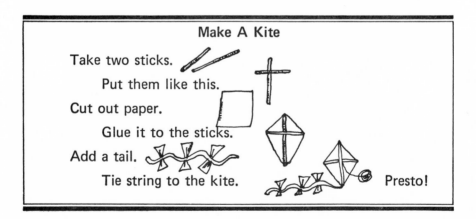

Figure 6.2. *An Example of a More
Directive Activity Card*

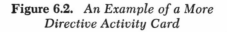

The Learning Center

Definition.   A physical space where materials are grouped with a learning objective in mind. It is also called a Learning Station or Instructional Center.

Use.   Learning centers provide an arrangement of space that encourages movement and interaction. If used in a conventional teacher-directed classroom as a supplement to the basic seatwork, it provides relief and a change of pace from routine instruction. If used as the basic classroom arrangement, it provides great flexibility of space and mobility of materials.

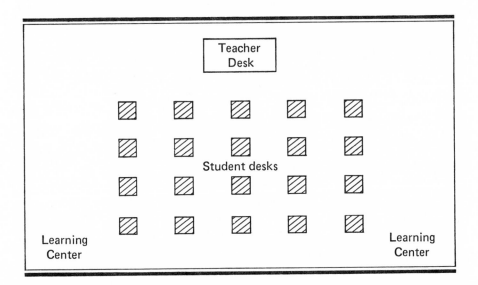

Figure 6.3. *Diagram of Learning Centers as Supplements to the Teacher-Directed Class*

In the predictable curriculum (Alternative One) classroom, learning centers are developed around an objective and provide particular steps for students to carry out. The center might contain activity cards, learning packets, or contracts. The center contains alternative approaches with materials of multimodal use. However, the end result always remains the same: the accomplishment of the objective.

In the unpredictable curriculum (Alternative Three) classroom,

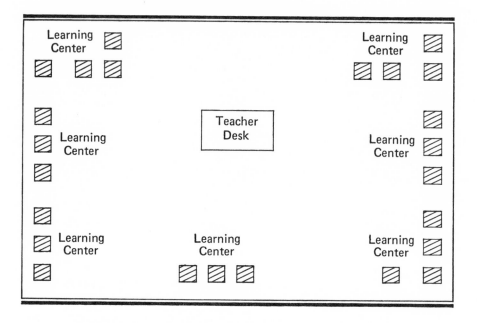

Figure 6.4. *Diagram of Learning Centers as a Basic Arrangement*

the learning centers are used only to get across minimum basic skills and are set up in the same way as in the predictable classroom. Alternative Two classrooms use learning centers extensively, in both directive and open-ended ways. The learning centers are a resource or supplement to the activity centers.

How to.   Learning Centers provide a logical sequence of individualized activities leading to the attainment of learning objectives. The activities are numbered according to their complexity so that students might easily follow from one to the next. At times, students may choose from more than one activity that promotes the same level of understanding. The final activity is a post-test to check student proficiency. An example of one learning center is illustrated in Figure 6.5.

Discussion.   Learning centers are an eye-catching and motivating way of teaching students' predetermined skills. Clear and simple directions are necessary for readers but directions via tape can be used for young children. In that a learning center uses various levels of activities, different modes for learning, and active student involvement, it provides a successful and exciting means for individualizing.

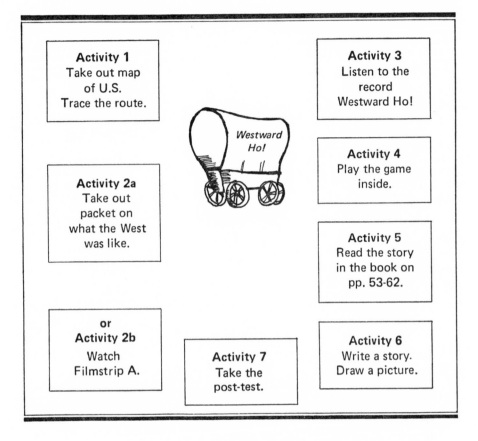

Figure 6.5. *An American Settler Center*

The Activity Center

Definition. A physical space where materials are grouped to encourage exploration and discovery. It may also be called an Interest Center.

Use. Activity centers are put out solely for the use of students so that they can pursue their own interests. They have no predetermined learning objective in mind. Learning comes about as a result of what takes place when the student works with materials, another student, or the teacher. In the unpredictable curriculum, this is the essence of learning. In the predictable curriculum, if used at all, it is used during playtime when all the serious learning activities are through.

How to.   The students or the teacher can group manipulative materials, art supplies, magazines, books, audiovisuals, living creatures, and miscellaneous units into different theme areas around the room. For example, some groupings might be machines, living animals, the universe, communications, etc. Some activity cards or leading questions can help stimulate thought. (In the machine center, a question might be overheard, "If you take it apart, can you put it back together?" In the communication center, you might hear, "How can you communicate with someone else without speaking? Use some of the things on the table to do so.")

Discussion.   Activity centers demand *activity*. For that reason, teachers need to be very firm in defining permissible and nonpermissible social behavior. Also, since these centers are predicated on the belief that students are curious and always learning, the teacher must be in constant movement—answering, questioning, rearranging, counseling, etc.

Spin-Off or the Experience Approach

Definition.   The introduction by the teacher of a stimulating activity that sets off a chain reaction of student inspired projects.

Use.   The spin-off approach is used to intervene with a child's present course of learning to expose him to other alternatives of study. This method is common in the unpredictable curriculum and uncommon in the predictable curriculum. It goes hand in hand with the activity-centered arrangement of materials.

How to.   Two examples will suffice. First, the teacher takes the class together as a whole. He tells them to close their eyes and then proceeds to open all the windows on a cold winter day. He then asks them to explain what has happened. Students talk about outdoor temperature, body warmth, the purpose of clothes, the school heating system, fire, insulation, etc. From this discussion they come up with a list of all the spin-off activities of projects which could be studied as a result of their initial experience. Each student picks one activity and heads off to pursue his own interest. Here is another example. The teacher calls Anne over and confers with her about what she's been doing. Anne tells him about the vegetables she is growing inside and the problems she is having. The teacher and Anne discuss various reasons for the problem—not enough sunlight, poor soil, inadequate water, wrong temperature, etc. As a result, Anne begins to study these possibilities by looking at books and filmstrips, having discussions with other classmates, and calling a plant store. She will report to her teacher later.

Discussion.   A curriculum that uses this method of instruction needs teachers who are trained in student cognitive development. They need to know the signs for appropriate intervention. They also need a different form of record keeping, having a knowledge of a broad range of skills, and ascertaining through observation and dialogue when more complex skills are essential and realistic to help extend the child's thinking. Also, the classroom must contain or have ready access to a multiplicity of resource materials.

Contracts

Definition.   A student commitment (usually written) to perform a specific project.

Use.   Contracts can be used in many ways. An independent student contract is simply a statement by the student in which he makes known what he will do, the resources he will use, and what the end results might be. A teacher-directed contract is usually given to a

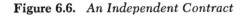

Student's name: _____ Date: _____

1. What will you do?

2. How will you do it?

3. What will be the end result?

4. How much time will it take?

We agree that the above is a worthwhile task.

_____   _____
        Student's name   Teacher's name

Figure 6.6. *An Independent Contract*

Contract IIIb
Title: Protozoans

Do the attached learning packet.

I agree that if this contract is done in three days with

at least an 80% on the posttest, the student will receive

3 points. 90% will receive 4 points.

(15 points for the semester is a B;

20 points for the semester is an A)

Student's name: _____

Figure 6.7. *A Teacher-Directed Contract*

student stating what the task is, how it is to be done, and how it will be evaluated. The student might negotiate the length of time and the reward, if any, to be given before signing. Another type of contract is similar in structure to the teacher-directed contract but is developed through negotiation from beginning to end.

Discussion.   Contracts are used to attain a commitment or promise from the student and thus to provide for greater involvement and responsibility for his work. The unpredictable curriculum uses only independent contracts and only for those few students who need greater self-direction and recognition for concrete achievement. In the predictable curriculum, contracts are teacher-directed and might be used extensively as a record keeping of the objectives being mastered. (Learning packets fit in perfectly with the concept of contracts.)

How to.   Some simple examples are shown in Figures 6.6, 6.7, and 6.8.

Simulation and Gaming

Definition.   A contrived situation that closely resembles and explores a real life problem.

Subject: Protozoan

1. Resources:

Packet, books, filmstrips, t.v. show, etc.

List:_____,_____,_____

2. Activities:

write a story, make a tape, oral presentation, diagrams, etc.

List:_____,_____,_____

3. Evaluation:

post-test, discussion on above culminating activity?

_____

4. Amount of Time: _____

5. Reward (if any): _____

_____   _____
Teacher's name   Student's name

Figure 6.8. *A Negotiated Contract*

Use. Simulation is used to foster empathy in students and to present strategies for dealing with problems in the real world. Simulation is usually based on group interaction in a problem-solving context. Some examples of simulation would be (1) a class meeting to discuss how one might feel and do if one had lost something belonging to another of great importance; (2) small groups participating in brainstorming sessions to come up with ideas on how to get the local town to conserve on energy; or (3) a play written and acted out by students to portray the issues behind the American Revolution.

How to. Simulation is still another teaching strategy that can be used in all types of curriculums. In the predictable curriculum, simulation is used occasionally to reinforce some content being taught, for example, by enacting a historical debate. The issues and actions to be taken are directed by the teacher with students guided towards a defined end. In the unpredictable curriculum, there are opportunities for children to fantasize, make up their own situations, and brainstorm solutions. The teacher serves as a facilitator of the discussion, allowing students to express themselves and listen to other ideas. In the Alternative Two, predictable-unpredictable classroom, it is a primary and much used method for social issues problem solving.

Discussion.   Simulation in the form of role playing or discussing ways to attack current community or social problems has been an acceptable practice in all forms of curriculum. The recent use of simulation where it evolves from student role playing to a social action (i.e., writing letters to the editor of the newspaper, forming picket lines around businesses that discriminate, and confronting government representatives) is obviously volatile. A staff has to make decisions as to what boundaries to keep between "pretended" and "real" issues.

Introspection and Value Clarification

Definition.   A method whereby a student attempts to "get in touch" with his inner feelings and values.

Use.   Introspection and value clarification methods are used by teachers to help students understand themselves, to express their beliefs, and eventually to act upon them.

How to.   For value clarification, the teacher asks students to answer different questions as to what they would do in certain moral dilemnas or to rank their current priorities and assess their life styles.

For introspecting, the teacher uses techniques such as meditation, yoga, and body movement so that the child may experience his own sensations.

Discussion.   Introspection and value clarification are hot issues. These approaches stem from the belief that a child should freely decide for himself outer issues based on his inner awareness. In other words, what is best for himself is alright. An Alternative One school would not make much, if any, use of this method in their curriculum. An Alternative Two school might use both methods only so that a child can learn to temper his desires and feelings and learn to work productively with others. An Alternative Three school would make much use of these approaches as the individual sensations, beliefs, and choices are an ultimate goal.

METHOD, MATERIAL, AND STUDENT INVOLVEMENT IN THE ALTERNATIVE MODELS

Alternative One

In the predictable curriculum, academic prescriptive learning is the core of instruction. Methods and materials are used largely to assure specific student learning outcomes. When a child has finished an activity, the teacher can be confident that another basic skill has been mastered. The culmination of any activity is an evaluation (test) which the child must pass before moving onto a more complex skill. Each activity builds upon the next in an hierarchical fashion (e.g., the child learns dictionary skills before learning encyclopedia skills, and even later learns library index skills). Therefore, methods and materials serve the purpose of arranging and then packaging activities in an orderly sequence of skills.

An observer walking into a fourth-grade Alternative One classroom might observe reading, mathematics, and spelling laboratory kits on the shelves. In each kit there are activity cards that may be leveled according to the colors green, yellow, blue, and red. The student must do ten of the green activities before going into the blue. Each child has textbooks in various subjects, moving through the pages at his own speed. The teacher gives daily instruction to small groups on basic concepts. There are audio-cassette machines in the small carrel area in the back of the room where students drill on listening comprehension. There is a sequence of tapes to go through.

When a child completes basic work in language arts, reading, and mathematics, he or she is assigned to work in one learning center, on one learning packet, and, if time allows, on a contract. One or two learning centers are in the room. The current center may be Social Studies, the theme being Canada. The center has all the direction and materials the student will need. He or she reads and follows the directions, beginning with Activity One and proceeding in order to the last activity. At the end, all children should be able to mark on a blank map of Canada all the major provinces and cities.

In a file cabinet near the teacher's desk are two drawers marked "packets" and "contracts." A child who has finished the third packet goes to the drawer and takes out the fourth. The child returns to his or her desk and follows the instructions. This packet may be about logical thinking. When the activities are finished, the child will take a post-test and pick all of the illogical statements out of twenty questions. He or she will put the post-test in a marked bin for the teacher to correct before going on to the next packet. The child then goes to the file cabinet and pulls out a contract which he or she has two weeks to complete. The contract may be on writing business letters to historical areas asking for their tourist brochures.

Alternative Three

In the unpredictable curriculum, free choice is the core of instruction. Methods and materials are used largely to stimulate alternative paths of pursuits for students. Activities are open-ended. The teacher cannot know for sure what a student will do with the materials or what he or she will learn. The teacher tries to structure the environment, and change materials in ways to encourage new individual learnings.

An observer walking into a fourth-grade Alternative Three classroom would find that activity or interest centers take up much of the physical space. There is an art center where miscellaneous paints, brushes, blocks, straw, yarn, easels, and paper are grouped. There is a "mechanics center" where an automobile engine, radios, clocks, and outboard motor in various semblances are being taken apart or put together. There is a 'library center' with books, magazines, records, and audio-visual materials arranged on shelves around a rug area. The "living center" is by the window where plants are growing and various gerbils, hamsters, snakes, and rabbits are wandering around in their cages. Above the centers are activity cards that ask questions about what can be done with the materials below. Probe packs are kept in boxes under the center tables to be used by students who might need some suggestions as to what they might do.

Near the exit is a box of blank independent contracts. If a child wants to do a project which entails using resources outside the classroom for an extended period, he or she is free to write his or her intentions and confer with the teacher before leaving. The child is back in the room for the last half-hour of the day when the classroom meeting takes place. At this time, the students discuss either their feelings about the class day or enter into some simulated value-clarification debates.

There are two other activity centers in the room, one in reading and the other in mathematics. The centers have many forms and types of reading and mathematics programs and materials. The child picks the program he wishes to work in and is required to spend some time at each center each day. This is Alternative Three's one concession to the societal concern of what children *have to learn.*

Alternative Two

In the predictable-unpredictable curriculum, there is a balance of sequential and spontaneous learning. There is an added stress on social problem solving. Some methods and materials are used to insure that basic, academic skills are learned while other methods and materials are made available to foster a child's individual pursuits. Methods and materials are arranged and packaged so that activities vary from open-ended to directive.

An observer entering a fourth-grade Alternative Two classroom would find the classroom contains permanent learning centers in current events, reading, and mathematics, and temporary learning centers that may be set up according to the themes of "Different Cultures," "Raising Food," and "Art." After closer inspection of two of the centers, it is obvious that they are quite different. In the reading center, students have to follow a sequence of activities, although the child often has a choice of two or three activities that get at the same skill. Some of the activities are just for fun with no evaluation intended. The reading center is used as a supplement to the individualized reading program that each student has been assigned. The Different Cultures center stands by itself; it is not a reinforcer of any directive instruction. Rather, the center has a sequence of activity cards that urge the student to look at pictures of various shelters around the world, to develop a hypothesis about what is common to all homes, and then look at more pictures and interview persons from different nations to test his hypothesis. The student's findings will be unique and somewhat unpredictable, yet his procedures are structured by the teacher in a deductive, problem-solving manner.

The room also contains learning packets for students to work on in teams of two or three. The instructional laboratory kits, leveled and in sequence, are also in evidence as is a drawer containing blank contracts. These contracts are for students who wish to write their own activities. However, before a child can begin, the teacher will negotiate with him the amount of work and time required. All students get together one hour before the school day ends to continue their classroom simulation of city management. For example, each student has been assigned a position of government responsibility—Health, Welfare, Sanitation, Business, etc. Their one month simulation has involved going out into the community, learning of the current problems in their respective government area, and finally negotiating how to allocate simulated city funds.

SUMMARY

We have described the various methods and materials of individualized instruction in this chapter. A school needs to pick and choose those activities which will foster the desired student learning. Our brief account of the observations that a visitor might make in each of the three alternative school classrooms has emphasized the relationship between curriculum and the use of methods and materials.

NOTES

1.   A quote from Dr. Lynn Canady of the University of Virginia in beginning his workshops on learning packets in August, 1976.

SUGGESTIONS FOR FURTHER READING

A sampling of various books that give a "how to" explanation of many of these methods and materials are listed below.

Activity Centers

Ingram, Barbara; Jones, Nancy; and LeButt, Marlene. *The Workshop Approach to Classroom Interest Centers: A Teachers Handbook of Learning Games and Activities.* Englewood Cliffs, N.J.: Prentice-Hall, Inc., 1976.
King, Joyce, and Katzman, Carol. *Imagine That: Illustrated Poems and Creative Learning Experiences.* Pacific Palisades, Calif.: Goodyear Publishing Co., 1976.
Lorton, Mary. *Workjobs: Activity-Centered Learning for Early Childhood Education.* Reading, Mass.: Addison-Wesley Publishing Co., 1972.

Contracts

Berte, Neal R., ed. *Individualizing Education Through Contract Learning.* University of Alabama Press, 1975.

Introspection and Value Clarification

Harmin, Merrill; Kirschenbaum, Howard; and Simon, Sidney. *Clarifying Values through Subject Matter: Applications for the Classroom.* Minneapolis: Winston Press, Inc., 1973.

Hendricks, Gay, and Willis, Russell. *The Centering Book: Awareness Activities for Children, Parents, and Teachers.* Englewood Cliffs, N.J.: Prentice-Hall, Inc., 1975.

Simon, Sidney B.; Howe, Leland; and Kirschenbaum, Howard. *Values Clarification: A Handbook of Practical Strategies for Teachers and Students.* New York: Hart Publishing Co., 1972.

Learning Centers

Blackburn, Jack E., and Powell, W. Conrad. *One at a Time All at Once: The Creative Teacher's Guide to Individualized Instruction without Anarchy.* Pacific Palisades, Calif.: Goodyear Publishing Co., 1976.

Breyfogle, Ethel. *Creating a Learning Environment: A Learning Center Handbook.* Santa Monica, Calif.: Goodyear Publishing Co., 1976.

Glasser, Joyce Fern. *The Elementary School Learning Center for Independent Study.* West Nyack, N.Y.: Parker Publishing Co., 1971.

Kaplan, Sandra et al. *Change for Children.* Pacific Palisades, Calif.: Goodyear Publishing Co., 1973.

Piechowiak, Ann B., and Cook, Myra B. *Complete Guide to the Elementary Learning Center.* West Nyack, N.Y.: Parker Publishing Co., 1976.

Voight, Ralph Claude. *The Learning Center Idea Book.* Invitation to Learning, vol. 3. Washington, D.C.: Acropolis Books Ltd., 1975.

Learning Packets

McLean, Howard W., and David L. Killian. *How to Construct Individualized Learning Pacs.* Dubuque, Iowa: Kendall/Hunt Publishing Co., 1973.

Russel, James D. *Modular Instruction: A Guide to the Design, Selection, Utilization and Evaluation of Modular Materials.* Minneapolis, Minn.: Burgess Publishing Co., 1974.

Ward, Patricia, and Williams, E. Craig. *Learning Packets: New Approach to Individualizing Instruction.* West Nyack, N.Y.: Parker Publishing Co., 1976.

Simulation

DeRoche, Edward F., and E. Gierl. *Creative Units for the Elementary School Teacher*. West Nyack, N.Y.: Parker Publishing Co., Inc., 1969.

Gibbs, G. *Handbook of Games and Simulation Exercises*. Beverly Hills, Calif.: Sage Publishers, 1974.

Section Four

Implementing the Student Management Dimension

7

Psychological Theories of Child Behavior

Undoubtedly, anyone who has worked in a school for more than twenty minutes knows that discipline and student management are major concerns. The student out in the hall, the waiting line by the principal's office, the teacher exploding with a reverberating shout, are all evidences of attempts to deal with misbehavior. As former teachers and principals, we know how draining, time consuming, and, at times, utterly hopeless the situation of correcting and developing long-lasting prosocial student behavior seems. For one of us the following anecdote from his own experience comes to mind:

> How vivid is the memory of blond haired, beatific looking, second grader Tommy. After two years of constant visits to the principal's office, teacher-principal-parent conferences, and a series of tried and failed plans to help Tommy from physically abusing other students—particularly little girls—at last improvement was detected. Tommy had not been sent off the playground for fighting for four consecutive days. His attention and cooperation with other students in class had been rather good. On the fifth day, Tommy's teacher and I gave each other wise smiles of self satisfaction as Tommy lead his class down the stairs, out to play. At the bottom of the stairs, beyond our vision, we heard a scuffle and then the sure tones of Tommy's strong voice yelling obscenities. Scurrying down the stairs, we saw Tommy with his red face and malice for all, biting and kicking one of the first grade *teachers*. The teacher had asked him to keep his line of students to one side of the stairs, so her class could pass. Tommy had taken offense and made this known in his not so subtle manner. Tommy's teacher and I looked at each other once again, this time with flagging spirits. As we separated I spoke feebly, "Well, at least now he's fighting people bigger than him."

We know full well that Tommy had yet to be really helped and that we somehow shoulder at least part of the blame.

Incidents such as these deflate and depress well-intentioned educators. What is to be done? Many teachers are facing populations of students that are foreign to their previous life experiences and professional preparation. School desegregation has brought tensions into the classroom among races, cultures, and economic classes. With the upsurge in heterogeneous grouping and the mainstreaming of children with emotional, physical, and cognitive disabilities, the schools are now places where educators must work with all types of children. We acknowledge this concern and are constantly reminded by other "outside of school" evidence. The National Education Association recently released a survey which indicated that more teachers are leaving the profession at a younger age than ever before.[1] One of the major reasons given was the teachers' perception of their inability to deal with students. The Gallup and Harris polls periodically survey the public about their concerns related to public schools. Cited as one of the top three concerns every year for the last twelve years was discipline.[2]

It is not coincidental that parents and educators, when looking at alternative schools, are as equally concerned with student management techniques as with curriculum. They go hand in hand. For example, a curriculum such as Alternative One, which bases individualization on learning certain prescribed, basic skills in an orderly way, would consistently have such an ordered, standard code and treatment of behavior. Popular back-to-the-basics schools are not only a return to the stressing of old fundamental rote skills but also an appeal for older forms of discipline. For a school staff to fully operate and maximize the development of students according to their philosophy and goals and objectives, there needs to be multidimensional consistency. There needs to be a congruence between the school aim in style of instruction, type of materials, activities, and the management and treatment of students. The illustration of such correspondence follows.

The illustration shows that if the school goal is to develop inquisitive individuals, then curriculum and management should flow from that purpose. Curriculum is planned around open-ended units. Methods and materials are geared for student activity and discovery. Student management also remains consistent with this school goal. Therefore, there are few fixed, absolute rules. Students are involved in determining the rules and discipline is used as an individual problem-solving activity so that the child might discover his own solutions to misbehavior. Chances of actually achieving a school's goals increase as more of the dimensions of school are placed according to purpose, plan, and consistency. Let's take a look at the

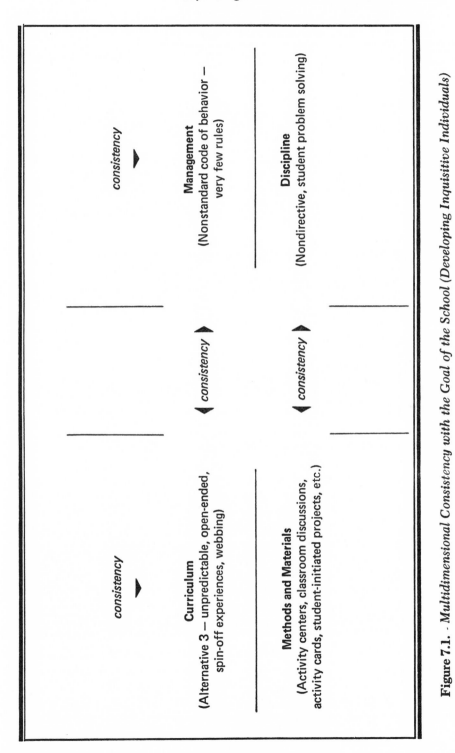

Figure 7.1. - *Multidimensional Consistency with the Goal of the School (Developing Inquisitive Individuals)*

major schools of psychological thought in dealing with children and see how they fit alongside our three alternative models.

MAJOR PSYCHOLOGICAL APPROACHES
TO CHILD BEHAVIOR

The various psychological views of the child and how he develops, provide the foundation for different educational applications. They can be roughly subsumed under three headings: the humanists, the interactionalists, and the behaviorists. The humanists view the child as intrinsically rational and capable of his own solutions. The interactionalists believe the child to be a social being who needs a reciprocal, give-and-take relationship with the outer environment in order to develop positively. The behaviorists perceive the child as being conditioned by outside forces that shape his future behavior. Although many of us involved in the daily reality of schools are not much interested in what appears to be a philosophical discourse seemingly as practical as "how many angels can dance on the top of a pin," it is our position throughout this book that a rudimentary understanding of such theory is essential if a school is to have purpose and power. After all, the educational reality of dealing with children comes out of a psychological and philosophical view of the child. One simply might look at the proliferation of best selling books on discipline for teachers, such as *Teacher Effectiveness Training* by Thomas Gordon, *I'm Ok, You're Ok—Transactional Analysis* by Thomas Harris, *Schools Without Failure* by William Glasser, and *Discipline Without Tears* by Dreikurs and Cassel, to support our contention. All of these step by step classroom application treatises, which are largely consumed by teachers, are written by psychologists or psychiatrists.

Without an understanding of the different theoretical psychologies of the child, school personnel are often using techniques of management that are at cross purposes with their professed school goals. With that in mind, let's look at the major theories.

The Humanists

The Humanists have the most optimistic view of the child. They believe that humans have tremendous capabilities for rational and creative development. The child is a born learner, constantly striving to improve himself. Within the child is an intrinsic self-motivation to learn more, to solve problems, and to grow to his fullest potential. According to the humanists, the reason that children become apathetic, rebellious, and negativistic is due to conditions of the environment that stifle or block this inner drive to excel. A. H. Maslow described this blocking as the result of an adult environment that deprives a child of progressive needs.[3] If these needs are met, then the inherent potential unfolds. Carl Rogers, perhaps the leading humanist, explained it in this way:

> Human beings have a natural potential for learning . . . this potentiality and desire for learning, for discovery, for enlargement of knowledge and experience can be released under suitable conditions. It is a tendency which can be trusted, and the whole approach to education . . . builds upon and around the student's natural desire to learn.[4]

The Interactionalists

This classification subsumes some major psychological theories that differ in many fundamental respects. However, psychoanalytical (Freudian) theory, social (Adlerian) theory, and cognitive developmental (Piagetian, Brunerian) theory all commonly believe that the child cannot be viewed apart from his environment. To explain a child's growth one must look at the corresponding tug of war going on between the child's needs and societal restrictions. It is only through this process that a child develops the kind of consciousness and reasoning to become a prosocial, cooperative being.

It must be noted here that we may be in hot water with classical Freudian company. However, we feel that the work of Erikson, Anna Freud, and Margaret Mahler puts psychoanalysis into this interactional mode. As Jerome Bruner wrote:

> One finds no internal push to growth without a corresponding external pull, for, given the nature of man as species, growth is as dependent upon a link with external amplifiers of man's powers as it is upon those powers themselves.[5]

The interactionalists do not believe in a pure inward goodness of the individual. Rather they believe that the child desires to manipulate his environment for his own needs (Freud's Id and Impulses; Adler's belonging; Piaget's Egocentrism). Yet the child develops as he runs into roadblocks to his own desires and eventually learns the system of behavior and actions within the parameters of societal boundaries.

The Behaviorists

The behaviorist rejects the humanist's idea of the inner rational drive or the interactionalist's idea of the individual's desire to manipulate and his manipulation by society. Behaviorists believe that all human behavior is a result of conditioning. A child acts the way he does because of rewards or punishment for previous behavior. For example, if a first grade child is overly loud, it is not due to an environment that suppresses his rational impulses, nor is it due to a child's desire to exercise his vocal chords without consideration of, or restrictions by, social constraints. Rather it is because that behavior has been rewarded in the past. Perhaps his parents smiled at him when he would speak in a big voice as a baby or perhaps the other classmates' giggles and laughs have given him reinforcement whenever he spoke loudly. B. F. Skinner, the most noted behaviorist, states it in this way:

> An experimental analysis shifts the determination of behavior from autonomous man to the environment—an environment responsible both for the evolution of the species and for the repertoire acquired by each member. . . . It is the autonomous inner man who is abolished and that is a step forward.[6]

Bandura has extended behaviorist theory by adding modeling to the explanation of a child being shaped by outside forces.[7] He believes that it is not only what forms of rewards or punishments a child receives when he acts, there is also an element of observation. When a child observes another person who is important to him behave in a certain way then he is likely to initiate or model that behavior. This modeling becomes even more obvious when the child observes this important person receiving rewards for the behavior.

CORRESPONDENCE TO ALTERNATIVES

To summarize, psychological theories of child behavior either view the child as an inherent self-improver, or behaving according to the resolution of his desires coming into conflict with the outside environment, or behaving only as the result of how the environment has previously rewarded or punished him.

These three positions of child behavior establish a framework for the various teacher techniques in managing a classroom and disciplining students. Each position and subsequent techniques to be discussed in the next chapter correspond to the three alternative models. We may illustrate this correspondence as follows:

Schooling Dimensions	Alternative 1	Alternative 2	Alternative 3
Curriculum	Predictable	Predictable/ Unpredictable	Unpredictable
Psychology of Child Behavior	Behaviorists	Interaction- alists	Humanists

In the predictable curriculum (Alternative One), the school staff wants to insure certain learning outcomes. The teacher is the authority. Instruction of knowledge is sequenced in steps for each student to master. The child is viewed as floundering without constant adult assistance of praise and reprimand. Behavior is viewed in the same context. A child, when left alone without continued outside reinforcement, will behave in an irrational manner. The role of the teacher is to have in mind a standard of acceptable behavior and to shape a student's actions accordingly.

In the unpredictable curriculum (Alternative Three), learning is viewed as a child's active exploration to discover for himself. The teacher helps move with one child's interests by adding materials, suggesting further activities, and probing with questions. He or she has an abiding faith in the child as a learner who, when left to his own doings, will develop novel responses. As to behavior, the rationale becomes that of the humanists. If the child is allowed to reflect on his own actions, then, with the help of discussion with the teacher, the child will realize the best course of action for himself.

In Alternative Two, the school staff has taken the position that a child needs the opportunity to discover for himself as well as learn certain skills that are felt to be essential in later life. Therefore, learning is at different times directed as well as open-ended. A child's behavior is viewed as a part of the process of learning. The child is allowed flexibility of action within understood boundaries. The teacher with this interactional view of the child is a delineator of boundaries, one who encourages self-reflection but also imposes and enforces the real societal limits.

NOTES

1.   "Who is the Classroom Teacher," *Today's Education* (Nov./ Dec. 1977): 11.

2. George Gallup, "Ninth Annual Gallup Poll on the Public's Attitudes toward the Public Schools," in *Phi Delta Kappan* (September 1977): 33-48.

3. A. H. Maslow, *Motivation and Personality.* (New York: Harper & Row, 1954).

4. Carl Rogers, *Freedom to Learn: A View of What Education Might Become* (Columbus, Ohio: C. E. Merrill, 1969), pp. 157–58.

5. Jerome Bruner et. al., *Studies in Cognitive Growth* (New York: Wiley, 1966), p. 6.

6. B. F. Skinner, *Beyond Freedom and Dignity* (New York: Alfred A. Knopf, 1971), pp. 214–15.

7. Albert Bandura, *Social Learning Theory* (Englewood Cliffs, N.J.: Prentice-Hall, Inc., 1976).

8

Alternative Methods and Strategies for Teachers

Mr. Johnson is an intermediate teacher who styles himself and is regarded by others as a progressive, open classroom teacher. His classroom is a constant buzz of activity. Students move freely to different activity centers and he is constantly mixing with them. He is now discussing a science project with Kevin, something about creating a relief map of the moon. Out of the corner of his eye, he spots Matthew with a hammer in his hand moving quickly towards Mary who has spent the entire morning painting a historic village. Mr. Johnson remembers the feud that Matthew has recently had with Mary. Without hesitation he yells, "Matthew, stop that. Sit over in this chair and the next time I have to talk to you, you will stay here for recess." Matthew sulks as he walks over to the chair, hangs his head down and the class which had become hushed, returns to its normal noise level.

A scene such as this happens often. If you asked Mr. Johnson to pick out, of our cited alternative models, which one he operates in, he would say Alternative Three. "I always stress spontaneity and creativity; learning must be turned over to the student. Only he or she knows what is of personal interest. Most schools restrict the type of learning that I encourage." A further question is asked. "Mr. Johnson, do you think that the way you handle discipline in the classroom such as in the case with Matthew is consistent with your instructional philosophy?" Mr. Johnson replies "Yes, I think so. After all, let's be realistic. I give the students so much freedom to learn that I need to crack down on those who abuse the freedom. If not, those few would ruin it for all of us. Specifically in Matthew's case, he would have ruined Mary's work, maybe started a fight, and the class would have been in an uproar." Okay, Mr. Johnson has made his case. Now let's look closely at the multidimensional consistency of philosophy, instruction, and student management to assess Mr. Johnson's effectiveness.

A. Mr. Johnson's philosophy is clearly Alternative Three. The goal of education is to enable the student to go beyond society as it now exists and to exercise free choice. The function of his classroom is to provide a supportive environment for the student to explore and progress according to his own interests and ability.

B. Mr. Johnson's instructional methods are also clearly Alternative Three. Activity centers are the core of instruction. Students develop their own projects, schedule themselves through the day, and learn the fundamentals of reading, writing, and arithmetic indirectly as a result of their projects. There are no groups for instruction. Mr. Johnson meets with students through the day. He checks what they are doing, suggests some further activities, and, when needed, gives instruction on an individual tutorial basis.

Therefore, there are no inconsistencies between philosophy and instructional methods. Now the Alternative Three disciplinary approach is based on a humanistic interpretation of behavior. The belief being that children are inherently rational beings. They need to realize and discover for themselves those forms of behavior which are most comfortable and acceptable to their emerging selves. In the same way that the classroom environment should encourage self-exploration to promote student's cognitive functioning, so should the environment be facilitative of a child's social and affective development. Now comes the rub. How does Mr. Johnson carry out the management function?

C. Mr. Johnson has stated that he views student misbehavior within the context of abusing freedom. In such a room as his, unless he deals directly to prevent disruption, one student will get the entire class going and ruin it for all. By being forceful, he is able to meet his philosophical goals.

You, as a reader, may be taking sides with Mr. Johnson, since you probably have an inkling that two college professors are now about to rip Mr. Johnson's approach apart piece by piece. You are correct to a point. We want to show the incongruence of Mr. Johnson's student management with his otherwise very sound and coherent running of the classroom. We are not questioning his effectiveness in dealing with students and we are not judging whether his approach is right or wrong. We are simply asking him and you to look at whether he is practicing what he preaches.

Since he really does operate an instructional classroom based on a child-centered approach to learning, what a confusing message it must be to his students when he deals with behavior. On one hand, he is saying, "I trust you students to learn and choose for yourself, I will help and encourage you. Explore, don't be afraid to fail. After all, you are the controller of your own learning." Yet, on the other hand, he is saying, "When you misbehave, I must correct you and tell you what to do. I am doing this for your sake and the class. If not, if left to yourselves, there would be anarchy." Maybe we have oversimplified, but his students are receiving two opposite messages at the same time.

If he does trust the children's desire to learn, then logically he should trust their desire to learn about controlling their own behavior. However, his habitual response of commanding and moving the student away from the situation saps any learning from the situation. Instead of the student being encouraged to reflect on his or her own behavior and to make choices as to what would be better, he or she becomes subservient to the teacher's authority. Now he or she behaves according to the consequences inflicted by the teacher (such as a stern word or isolation) and not because of the situational consideration of the feelings, physical hurt, or individual rights of others.

Mr. Johnson's typical method of discipline is aligned with behaviorist theory and more indicative of Alternative One philosophy and instruction. To our thinking, he is somewhat negating the effectiveness of reaching his goals for students. If one views each dimension as having a consistency rating of one unit of effectiveness. Mr. Johnson's rating would look like this.

Mr. Johnson's Multi-Dimensional Consistency Pattern
Philosophy — Alternative 3

1 unit	no unit
▼	▼
Instructional methods	Discipline
(Alternative 3)	(Alternative 1)

Out of a possible score of two units, he receives one.

You, as an educational leader, should be able to gauge the consistency of your teachers' management style with your school's goals. A specific description will follow of what teacher behaviors to note as indications of each of the three alternative modes. In the subsequent chapter, we will take a similar look at what the principal's behaviors are indicative of in dealing with students.

ALTERNATIVE ONE— PREDICTABLE PRACTICES

Behaviorist Approach

In this alternative, the goal of education is to prepare the student to fit into society. Individualized instruction in such a school classroom is a systematic approach of moving a student through a linear progression of content. Students are managed according to specific, clear standards of behavior. The teacher explains the rules of the classroom and his or her procedures for dealing with wrong doers. If a student is a chronic behavior problem, then the teacher plots a sequential plan for eliminating the undesirable actions and at the same time promoting the desired standard. Some of the teacher behaviors are as follows:

> Direct Commands—The teacher tells a child in a stern manner to stop what he is doing and tells him what he is supposed to be doing.
>
> Physical Intervention—When direct commands are not working, the teacher puts a firm hand on the student and shows him what to do. Usually this is accompanied by repeated commands.
>
> Isolation—The teacher verbally commands or physically removes the child to a place removed from the other students. The student is told to sit there and not to return to the class until told to do so. The isolation area is kept bare of any form of stimulation.
>
> Dire Consequences—The teacher states to the child that if he or she continues the deviant action, there will be a painful result (i.e., he or she will be sent to principal's office; a note will be sent home to parents; he or she will have to stay in at recess or after school, write something 100 times, etc.).
>
> Reinforcing Proper Behavior—Through either verbal praise ("I'm so proud of you." "Good job." "That's the way a good student acts."), material rewards (candy, an extra drink, tokens that can be redeemed for such desired items as comic books, pencils, and games), or situational rewards (extra free time, longer recess, appointment to teacher helper), the teacher reinforces the correct behaviors when they occur.
>
> Ignoring Misbehavior—Usually done in conjunction with reinforcing, the teacher gives no attention to the deviance but instead waits for the student to act in an acceptable manner, then gives reinforcement.

An Example of a Behaviorist Teacher

Ms. Shaper tells her second grade class at the beginning of the year that these are the rules:

1. Everyone is to come into class, sit down without talking, and wait for class to begin.

2. There is to be no gum chewing.
3. No talking.
4. No fighting or ruining property.
5. Everyone is to stay in one's seat unless permission is received from the teacher.
6. At recess, lunch, and in the hall, students must remain in line without pushing or shoving.

She then states that anyone who does not follow the rules will first be talked to; a second time, will be moved to a corner; a third time, will stay in at recess; and a fourth time, will go to the principal's office. She has now set the stage for the year. Behavior has been explained along with the procedural matters of discipline.

Ms. Shaper, true to her belief that she must follow through with her rules, treats her students according to the disciplinary steps. After six weeks, Elsie, a misbehaving child, has been to the principal three times. The teacher realizes that her procedure is not working and that she needs to focus on the most undesirable behavior first. Ms. Shaper feels that if Elsie could only calm down and get to work right away in the morning, the rest of her day would be smoother. She recollects all of the times Elsie has been involved in a shoving match during morning milk money collection and talking during attendance taking. With this in mind, and knowing that Elsie loves to be the leader, she and Elsie meet after school. Ms. Shaper says, "Elsie you have been to the principal's office three times already and you are always in trouble. I know that you would like to do better. I have a plan for you. Starting tomorrow, if you can come into class in the morning, sit down immediately, do not talk, and keep your hands folded, then, after I take morning attendance, you'll get a gold check. When you have earned five checks, you can bring the milk money to the office. Of course, if you don't behave you will still be treated the same as before." The next morning, Ms. Shaper notices Elsie trying to be good, a few times she turns to talk but the teacher tries to ignore those slips. When Elsie sits back upright, she tells her how well she is doing and to keep it up just for a few more minutes.

ALTERNATIVE THREE—UNPREDICTABLE PRACTICES

The goal of education is to promote individual creativity that goes beyond the conventions of society. The premise is that if students can think in nonconventional ways, then, as adults, they will have the capacity to solve problems that have defied conventional thinking. This capacity of creative and rational problem solving is believed to exist within each individual. The teacher's role in instruction is to provide hands-on, open-ended materials that will require the student to tap this inner reserve. Along with an activity-centered instructional approach is a humanistic orientation of regard for individual codes of behavior. Behavior is not judged to be appropriate or inappropriate to classroom standards, but rather whether the behavior has value to the student in developing his or her inner potential. In other words, if a student is a daydreamer who drifts around the classroom in a perpetual fog, the teacher does not judge this to be deviant. As long as the student is not putting himself or herself into danger or interfering with others, and is able to carry out his or her own learning, then the actions are okay. The humanist teacher, when observing that the child's behavior is interfering, takes a nonjudgmental position of helping the student clarify his actions and come up with his own solutions.

Some of the teacher behaviors are as follows:

Glancing or Looking at the Child—The teacher simply observes the behavior without comment. The glance is not one of threat or intimidation, but simply one that nonverbally says, "I see what you are doing, you can take care of yourself but if you wish my help, I am here."

Reflective Statements—The student's behavior is clarified by the teacher according to its effect. Again, it is nonjudgmental with the teacher conveying empathy and trust that the child is capable of his own correction. For example, Stevie throws his book, the teacher says "Stevie, you have thrown your book, you must be very mad to do that."

Helping Statements—The teacher does not scold or tell the student what to do, instead he or she asks the student if his or her help is needed to correct the situation. This might be done after a reflective statement in which the child continues to vent his or her anger.

Conference—The teacher and the child discuss on a one-to-one basis what is troubling the child. The teacher spends most of the time listening, rephrasing the student's opinions, nodding sympathetically, and asking questions that prod the student to find a solution to the problem. The teacher does not interject with his or her own opinions or solutions. Only if the child asks, may the teacher do so.

An Example of a Humanist Teacher

Ms. Sympatico opens her first day of class, sitting in the rug area with her primary grade students. She asks them what kinds of interests they have, how they wish to arrange the room, and what materials they might bring from home. After explaining about the various activity centers, particularly the one labeled "Communication," which has a C.B. set and several activity cards listed on ways to use the set, she asks the class if there are any rules for the classroom that they would like to make. She says, "Let's only have a few rules that we can all agree are important." The students suggest and agree upon three: (1) Don't fight; (2) Don't scream; and (3) Let's be friends. With this, the year has begun.

How is Ms. Sympatico to carry out her humanistic philosophy of discipline? She believes that discipline is a self-responsibility for students to realize and carry out for themselves. The first three days proceed smoothly with only a visual look or reflective word needed here and there for the children to stop screaming or fighting. On the fourth day, a potentially explosive situation occurs. Tony, who is quite large for his age, gives a yell and runs across the room at little Mollie. Ms. Sympatico's visual look has no influence on the charging boy. She quickly intercepts Tony and standing between he and Mollie says "Tony, you are yelling and running at Mollie. You would think that she has done something to you." Tony keeps trying to get around to Mollie. Ms. Sympatico holds him off with these words: "It looks as though you need my help to solve what is bothering you. Let's you and I go to the conference area and have a talk. After you have quieted down, Mollie can join you in solving this problem."

By handling the situation in this way, Ms. Sympatico has left the thinking about and solution of the problem with Tony—a problem he may later work out with Mollie.

Ms. Sympatico's reasoning is that it is not the teacher's problem, it is Tony's and possibly Mollie's. Since self-discipline is her goal, she does not wish to control or solve his problems. After all, if she steps in and tells Tony what to do, then he will learn to follow what others tell him, instead of considering consequences and learning what is the best action for himself. Ms. Sympatico feels that people should make their own decisions. If they act only in accord with authority, she fears that they will not be responsible when authority is absent. Besides, she thinks that such unquestioning individuals have been the cause of some of the great atrocities in history.

The conversation begins.

> "Tony, you looked so mad."
> "Mollie spit at me."
> "Mollie, spit at you?"
> "Yeah, hit me in the hair."
> "You got mad when that happened?"
> "Yeah, she's always picking on me."
> "You think that Mollie doesn't like you."
> "Yeah, yesterday she . . ."

ALTERNATIVE TWO—UNPREDICTABLE
AND PREDICTABLE PRACTICES

The goal of education in Alternative Two is to prepare students to become flexible enough to adjust to society, as well as to delineate and solve problems. This person is thus able to work within the system to promote reform. The school places equal emphasis on rudimentary, directive skill training, as well as problem-solving exploration. Interactional psychology, which is the basis of discipline in Alternative Two, holds the assumption that the individual grows within the context of the outer world. It is when the individual asserts his or her egocentric desires against the will of others that he or she becomes socialized. It is with this growing awareness of other people's rights and societal restraints, that one acquires a consciousness. This developed consciousness can later save the person the actual pain of testing the limits of society by knowing the probable consequences of the contemplated action. The teacher plays a crucial role in the child's developing conscience by making clear the boundaries of behavior and using logical consequences when transgressions occur. Unlike the behaviorist, the teacher does not shape uniform behavior through conditioning. Instead, he or she is concerned with the child's internalization of discipline and uses clarification, discussion, and problem solving methods. However, unlike the humanist, he or she is not satisfied with any form of behavior chosen by the student. He or she does not take a nonjudgmental attitude. Solutions are arrived at that must be agreeable to the teacher. Student input is solicited, and the teacher enforces the plan of action.

Some of the teacher behaviors are as follows:

Confronting with Clarification of Consequences—The student is told what his behavior is doing to others.

Questioning Consequences—The teacher asks the student to tell what he or she is doing and in what ways the student's behavior is helping or hurting him or her, as well as others.

Having Others Confront the Student—The teacher convenes a small or large group meeting composed of the student and those that the student has bothered. The teacher guides the discussion so that the other students tell the offender to his face what effect his behavior has upon them.

Pressing for Solution—After an individual or group session with the offending student, the teacher asks the student to come up with a solution. If none is forthcoming, the teacher suggests a few possibilities. If the student still does not respond, a teacher solution is imposed.

Commitment to the Solution—Once a solution is agreed to or imposed, the student makes a pledge, either written or oral, to the teacher or group to carry it out.

Enforcement of Commitment through Logical Consequences—The teacher enforces the solution by making the student responsible for his or her commitment. If the student does not follow through, then a logical consequence takes place. A logical consequence is tied to the immediate breakdown of behavior. This concept will be explained in the example of an interactional teacher.

Example of an Interactional Teacher

Mr. Ilg begins the first day of school meeting with his class of fourth graders. He tells them about the schedule of reading, writing, and mathematics during the morning and activity and project centers in the afternoon. He explains the need for rules so that all students can live together, be comfortable with each other, and do their best work throughout the year. He then tells the students that he has a few rules that must be followed and would like some suggestions as to other rules that might be important. Before putting his rules on the board, he divides the chalkboard with a line and solicits student suggestions for rules. He writes the seven rules that are suggested on one side of the board and then on the other side he writes his required four rules. The board looks like this:

Class Rules	*Required Teacher Rules*
1. Don't Swear.	1. Come into the room quietly at all times.
2. No running in the halls.	
3. Don't Hit.	2. Let other students do their work without interruption.
4. No bringing in jack knives.	
5. Don't sass the teacher.	3. If someone needs help, help him or her.
6. Don't yell.	
7. Raise your hand to go to the bathroom.	4. Put back any materials that you use.

Mr. Ilg now explains how some of the student rules would fit under his rules and collapses both lists into one set. The new list is as follows:

Class Rules

1. Come into the room quietly at all times (no running in the halls).

2. Let other students do their work without interruption (don't swear, don't hit, don't yell, don't sass).

3. If someone needs help, help him or her.

4. Put back any materials that you use.

5. Raise your hand to get the teacher's attention during seatwork.

6. Do not bring to school any sharp or hard objects without me knowing about them.

With this done, the teacher explains how he and the other students will try to help anyone who has trouble following the rules. The school year has truly begun, when two weeks later, Francisco has taunted the other three children in his reading group to the point where Bubba complains to Mr. Ilg that no one can get any work done. Mr. Ilg has noticed Francisco's constant monologue, jokes, innuendos, and high drama. Up until this point he handled the situation by telling Francisco to stop what he was doing and to get back to work. Now that Mr. Ilg is aware of Francisco's enlarging sphere of irritation, he moves more forcefully into the situation. When the next smart remark is heard, the teacher says, "Francisco, when you say that, I have to stop my work and it bothers me and it bothers the other children. Would you please stop!" This is sufficient for ten minutes, until Julie topples to the floor with a crash. Francisco has just pulled the chair from under her. Mr. Ilg calls the boy over and questions him, "How does bothering Julie, help you? What good is it doing for you?" The lad looks sheepishly down, says that he is sorry and will be good, and returns to his seat. That afternoon, Leon is tripped by Francisco's nonchalantly placed foot which happens to be stretched out a full yard. Mr. Ilg pulls the furious Leon off Francisco. Bubba, Julie, and Leon are muttering about how they are going to "get" Francisco. Mr. Ilg says that he wants to speak to all four of them at recess time.

The meeting begins with all participants seated in a circle, facing each other. Mr. Ilg begins, "Francisco, you have been annoying me and the others in your group. We need to do something about your behavior. I want to go around to everyone and have each of you tell Francisco exactly what he does to bother you and how it makes you feel." One at a time, each speaks. Much emotion is expressed. Mr. Ilg carefully guides the encounter so that statements are directed to Francisco about his behavior and its effect. He does not allow any statements or words as to Francisco's character (such as stupid, mean, ugly, or obnoxious). Finally, everyone has had their turn including Mr. Ilg. Francisco is obviously uncomfortable, head down with eyes beginning to water. Finally, Francisco is asked if he has anything to say about his behavior and what effect it is having on him. With a few mumbled words of being sorry and then silence, Mr. Ilg continues the meeting. "Our job now is to suggest ways that Francisco can behave better and ways that we can help him." A plan is developed that calls for Francisco to work at his desk removed from the group for the first twenty minutes of each reading period. If he keeps to himself and is quiet, he can then move back to the group for the last ten minutes. One student each day will check with Francisco twice during his removed time to see if he needs any help with his work. If the plan works then each week Francisco will have five additional minutes with the group. Francisco agrees to the plan, it is written up as a contract and he signs it. Mr. Ilg will enforce Francisco's commitment. If Francisco does not carry out his pledge to quite bothering his group mates when he joins them, then the logical consequence will be to extend his time away from the group. (For clarification purposes, a nonlogical consequence would be to send a note to his parents, keep him after school, take away his free time, etc. As one can see, punishment of this nature has no immediate relationship to the misbehavior.) The next three days Francisco does very nicely in his fifteen-minute removal time. Upon returning to the group, on the fourth day, all goes well until an awry paper plane hits Francisco in the face.

TAKING ISSUE

One might scratch his or her head and feel that the three distinct approaches to discipline are not so clearly distinct in real life. In looking at a particular teacher, some teacher behaviors that may come to mind are commands, personal conferences, and praise. They seem to smack of both behaviorist and interactional psychology. How does a school leader categorize this teacher? To fully answer this important question requires many levels of understanding.

First, very rare are the times that real behavior fits exactly into theoretical categories. Theoretical categories such as humanists, interactionalists, and behaviorists are attempts to conceptualize the different approaches to viewing and treating children.

Secondly, what the theoretical categories provide is a perspective to view *the role* that each party in the student-teacher relationship plays and the *intent* behind the teacher behavior. The humanists have the intent of giving the child maximum control over his own behavior. The behaviorists have the intent of giving maximum power to the teacher to control the child's behavior. The interactionalists have the intent of sharing the power between teacher and child.

Thirdly, a teacher who uses cross techniques (and many do) must be assessed according to the intent. Does he or she have a specific intent to maximize or share power? If there is no intent, then the teacher is simply using whatever techniques or strategies available to survive on a daily basis. There is no thought to goals and ultimate effectiveness. There is no thought as to the implied consequences of tactics or the desired direction of individual growth. Therefore, this teacher could use strategies from all three psychological camps but the application is truly "mindless."

However, if the teacher does have a reasoned intent behind his or her tactics then he or she again may use behavior from all three psychological camps. The application is directional and purposeful. For example, a teacher who wishes each student to have the capacity for total self-responsibility (humanistic belief), might use behavioral or interactional behaviors with some children (such as reinforcement, encountering, and contracting) because nonjudgment techniques are not working. However, the teacher will plan to use more humanistic techniques with the child after he has responded to the other approaches. His or her intent is to ultimately use strategies of less teacher control that maximize the student's ability to acquire greater freedom to solve his own behavioral problems. Therefore, a teacher may use an eclectic approach, but if he or she has a commitment to a goal of education and thus a purpose for discipline, he or she will constantly be moving approaches towards that psychological model consistent with his or her philosophy.

Perhaps this explanation has clarified the type of teacher or teachers that you have on your staff. Following are some additional questions that you might ask yourself.

1. Do your teachers have a conscious intent in disciplining students?
2. Is it consistent with your school goal and alternative model (i.e. predictable curriculum with behaviorism, unpredictable and predictable curriculum with interactionalism, unpredictable curriculum with humanism)?

If the answer to question number one is no, then you need a series of consciousness raising sessions about the psychological consequences and implications of various disciplinary approaches. (Perhaps having the staff read this chapter and excerpts from some of the suggested books would be a springboard to discussion.)

If the answer to question number one is yes, and the answer to two is uncertain—then review your school goals and your alternative model and decide which orientation to managing students is congruent.

If the answer to question number one is yes and the answer to two is no, have brainstorming sessions as to what typical classroom teacher behaviors should be tried out on misbehaving students to be more congruent with school goals and model. Also what are the actions that the principal, supervisor, and special personnel would engage in when treating students that would correspond (this will be discussed in the next chapter).

If the answer to question numbers one and two are yes, then you need no advice. (Perhaps you could give us some help in further clarifying this issue.)

SOME OBSERVATIONS ON TEACHER BEHAVIOR

Regardless of philosophical and psychological persuasion, in our review of the multitude of popular approaches to managing students, we have not come across any psychological rationale for some common teacher actions that exist in many schools. In any school that is ready to reappraise itself and to make changes for greater effectiveness, a hard look must be taken at the following teacher behaviors.

Guilt Inducing Statements—The teacher tries to change the child by telling him or her what a disappointment the child is to the teacher and the class. Such statements that play on guilt are these: "Here I thought that you were such big students and could be left alone. I've spent so much time doing things for you and this is what I get."

Humiliation—The teacher embarrasses the student in front of the others by placing the child in front of the classroom to stand, or in the corner with a dunce cap, or to sit in a refrigerator box, etc.

Ridicule—Statements to the child, such as "How can anyone be so dumb?" "Don't you ever think?" "That was ridiculous," "You act like a baby," all accomplish this purpose.

Sarcasm—Adult use of sarcasm can be found in expressions like "That's terrific, you're really a smart kid to do that"; "You're going to make yourself really popular acting that way."

Screaming—The teacher blows up at a child and slams a book down, pounds his or her hand, and yells loudly. This initial episode usually frightens that student into momentary submission.

Inflicting Physical Pain—Slapping, pulling by the ear, pressured grips, and hitting with a ruler or paddle are only a few of a numerous ways to inflict pain.

Behaviorists, interactionalists, and humanists despite their multitude of differences, all concur that the above techniques are ineffectual. At best, they make a child momentarily submit, at worst they give the child a model of how to act when he or she has power over others. In between are levels of resentment, revenge, and passive disobedience. On grounds of effectiveness alone they should not be used (not to mention such other rationales as human rights and dignity).

One of us remembers the afternoon when an irate parent called to inform the principal that Ms. Queen, the fourth-grade teacher had slapped her child across the face. Knowing Ms. Queen as one of the most composed and gentle of teachers, the principal blithely remarked "I'm sorry, you must be mistaken, Ms. Queen would never do such a thing. Let me talk to your child." He then asked the child to give his side of the story. The child nervously said that he had been out in the hall, playing the piano with his feet when Ms. Queen came out of her room and asked him to stop. She came back a few minutes later, pulled him down and slapped him. Listening rather incredulously to the story, the principal asked to speak to his mother again. He told her, "I'm not saying you're son is telling an untruth but he might be distorting the episode in some ways. You can be assured that Ms. Queen would not do such a thing. I'll talk to her and call you right back." The principal walked in to Ms. Queen's classroom and saw a rather dejected figure. He asked her what was wrong. She looked up and said, "You wouldn't believe this, I still don't believe it, but this afternoon I completely lost my cool and slapped a child." So much for the principal's credibility with this one parent! However, the point being made is that it is relatively easy for us to analyze and suggest teacher behaviors as appropriate and to reject others as simply unsound. It is another matter to accept that we as humans do sometimes explode and "lose our cool." We accept and expect this, but we also view this as an extraordinary occurrence of error, not to be used as a pattern for dealing with students.

SUGGESTIONS FOR FURTHER READING

Behaviorist Approaches

Axelrod, Saul. *Behavior Modification for the Classroom Teacher.* New York: McGraw-Hill, 1977.

Blackham, Garth, and Silverman, Adolph. *Modification of Child and Adolescent Behavior.* 2d ed. Belmont, California: Wadsworth Publishing Co., 1975.

Dobson, James. *Dare to Discipline.* Wheaton, Illinois: Tyndale House Publishers, 1970.

Engelmann, Siegfred. *Preventing Failure in the Primary Grades.* New York: Simon and Schuster, 1969.

Homme, Lloyd. *How to Use Contingency Contracting in the Classroom.* Champaign, Illinois: Research Press, 1970.

Walker, James E., and Thomas M. Shea. *Behavior Modification: A Practical Approach for Educators.* St. Louis: C. V. Mosby, 1976.

Humanist Approaches

Axline, Virginia M. *Play Therapy.* New York: Ballantine Books, 1969.

Gordon, Thomas. *T. E. T.: Teacher Effectiveness Training.* New York: Peter H. Wyden, 1975.

Moustakas, Clark. *The Authentic Teacher.* Cambridge, Mass.: Howard A. Doyle, 1972.

Raths, Louis E.; Harmin, Merrill; and Simon, Sidney B. *Values and Teaching: Working with Values in the Classroom.* Columbus, Ohio: Charles E. Merrill, 1966.

Rogers, Carl R. *Freedom to Learn.* Columbus, Ohio: Charles E. Merrill, 1969.

Interactional Approaches

Babcock, Dorothy, and Keepers, Terry. *Raising Kids O.K.* New York: Grove Press, Inc., 1976.

Berne, Eric. *Games People Play: the Psychology of Human Relationships.* New York: Grove Press, 1964.

Dreikurs, Rudolf, and Cassel, Pearl. *Discipline Without Tears.* New York: Hawthorne Books, Inc., 1972.

Freed, Alvyn M. *TA for Kids (and Grown Ups, Too).* Los Angeles, California, Jalmar Press, Inc., 1971.

Glasser, William. *Schools Without Failure.* New York: Harper & Row, 1969.

Harris, Thomas A. *I'M OK—You're OK: A Practical Guide to Transactional Analysis.* New York: Harper & Row, 1969.

Redl, Fritz and Wineman, David. *When We Deal with Children: Selected Writings.* New York: Free Press, 1972.

9

Alternative Methods and Strategies for the Administrator

What's happening in the principal's office?

Third grader, James, is sent to the principal's office for misbehaving. He walks in hesitantly, lower lip trembling, and eyes on the verge of tears. The secretary tells him to wait, Mr. Stern will see him shortly. James takes a seat, cowers in the corner, and keeps his head lowered. A few minutes later, the office door opens, Mr. Stern, with a look of anger, beckons him to come in. The door closes behind them. An angry man's voice is heard punctuated by stern statements. The only sound on the boy's part is an occasional whimpering, "Yes, Sir" and "I'm sorry, Sir." The door opens and James leaves. His eyes are red with tears. In the hall, he averts everyone's glance by keeping his head bowed and his eyes covered by the crook of his elbow. A few teachers notice what has transpired and one is overheard saying, "Mr. Stern is too hard on children. He has no feelings for them. No wonder they're so afraid of him. I feel so guilty when I send a child to the office."

Is Mr. Stern correct in his role as disciplinarian?

Third grader, Josué is also sent to his principal's office for misbehaving. He walks in still angry from what has happened to him in a fight. However, his step is sure, no hesitancy, almost as if he was looking forward to seeing Mr. Condon. He walks directly into the open door of the principal's office which opens into the hallway. Josué says, "Mr. Condon, the teacher thought that I had better talk to you." Mr. Condon closes the door. The boy's voice is heard often, only interrupted with an occasional adult question. The meeting ends with Josué leaving the office with a smile on his face and a farewell. "See you later Mr. Condon. It was good talking with you." A group of teachers sitting in the adjacent lounge have noticed the goings on. One teacher remarks to the others, "Mr. Condon is such a pushover. He never does anything to children sent to his office. Why, the students love to go talk with him."

Is Mr. Condon correct in his role as disciplinarian?

Third grader Darryl has been caught cheating and has been directed by the teacher to go immediately to the principal's office. Darryl moves along, with no great eagerness towards. Ms. Ernest's door. He is obviously embarrassed. The secretary has him sent immediately into the inner room. Ms. Ernest, in a businesslike manner, says hello to him and closes the door. Considerable discussion takes place. The voices of Darryl and Ms. Ernest are heard about equally. There are no variations in sound levels. A serious matter of fact tone to both voices continues throughout. The principal eventually comes out and asks the secretary to get Darryl's teacher. After she arrives, and further discussion takes place, all three leave the office. Darryl returns to his class looking serious but unbowed. Darryl is clutching a piece of paper in his hand. Two teachers passing through the hall at this same time are shaking their heads vigorously at each other. One has said, "Ms. Ernest needs to be less serious with kids. She makes them feel like they have to carry the world on their shoulders. After all, they're just kids. She should loosen up and relax." The other counters with, "I can't believe you think that. She already is too loose. She never gets mad at them. She needs to tell them off and make them mind."

Is Ms. Ernest correct in her role as disciplinarian?

WHAT IS THE CORRECT ROLE?

The answer must be sought in the school's desired goals and purposes. No one can put up incontestable empirical validation that one role is more advantageous than another (although researchers have certainly tried). For example, if the role of Mr. Stern is part of the predictable behavioristic goal of the school (Alternative One), then there is a complementary match. Mr. Stern is reinforcing what the teachers do and vice versa. On the other hand, if Mr. Stern is part of an unpredictable, humanistic school (Alternative Three) or an unpredictable-predictable, interactional school, then the staff and he are at cross-purposes. If the school has no direction, then anything is legitimate and Mr. Stern as well as each staff member can continue doing their "own thing." Any effect on children is chaotic and cancelled out as the student travels from person to person.

The only way to determine if the principal is effective as a disciplinarian is to peg that role into the fabric of the school. Each dimension of schooling should reflect back to an overall purpose. As stated before, power increases in having students become what is desired as the various dimensions of schooling are congruent with the desired outcome. This is illustrated in Figure 9.1.

Without such clarity there will always remain some bothersome questions about the role of the leader as a disciplinarian. The principal is a disciplinarian, this is an indisputable fact. Let's not kid ourselves about the reason that such a huge, disproportionate number of males hold the principal's position. This is because of an antiquated and chauvinistic but still persistent belief that authoritarianism and maleness go together. The principal is often likened to a blustery sea captain with the school as his ship. One often hears principals referred to by lay persons as a captain running a tight or loose ship. Whether a person in this leadership capacity desires it or not, the community expects him or her to be responsible for the overall behavior and order of students. Therefore, it is not an issue of whether to be or not to be a conveyor of order (a disciplinarian) but rather what kind.

Without an overall consensus of school purpose which would illuminate the correct form of discipline, the principal must grope and rationalize for himself. When a child is sent to the principal's office, what has top priority? Does one have to unwaveringly support the teacher's position, punish the child, and ignore the child's side of the issue? After all don't teachers need to know that the principal is there to back up their dictates and classroom regulations? Yet, what about the child, isn't he entitled to be heard out? If the child has a more plausible explanation than the teacher's, shouldn't the truth fall where it may, even if it means siding with the child against the teacher? What does that do for staff morale? What about all the reading one does about the importance of a child's self-concept and not setting up failure situations that might emotionally bruise a student for life? These are profound questions the principal so often must answer for himself.

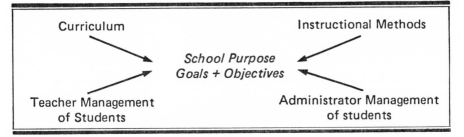

Figure 9.1. *Congruence between the Dimensions of Schooling and the Desired Outcome*

If the school has no congruency and thus no consensus of purpose, the principal knows that regardless of his or her actions, he or she will be undermined and criticized by some, praised by others, and ignored by the rest. It is little wonder that a principal, after being pinned to the office hours on end by a parade of teacher-sent students, can become bitter. The principal resents the teachers' expectations of him or her as a miraculous curer of their failures. He or she might think, "What does Mr. H. expect for me to do in a fifteen-minute office session with Clarence Bad News when he hasn't been able to do anything with him all year. He must think that I have a messianic touch. Why can't he take care of his own problems?"

Providing specific guideposts as to how the principal should function is of little use without knowing the schools direction. Of course, we could list some general do's and don't's that we favor (i.e. be patient and calm, treat each child as an individual, listen to all sides of the issues, etc.), but these are holisms and not practical applicators. Practical applicators can be prescribed in terms of consistency with a particular school model. It is within the context of the described three school models that we can propose consistent modes of operation that a principal can use with students and thus complement and reinforce the strategies being used by staff. The staffing procedure in chapter 20 will provide a handle for staff involvement and support for dealing with individual students.

ALTERNATIVE MODES OF DEALING
WITH STUDENTS

In this section, we will proceed through the behaviorist (Alternative One), humanist (Alternative Three), and interactionalist (Alternative Two) approaches to discipline as applied to the principal. We will return to the cases involving Mr. Stern, Mr. Condon, and Ms. Ernest as examples of the three positions and provide a detailed explanation of what actually might transpire between student and principal. We are now assuming that Mr. Stern, Ms. Ernest, and Mr. Condon are using tactics that are consistent with their school's goals and objectives.

Behaviorist Approaches

Description.   Mr. Stern is the principal of a school which is committed to basic academic excellence. Learning the skills required to be successful in society are stressed along with those age-old values of respect for elders, loyalty, and obedience. The school is rooted firmly in Alternative One. The curriculum is prescribed, regulated, and sequenced for each student. Misbehavior is viewed as a deterrent to learning and is dealt with quickly so as to get the student back on the right track. Mr. Stern and his staff use a behaviorist approach to discipline. There are clear standards of acceptable behavior and they use a system of reinforcement and punishment to help students act appropriately.

Guideposts for dealing with students. The behaviorist principal makes his or her authority apparent. Being sent to the principal's office is a serious matter in itself. The student is to view such a teacher action as a serious form of punishment. The student does not receive any form of positive reinforcement during the visit. He or she is spoken to in a stern manner. The student is told what he or she has done wrong, what he or she needs to do in order to behave correctly, and what the consequences of continued misbehavior will be in the future. The principal may use one or a combination of the following: contingency contracting, reinforcement, extinction, isolation, or punishment in developing the plan of correction. Briefly, contingency contracting is telling the student that if he or she behaves in a prescribed, appropriate way for a certain amount of time he or she will be rewarded. Extinction is a plan whereby the student might receive immediate payoffs for each appropriate behavior and any occurrence of the inappropriate behavior is ignored. The principle of extinction is that if a behavior goes unrecognized, it will eventually cease all together. Isolation is used as a form of nonreinforcement whereby, if an inappropriate behavior occurs, the student is removed from all outside stimuli. Finally, punishment or negative reinforcement is making the consequences of a behavior more unpleasant than any temporary satisfaction. (For a fuller treatment of each method, you might wish to reread the behaviorist section in chapter 8 and some of the resource books.)

An Example of a Behaviorist Principal

James walks into Mr. Stern's office. He is obviously upset and frightened. Mr. Stern's office is arranged with his desk out from the wall facing the door. It is like a barrier that demarcates the zones between subordinate and superior. Mr. Stern walks behind his desk, sits down and tells James to stand up. He asks for the note and reads silently. James fidgets. Mr. Stern puts the note down, looks up and begins.

Step One: Making the Inappropriate Behavior Clear

James, your teacher says that you were using swear words in class. She told you three times to stop using such words in class. She warned you twice and said that if you continued, you would be sent to the office. Yet you continued.

Step Two: Making the Standard of Behavior Clear

We have a rule in this school that we do not use swear words and that we do what adults tell us. You know these rules, I've explained them to everyone in assembly, and your teacher has gone over them in class.

Step Three: Make the Consequences of the Behavior Known

Since you have not followed the rules, you are to sit in the isolation room across the hall until your teacher comes for you. I will call your parents about your behavior. You will go back to your room and apologize to your teacher and the class.

Step Four: Make the Future Plan

In the future, I don't want you using foul language again. . . . You will bring me a written note after school for each of the next five days from your teacher telling me about your behavior. If I get five good notes then I will send a note to your parents telling how you've been improving (contingency contraction). I will stop in your classroom each day to see how you're doing. If you're doing well, I'll tell you so (positive verbal reinforcement). However, if you've been using bad language, then at recess time you will sit in the isolation room (negative reinforcement). After each day that your teacher feels that you have been using good language and following her orders, you can collect the school attendance forms. If you are not doing as she wishes, then no collection round for you (contingency contracting, positive reinforcement, extinction). [In this case only the correct behavior is being recognized by a reward, the incorrect behavior is being ignored with no reward or punishment.] If you are sent to my office one more time for this then you will be sent home and you will not return until I come over to your house and speak to your parents (negative reinforcement).

Discussion.   The control and authority of the principal is evident throughout all of the above. The principal usurps all student power or decision making to "call the shots." The student is learning that one does not challenge authority or rules lightly. Furthermore, he is learning that adults possess much greater experience and wisdom and should be listened to.

Humanist Approaches

Description.   Mr. Condon is the principal of a school which is committed to student discovery. He believes that children are natural learners who have an infinite capacity for creativity and openness. The school is of the Alternative Three mode. The curriculum is not prescribed, students seek out their own activities based on interests. The teachers enhance the environment with new materials and stimulate the students' thinking with questions. Misbehavior is viewed as an opportunity for further learning. Students have few imposed rules to follow and the teachers only intervene when there is the possibility of bodily harm or severe property damage. Mr. Condon and his staff use humanistic strategies when such incidents do occur. The key techniques are visual empathy, reflective statements, and nonjudgmental questions.

Guideposts for dealing with students. The humanistic principal divests himself or herself of the paraphernalia of positional authority. He or she wants to be regarded as a person with the same strengths, weaknesses, and individual dignity as any other person. To be wrapped in a shroud of authority would rob him or her of the chance of meeting students on an equal footing. The humanistic principal wishes to cultivate a ready accessibility and comfort with all children. The principal's office, if he or she possesses one, is conspicuous in its lack of pretentiousness. There is a small desk tucked in the corner of the room. The eye catches the informal lounge-like atmosphere of soft chairs, coffee table, home lamps, braided rug, and curtains.

When a student is sent to the principal by a teacher, it is with the expectation that the principal will be calm and give undivided attention to the student's plight. He or she will sit or kneel at eye level and listen to the child. The principal might nod or give a guttural acknowledgement of understanding. He or she may ask a question or make a nondirective statement to extend the student's discussion. The most obtrusive the principal might become is in relating personal feelings to the situation. The student, after having relived, clarified, and come to terms with his or her own actions, will then move back to the classroom. The ideal outcome would be cathartic. The student would have owned up to what has happened, and, ridded of the ensuing frustration, guilt, or anger, will have decided upon a better solution for the future.

An Example of a Humanistic Principal

Josué, still red in the face from the free-for-all in the classroom that resulted in the tearing of Bruce's sweater, walks into Mr. Condon's office. The principal turns from his chair and greets Josué.

Step One: Putting the Child at Ease

MR. CONDON: Josué you look angry. Why don't you come sit down on the couch with me.

Step Two: Attentive Listening (If Necessary, Initiating the Student's Narration of the Event)

·Mr. Condon and Josué sit on the couch at eye level. Mr. Condon looks directly at the child and waits for him to begin telling the circumstances for his apparent anger. After a lengthy silence, Mr. Condon speaks.

> MR. CONDON: Josué, what happened? Would you tell me about it.
> JOSUÉ: I was playing with a toy that I brought from home when Bruce came over and took it from me. That's it.

Step Three: Reflection (Nondirective Statements to Clarify the Child's Thinking)

> MR. CONDON: You didn't like it when Bruce took your toy.
> JOSUÉ: No, it's my favorite model plane and my Dad told me to be careful with it. Bruce was going to wreck it and my Dad would have given me heck.
> MR. CONDON: Bruce was going to break your plane and get you in trouble.
> JOSUÉ: Yes, if I hadn't slugged him, he would have broken it.

Step Four: Nonjudgmental Questions to Extend the Child's Thinking of Consequences

> MR. CONDON: What happened when you slugged him?
> JOSUÉ: We started rolling on the floor. Bruce tried to get away and I grabbed him and tore his sweater by mistake.
> MR. CONDON: You tore his sweater by mistake?
> JOSUÉ: Yeah, it was a mistake. I was mad and didn't mean to do it.

Step Five: Probing Nonjudgmental Questions Aimed at Alternative Solutions

> MR. CONDON: Did Bruce know that it was a mistake?
> JOSUÉ: No, I was too mad to tell him.
> MR. CONDON: How did you know that Bruce was going to break your plane?
> JOSUÉ: Because he snuck up behind me and made a grab for it.
> MR. CONDON: How could you have gotten him to stop?
> JOSUÉ: By slugging him.
> MR. CONDON: Any other way?
> JOSUÉ: Aaah, I could have told him to stop or called the teacher.
> MR. CONDON: Anything else?
> JOSUÉ: I guess I could have asked him what he was going to do before I hit him.

Step Six: Questioning for Further Solution

MR. CONDON: Now that you've thought about it, what are you going to do when you get back to the classroom?

JOSUÉ: Tell Bruce that I'm sorry for tearing his sweater and that he'd better keep his hands off my plane.

MR. CONDON: What if he touches your plane again?

JOSUÉ: I'll tell him to cut it out or ask him what he wants. If that doesn't work I'll call the teacher. If that doesn't work then I'll slug him.

This might conclude the session but the principal might want to personalize the session with step seven.

Step Seven: Personalizing the Situation

MR. CONDON: O.K. Josué, you've thought about it. When you come to me, I have to stop what I'm doing. Next time maybe you could try out your ideas before fighting. You can solve many of the problems right then and there in the classroom by using your head.

Discussion.   The absence of control and authority is evident throughout this dialogue. The student is the problem solver. The principal helps the process through empathetic listening and verbalization that extends and probes the child's thinking. The solution that the student arrives at may not be acceptable by many adults outside of this type of school. For example, Josué deciding to talk to Bruce first before slugging him would not be allowed in other schools (Alternative One and Alternative Two) or in any segments of society that do not tolerate physical conflict. The point, however, is that in this school Josué must learn for himself. The staff will not allow him to hurt Bruce. When conflict does erupt, some adult will step in to protect them both. However, this stepping in does not restrict the child from devising solutions that admit of unconventional possibilities. It is expected that in the long run, physical conflict will be seen by the child as not a good solution to the immediate problem but rather as perpetuating the problem. The principal and staff believe that only when one experiences the reality of violence as getting one nowhere does the child internalize the use of rational, nonviolent means. The child, therefore, acts out of consideration of past events and uses rational analysis to arrive at decisions. This is the basis for education in the Alternative Three school.

Interactionalist Approaches

Description.   Ms. Ernest is the principal of a school which believes in a balance of basic instruction with exploratory learning. A child must be adaptable and flexible. The child must at times be able to make independent decisions and at times must learn to conform to the will of others. Schooling is a microsphere of the real world. No one can expect to do whatever one wishes but at the same time there is flexibility to make choices. When one works on the job, in order to keep the position, one must learn to follow orders from the upper echelon. However, if one is to rise in position then one must also be capable of tactfully pointing out ideas for improving the organization. The person must display proficiency in rudimentary skills as well as leadership in carrying out tasks and facilitating change. The school is committed to the Alternative Two model of using both predictable and unpredictable approaches to learning and thus an interactional basis for the management of students.

Students are expected to follow rules that have been laid down by the staff and the majority of students. They are confronted by adults when misbehaving and are made to be responsible for correcting their behavior. The adult plays an active role as facilitator and enforcer of student behavior. The key techniques used by the principal when confronting a student are the use of clarifying questions, authority, input, joint resolution, and enforcement.

Guideposts for dealing with students. The interactional principal retains an authoritarian presence. His or her office is attractive and functional. The desk is against the wall. Filing cabinets and bookcases make up most of the furniture. Two chairs are against the wall on the desk side. When conferences are held, the principal swivels a chair around to face the students. The interactional principal wants students to be aware of the principal's enforcement powers. At the same time he or she acknowledges that students have the right to work out their problems as long as the solutions are acceptable to school guidelines. The principal treats students in a kind, matter-of-fact manner, and does not wish to be viewed as either a buddy or as a feared character. He or she wants students to know that they will be treated fairly, will be listened to, will be helped to correct their misbehavior, and will be required to act appropriately. Students must make a commitment to implement any agreed upon plan. If they do not carry out the plan, no excuse is acceptable and they will have to face the consequences.

When a conference begins, the principal has one goal in mind. The student, the teacher, and the principal will agree upon what needs to be done to improve the behavior in question. The plan will be clear, and easy to assess in terms of compliance. The student will know exactly where he or she stands. If the plan is not followed, it will be done with student knowledge and the consequences will be self-inflicted. In other words, the responsibility will be the student's to implement the agreed upon behavior. If the student fails to do so, then the punishment will not be a result of what others do but rather the conditions that he or she has agreed to abide by.

The discussion that leads to such a result is a lively exchange. The principal leads the discussion, asks questions, and gives opinions. If the student attempts to avoid the issue or make excuses, the principal does not allow the student to wander. The principal stresses the child's inconsistencies and mistakes. He or she does this in an objective manner avoiding carefully any personal language that would debase or humiliate the child. The principal is like a manager talking to a wayward employee and putting the facts on the table. Towards the end of the discussion, the student is pressed for a commitment to change. If none is forthcoming, the principal mandates one. If the teacher is intimately involved as an overseer or participant in the plan, the teacher is brought in and the three go over and agree to the specifics.

An Example of an Interactionalist Principal

Darryl follows Ms. Ernest into her office. The door is closed behind them. Ms. Ernest tells him to be seated as she sits and faces the youngster. Darryl hands the clutched note to the principal. The principal reads and then begins.

Step One: Airing the Issue

MS. ERNEST: Darryl, I read that Ms. B saw that you were copying from Patricia during the spelling test. She told you to stop and you said that it wasn't true. Ms. B looked at Patricia's paper and yours and both had the same spellings for each word. You continued to argue and she sent you to me. What do you have to say for yourself?

DARRYL: I didn't cheat. I didn't look at Patricia's paper. I didn't do anything wrong.

MS. ERNEST: Did Patricia copy from you?

DARRYL: Naw, she's too smart to look at my paper.

MS. ERNEST: Then why are your words, even those spelled wrong exactly like hers?

DARRYL: [shrugs shoulders]

Step Two: Stating the Problem

MS. ERNEST: Darryl, all the evidence points to you. You might still say you weren't doing anything wrong but from everything I've read and you've said, it is obvious why Ms. B told you to stop. You shouldn't have been looking at Patricia's paper in the first place and when Ms. B told you to stop, you should have gone back to your own work. You disrupted the entire class.

Step Three: Asking the Student for the Immediate Consequences
of His Actions

> MS. ERNEST: Does it help you to look at Patricia's paper and to argue with the teacher?
> DARRYL: No.
> MS. ERNEST: What happens when you do?
> DARRYL: All the kids laugh and I get in trouble.

Step Four: Clarifying the Consequences

> MS. ERNEST: You might like getting all that attention from the kids but you don't like getting into trouble.
> DARRYL: No, I don't spell very good and the kids think that I'm stupid and dumb.

Step Five: Restating the Problem and Pressing for a Solution

> MS. ERNEST: It is wrong to look at someone else's paper during a test and it is wrong to argue with the teacher. What are you going to do about this?
> DARRYL: I'll tell the teacher that I'm sorry and not look at Patricia's paper any more.
> MS. ERNEST: Or anyone else's paper, right?
> DARRYL: Right.

Step Six: Working Out an Agreement

> MS. ERNEST: (thinking that one of Darryl's motives was to gain social acceptance) That sounds like the right thing to do. Let's work out a plan. Maybe Ms. B can have you pick two kids to study with for the next spelling test. If you pass the test, all three of you can get an extra ten minute recess. We'll have to see if Ms. B thinks this is a good idea. What do you think?
> DARRYL: That sounds great.

Step Seven: Stipulations

> MS. ERNEST: You have to live up to the agreement. If you get in trouble again for looking at papers or talking back to Mrs. B, what should happen to you?
> DARRYL: You can take away my recess for the whole month.

Step Eight: Commitment

> MS. ERNEST: Let's make it for the week. That sounds like a good bargain to me. Let's see what Mrs. B thinks. If she agrees, we'll write this all down on a piece of paper and you will sign the paper that reads: "I agree not to look at anyone's paper next week or talk back to the teacher. If I break this agreement then I will lose all recess privileges for the week."

Discussion. The responsibility for action shifts from the teacher (sending the child out) to the principal (airing and stating the problem), to finally the child (agreeing to a plan). If the child does not respond, then the principal frames the plan for him. At the end, the child is held accountable for the implementation. Interactionalists do not concern themselves with the past. They want to know what has happened and, more importantly, what the child is going to do about the misbehavior in the future.

A PRAGMATIC EXPLANATION OF THE USE OF BEHAVIORIST, HUMANIST, AND INTERACTIONAL APPROACHES

Must the principal of an Alternative One school always use behavioristic plans of contingency contracting, reinforcement, extinction, and nonreinforcement? Must the principal of an Alternative Three school always use the humanistic techniques of listening, nonjudgmental statements and extending questions? Must the principal of an Alternative Two school always use interactional strategies such as probing, clarifying, and forcing a resolution? The answer is no. We have in our minds a goal of what we wish our students to become. We then use that approach which will be most effective in realizing that goal. Yet, if that approach is not working with an individual student, it is useless to repeat it. For example, if we have a student in a humanistic school who runs wild, does not respond to self-clarification, and only responds to commands and reinforcement then we must at first deal with that student at his or her level of understanding and use behavioral or interactional strategies. The same is true for a student in a behavioristic school who outrightly rebels against any form of authority. We then begin with nonauthoritarian humanistic approaches. What is important is that, first, we reach the student where he or she is capable of being helped and, secondly, we move gradually off the approaches that do not accomplish our ultimate school purpose towards those that do.

Keeping Anecdotal Records

It is most helpful for the administrator to keep a brief record of each student's visit to his office. Often many students will come and go in a relatively short span of time. It is easy to forget how often a particular child has been sent and for what reasons. When the student population of a school numbers over three hundred, it becomes almost impossible for the principal not to confuse students.

A record of this sort also aides in evaluating a student's performance. For example, it might be useful to know that a student who has been coming to the office almost daily, now is coming once a week. Perhaps a particular plan is working for a longer duration with this student. If the principal knows that the duration between visits is lengthening he or she might be less quick to anger and can refer back to the anecdotal record book of the previous visit, see what plan was employed, and reuse a similar version.

When parent conferences are held to discuss a particular troublesome child, specific dates and incidences are vital to move the discussion from an emotional, defensive level to an objective presentation of the facts. We all have had experiences with the furious parent who calls the school about the teacher and principal "picking on a child who never does anything." In such a case, unless records are kept, the principal is often at a loss as to what the parent is talking about and mumbles something to the effect "I'm sorry you're so upset, there must be a misunderstanding. I'll call you back." The parent only becomes angrier and justifiably questions, "What kind of principal and school is it that does not know what they are doing with their own students?" It is much more credible for the principal to have a record of each student visit to his office. When such an irate call comes in he or she can say, "Yes, Mr. or Ms. X your child was sent to my office last Tuesday for pouring paint on the floor. . . ." or "No, you must be mistaken, I have not seen your child in my office in over a month."

An anecdotal record for each child should be quick and easy to fill out. It could be accomplished in about thirty seconds, immediately after a student visit. We have found a loose leaf secretarial notebook as good as any. Each page is titled across as illustrated on page 105.

The information kept should contain the student's name, date, time of incident, reason for visit, and action taken. Confidentiality of this report is a sticky issue. In our opinion, it should be kept only as a private record for the principal. It should not be read or used by teachers or other staff members. If it is used by others, then according to the interpretation of the Family Rights and Privacy Act, a parent has the right to see the record. This is an individual matter for the principal to decide. There may be nothing in the record that would keep a principal from allowing parents access. In our use of this record though, we often would jot down information for ourselves that might be liable to misinterpretation. Unless one is consciously writing with parents in mind, one might put down something hurriedly that is sloppy, ungrammatical, and subjective. One last comment. The record should be destroyed after the school year. It should not be transferred to a student's permanent records. A new school year should begin with a clean slate.

Anecdotal Record of Student Visits to Office for Misbehavior

Jennifer Grabowski, Sept. 28, 12:30

> Throwing food in the cafeteria. She said that she wouldn't do it anymore and was sorry. Left it at that.

Jamuel Cristie, Sept. 28, 1:10 a.m.
Nathan Citino
Rachel Gumber
Andy Bratt

> All sent in from playground for taking balls away from kindergarten child. Warned twice by playground supervisor. They were told that if they were sent in again then they would lose lunch recess privilege and would have to sit in their rooms.

Bernard Finkle, Sept. 29, 9:00 a.m.

> Sent in for bringing a jackknife to school. He gave me the jackknife and I told him to pick it up after school.

SUMMARY

In this chapter, we have looked at the alternative strategies that a school principal might use in dealing with students. We have focused on students being sent to the office as one of the most common situations that the school leader faces in dealing with children. Strategies that the principal most often uses should complement those techniques that the staff employs. The use of record keeping was discussed and an explanation of individual treatment of students was given.

Section Five

Implementing the
Supervisory Dimension

10

Supervision of Staff

As stated previously, our premise is that schools will become more powerful and effective when there is consistency across the various dimensions of schooling. The authors of texts and articles concerning the supervision and evaluation of staff concern themselves with differing strategies and methodologies. However, there does not appear to be much focus or emphasis as to the relationship between the method of supervision and evaluation and the previously discussed other dimensions of schooling. In other words, is the way in which staff are supervised consistent with the overarching school philosophy? It is probably safe to say that these authors have assumed that we, as administrators, know what supervisory styles and methods of evaluation are congruent with specific school goals, curriculum, management, etc. Our belief is that this "assumed assumption" is fallacious.

Numerous supervisory models exist. Harris; Eye and Netzer; Feyereisen, et al.; Burton and Brickner; Marks, et al.; Purple and Mosher; Sergiovanni and Starratt; Cogan; Goldhammer; Wilson, et al.; Hawthorne; Popham; Lucio and McNeil; Wiles; Alfonso; Firth and Neville; Unruh; Turner; and Oliva are but a few who have presented various supervisory conceptualizations, strategies, and methods. Most authors have also defined supervision. Each definition implies a difference in the behaviors that one would demonstrate. For example, the following are some of the existing definitions of supervision. As the reader studies each definition, it is clear that the ways in which administrators and supervisors would supervise staff can certainly be different.

Definitions of Supervision

Supervision is a process used by those in schools who have responsibility for one or another aspect of the school's goals and who *depend directly upon others* to help them achieve these goals.[1]

T. J. Sergiovanni and R. J. Starratt

Emerging Patterns of Supervision

General supervision subsumes supervisory operations that take place principally outside the classroom and includes such activities like the writing and revision of curriculums, preparation of units and materials of instruction, etc., and such broad concerns as evaluation of the total education program.[2]

M. Cogan

Clinical Supervision

Supervision can be defined as the effort to improve professional procedures and is reflected in the development of the student.[3]

J. R. Marks et al.

Handbook of Educational Supervision

Supervision is most accurately defined as what the particular supervisor does or says he does.

Supervision can be defined as teaching teachers how to teach, and professional leadership in reforming public education—more specifically, its curriculum, its teaching, and its forms.[4]

R. L. Mosher et al.

Supervision: The Reluctant Profession

Supervision can be defined as the ability to perceive desirable objectives and to help others contribute to this vision and to act in accordance with it.[5]

W. H. Lucio and J. D. McNeil

Supervision: A Synthesis of Thought and Action

Supervision is what school personnel do with adults and things for the purpose of maintaining or changing the operation of the school in order to directly influence the attainment of major instructional goals of the school.[6]

B. Harris

Supervisory Behavior in Education

Supervision is that phase of school administration which deals primarily with the achievement of the appropriate selected instructional expectations of educational service.[7]

G. G. Eye and L. A. Netzer

Supervision of Instruction

School supervision is instructional leadership.[8]

K. Feyereisen et al.
Supervision and Curriculum Renewal:
A Systems Approach

Supervision is defined as the art and science of designing the educational environment.[9]

L. C. Wilson et al.
Sociology of Supervision

... Supervision can be defined as an expert technical service primarily aimed at studying and improving cooperatively all factors which affect child growth and development.[10]

W. H. Burton and L. T. Brueckner
Supervision

Supervision can be defined as all the activities leading to the improvement of instruction, activities, related to morale, improving human relations, in-service education, and curriculum development.[11]

K. Wiles and J. T. Lovell
Supervision for Better Schools

There does appear to be a degree of congruence with the definitions of supervision and each of the respective approaches to education. Our intention in this chapter is to present three differing approaches to supervision. We will discuss the three approaches in terms of differences in (1) conceptualization of the role; (2) behaviors, practice, and methods; (3) skills and understandings needed by administrators and supervisors; (4) supervisory strategies; and (5) observable classroom practices. Strengths and weaknesses of each approach are also presented.

THE ALTERNATIVE ONE APPROACH TO SUPERVISION

Conceptualization of Role

As with any approach one chooses to incorporate, the supervisory strategy and methods are based upon one's conceptualization of the role of supervisor and the purposes of supervision which he or she acknowledges. An individual behaving in a supervisory role seeking congruence with Alternative One has a unique set of goals, purposes, skills, strategies, and methods. These supervisors conceptualize their role as teaching teachers how to teach. They see the process of supervision as including the functions of leading, controlling, and directing. Based on many years of experience (as teachers and learners), they have a very definite idea as to what constitutes the behavior of an effective teacher.

It is their assumption that behavioral change in the teacher will directly lead to change in student behavior. They are most concerned with product evaluation and believe that efficiency results from arranging the conditions of work in such a way that the human variables have only minimal interference. Their leadership style is task oriented. In regard to certain behaviors, using a scale with the multiple choice answers of always, frequently, occasionally, seldom, or never, they would probably answer the following questions in these ways.

1. I would most likely act as a spokesman for my teachers. (always, frequently)
2. I would allow my teachers complete freedom in their work. (seldom, never)
3. I would encourage the use of uniform procedures. (always, frequently)
4. I would keep the work moving at a rapid pace. (always, frequently)
5. I would decide what shall be done and how it shall be done. (always, frequently)
6. I would push for increased production. (always, frequently)
7. I would permit my teachers to set their own pace. (seldom, never)
8. I would ask that teachers follow standard rules and regulations. (always, frequently)[12]

Their behavior would be guided by the assumption that supervisory behavior involves working on others to help improve them. Their conceptualization of the word "help" might be interpreted to mean, "Let me help you get to where the school system and I think you ought to be." Their control over teachers is based in the authority of legitimacy (law, policy, administered codes, rules, regulations, manuals, governing boards, etc.) and position. (For a more detailed description of supervisory power and authority bases, see Sergiovanni and Starratt, 1971.) They might also feel that the status of their relationships with teachers is more important than what the teachers think of them. In other words, because they are called supervisors, they are automatically viewed by teachers as authorities. Generally speaking, they conceptualize supervision as including all of those tasks in which they are engaged. Supervision is a role, with certain role expectations, carried out by an individual who is occupying that status position. The supervisor's success is a function of the extent to which he or she fulfills those role expectations as evaluated by his or her superiors.

Behaviors, Practices, and Methods

Supervisors behaving in ways congruent with Alternative One use certain practices and methods. Their approach with all teachers is standard. They assume that they can elicit the same kinds of behaviors with individual teachers by presenting them with similar stimuli. They determine, on the basis of past teacher performance and school system goals, individual teacher objectives which will facilitate the accomplishment of school goals. These goals and objectives would be communicated to all of the teachers for whom they are responsible. They would help teachers develop specific performance objectives that detail teacher behavioral change. They establish some kind of reward structure for teachers and attempt to determine ways in which teachers can be best motivated. In order to get teachers to behave in appropriate ways, they may set up rewards based upon internal or external motivational factors and use either positive or negative reinforcement strategies. With clearly stated behavioral or perform-ance objectives, they can develop observational methodology that would facilitate the collection of data. They would use structured types of observational tools which have predetermined frameworks, and quantify and analyze these data for the purpose of making value judgments about a teacher's performance. Objective attainment and the development of future teacher objectives would be based on this analysis. Action plans for attainment of objectives would be designed by supervisors for teachers. In essence, supervisors rate teachers.

The supervisors' behavior with teachers would be direct. They would do a lot of telling and giving opinions about teaching practices. They would make suggestions that teachers do things in specific ways or, in fact, tell teachers specifically what to do. They would be critical of teaching behavior. Their major concerns would be with controlling teacher behavior, excluding teachers from problem solving and evaluating their own performance. Blumberg has stated that super-visors using these more direct types of behavior would hold the following assumptions:

1. The control of the situation is based on the authority of one's position in an organizational hierarchy.

2. People in higher organizational positions have more expertise.
3. People in lower organizational positions can best be evaluated by those who are higher.
4. The most important external rewards of a job come to a person primarily from a person who holds a higher position.
5. Empathetic listening to the teacher is not a necessary dimension of helping.
6. People learn best by being told what to do by someone in a higher organizational position.
7. Work is rational; there is little place in supervision for discussion of feelings or interpersonal relationships.
8. Collaborative problem solving between supervisor and teacher is not a critical concern in supervision.
9. Teaching as a skill can generally be separated with the right and wrong ways of doing things.[13]

The supervisors' repertoires would include a catalogue of teaching practices which they have judged to be ineffective. They might suggest a technique or practice to model for effective teaching. They also might identify teachers within the school or school system who are judged "effective" and arrange interclassroom visitation so that staff members might be able to observe these teaching practices. Other activities they would engage in would be planning and arranging in-service programs and workshops based upon their identification of teacher weaknesses; formulating school. policy; selecting textbooks; orienting new teachers to school philosophy, goals and objectives; developing school curriculum guides; and evaluating student progress.

Skills and Understandings

In order to function effectively, supervisors behaving in ways congruent with Alternative One also possess certain skills and understandings. They demonstrate an understanding of behavior modification and are highly skilled in employing its techniques. They are skilled in goal setting and the ability to translate educational goals into clearly defined objectives (instructional objectives, behavioral objectives, performance criteria, etc.). They possess a sound understanding of observational methodology and the skill to categorize behaviors accurately. They have at their disposal and are competent in using standardized observational techniques, such as Flander's Interactional Analysis.[14] They are familiar with research identifying effective teaching behaviors and are competent in the area of research design and statistics. They are skilled in the area of data analysis and in the use of audio-visual media. They have learned how to categorize data into pictorial patterns.[15]

Example of a Supervisory Strategy Consistent with the Alternative One Approach

James Popham, a leading proponent of the accountability movement in education, has proposed and developed a strategy for the supervision of instruction which captures the essence of the Alternative One approach. He has entitled this strategy "Criterion-Referenced Supervision." Popham states that the major purpose of this strategy is to improve the quality of other people's teaching. Supervisor focus is on ends rather than means and is concentrated on the effects of teaching behavior on student outcome.

The strategy is straightforward and consists of two major supervisory functions and suggested steps for supervisors to engage in. The strategy is presented as follows:

Function 1: Assist teachers in developing the most defensible instructional objectives.

Suggested Procedures for carrying out Function 1:

1. Identify any curricular restraints related to instructional objectives (local regulations, state or district mandates).
2. State all objectives in terms of observable behaviors. Ask question, "What do I want students to become?"
3. Encourage teacher to consider alternative objectives.
4. Evaluate the worth of each objective asking the question, "Is this the most worthwhile behavioral change?"

Function 2: Help the teacher in attaining educational objectives.

Suggested Procedures for carrying out Function 2:

1. Determine objectives to be evaluated during classroom observation.
2. Collect evidence relating to objective accomplishment.
3. Look for undesirable side effects.
4. Suggest alternative instructional strategies if objectives are not attained.[16]

Example of a Supervisory Visit to a Classroom

Mrs. Jones (principal) and Mr. Howard (teacher) have met earlier in the week to discuss Mr. Howard's objectives for the year. Based on

Mrs. Jones' assessment of his teaching last year and the school systems goal stating that teachers shall improve in the area of questioning strategy, she has given Mr. Howard objectives which he should strive to accomplish. One of these objectives is to develop and use questioning techniques that require pupils to employ the higher cognitive processes as well as to demonstrate retention and comprehension. Mrs. Jones tells Mr. Howard that she will visit his classroom sometime during the hours of 9:00 and 12:00 on Thursday.

Mrs. Jones enters Mr. Howard's classroom at 9:50. His language arts section will be completed in forty minutes. She carries with her a mimeographed sheet of paper which is labeled, "Questioning Strategy—Frequency of Questions Asked." Along the left side of the sheet are descriptions of six types of questions. Across the top are the numbers from one to twenty. Mrs. Jones finds a seat near the back of the room and proceeds to place a check mark in the appropriate box whenever Mr. Howard asks a question.

After forty minutes of observation, the language class is dismissed. As another of Mr. Howard's classes is entering the room, Mrs. Jones finishes her writing and walks to the front of the room. She informs Mr. Howard that she will see him tomorrow morning during his free period to discuss the observation.

The next morning she meets with Mr. Howard and informs him that during the forty minute observation, he asked 10 questions in category one, 3 in category two, 2 in category three, and none in the remaining three categories. Her evaluation is that he should attempt to begin asking more questions in the last three categories since the majority of his questions were in lower level categories. She gives him a book entitled *How to Improve Your Questioning Strategy* and suggests that he call on her if he needs any more help. They set up another date for classroom observation and Mr. Howard arranges to meet with some other teachers from whom Mrs. Jones has said he might get some additional help.

Strengths of Alternative One

This approach to the supervision of instruction adds preciseness and clarity not only to the area of teaching but to that of supervision and evaluation as well. It forces both supervisors and teachers to be clear about educational goals, the relative success of different classroom activities, and judgments made of those activities.[17] Objective attainment is measurable and may be quantified. As Richard Smith has stated, the more precise we are about what we are trying to accomplish, the more precise we can be when measuring our accomplishments.[18] The Alternative One approach may help us to think more clearly and act more efficiently.

Some teachers may feel more comfortable with this approach because expectations for them are defined. Knowing the objectives on which they will be evaluated and the methodology which will be used to collect evaluative data may lower teacher anxiety. The process of evaluation congruent with Alternative One is more objective. Teachers also would be provided with data describing what is actually happening in the classroom. The use of predetermined frameworks for observation and precise data related to categories allows teachers to focus clearly. Also, the approach is quite consistent with the financial accountability movement and over a short period of time, teacher production may be increased.

Weaknesses of Alternative One

Supervisory strategies based on the Alternative One approach imply that teacher and student perceptions are not of immediate concern. This may present significant problems in teacher morale. Since defining behavioral objectives related to affect is difficult, evaluation of teaching behavior may be somewhat limited. All that educational leaders and teachers seek to accomplish may not be directly observable, definable, or measurable. Variables not easily described may be lost in the attempt to be accurate and scientific. Teacher evaluation solely by supervisor judgment may be seen as unfair. Teachers may want more input in their own evaluation. This approach assumes that the individual in the supervisory position possesses superior knowledge and teaching skill, in other words, knows what's best. In some instances, this assumption may be erroneous. Finally, this approach implies a mechanistic view of both supervising and teaching that some teachers might rebel against.

THE ALTERNATIVE THREE APPROACH
TO SUPERVISION

Conceptualization of Role

Supervisors behaving in ways consistent with Alternative Three see the purpose of supervision to be that of facilitating the personal growth of teachers. They view supervision as a service function which seeks to establish a helping relationship. Since they view individuals as unique, they feel that there is no best way to teach. They assume that as teachers grow personally, there will be equal growth and improvement in the classroom. They are most concerned with process evaluation and strive to help teachers in the process of self-evaluation.

They try to know teachers on a personal level and their leadership style is people-oriented. In assessing behavior, using a scale from always, frequently, occasionally, seldom, or never, they would probably answer the questions which follow in these ways:

1. I would allow my teachers a high degree of initiative. (always, frequently)
2. I would schedule teacher work to be done. (seldom, never)
3. I would turn teachers loose on a job and let them go to it. (always, frequently)
4. I would be reluctant to allow teachers any freedom of action. (seldom, never)
5. I would trust the group members to exercise good judgment. (always, frequently)
6. I would push teachers for increased production. (seldom, never)
7. I would allow teachers complete freedom in their work. (always, frequently)[19]

Based upon the notion that the task of educators is to help people find out what's already inside them, rather than to reinforce or shape them in a prearranged form, supervisors would value a supportive environment that would allow the individual teacher to experiment. Therefore, their major task is to provide opportunities for teachers to become increasingly aware of their own perceptions, goals, wants, and desires. Operating from a humanistic psychological base, they believe that they cannot alter teacher behavior directly, but can only help to create environments in which teachers may change themselves. They believe that by providing teachers with new experiences, their perceptions will be altered and hence they'll behave in different ways. They also believe that teacher self-concept is crucial and focus much emphasis on teachers knowing themselves. They believe that helping teachers analyze their own behavior in light of their own intentions is a primary role function.

In this position they operate from no authority base other than respect. In order words, teachers have granted them the power to supervise. Generally speaking, they conceptualize supervision as a process and a set of behaviors which facilitate teacher growth in a nondirective fashion. They are successful when they live up to the role expectations which teachers have for them.

Behaviors, Practice and Methods

Emanating from a humanistic point of view, supervisory behavior is aimed at helping teachers achieve the goals and objectives which they have set for themselves. The behaviors the supervisors practice, and the methods that they use are totally personal and individual. In other words, their actions start from the reference frame of the teacher. They initiate contact with teachers based upon the teachers' concerns. They help teachers to become aware of their own objectives and attempt to collect information and secure resources that would provide teachers with data for self-evaluation. Since they assume teachers are self-motivated, they are not concerned with developing motivation strategies. They believe that teachers who see a need will work toward improvement; every person wants to be better.

Supervisory behavior is aimed at building trust between self and others so that teachers can spread their wings and fly. Humanistic supervisors attempt to behave in ways which communicate feelings of unconditional regard and empathy to the teacher. Their behavior is aimed at improving teacher attitudes toward their job, peers, and students, increasing levels of job satisfaction, and increasing teacher control over their environment.

They encourage experimentation and see conflict as necessary and, in fact, healthy. Their behavior communicates that supervisors are not experts. Their behavior is both supportive and most importantly nonjudgmental. What they communicate to teachers is the idea that teachers possess the power and potential to solve their own problems. They realize that a positive value judgment on their part, is, in the long run, as potentially dangerous as a negative one. In both situations, they would be implying a standard of behavior.

Their behavior with teachers would be indirect. Their methods would include accepting and clarifying questions about teaching problems, asking uncritical questions about teaching behavior, asking opinions about how to overcome teaching problems, and discussing teacher feelings about the productiveness, ease of communication, threat, etc. in the supervisor-teacher relationship. Blumberg has stated that supervisors using these more indirect types of behavior would hold the following assumptions:

1. Control of the situation depends on the demands of the problem. The problem determines the direction that events take.
2. Expertise is a function of knowledge and experience, not necessarily of organization position.
3. The important rewards of teaching are intrinsic to the job, ...
4. People learn best by being confronted with a situation and with help, finding their own situation.
5. It is important for teachers to feel that they have been listened to and understood.
6. Work is both rational and emotional; discussion of feelings and interpersonal relations may be as important as discussion about the job.

7. Collaborative problem solving between supervisor and teacher is an important concern of supervision.
8. Teaching is a complex process and what works well for one person may not for another, so that most of what goes on in a classroom needs to be viewed experimentally.[20]

Through sensitive observation, supervisors attempt to see through teachers' eyes what is happening in the classroom. The teachers, in many instances, develop the plan for observation and ask supervisors to focus on actions which have been identified as being important. Supervisors collect their observations and present them to teachers without judgment. After presenting teachers with this information, they do not indicate a plan of action for teachers to follow unless asked. They assume that on the basis of the information, teachers will make the best decisions. They employ a questioning strategy which enables teachers to become more aware of their own beliefs and actions, and they consistently demonstrate a respect for the teacher as an individual of worth and dignity, as professional persons qualified to do the job for which they were hired. Other activities or tasks these supervisors might perform are assisting teachers in the location, selection and interpretation of materials; collecting and disseminating current curriculum materials; and helping teachers plan and arrange their own in-service programs.

Skills and Understandings

Supervisors behaving in ways congruent with the Alternative Three approach have a solid understanding of perceptual psychology and self-concept theory. Their listening skills are superior and they are able to see things from another's point of view. Their skill in observation allows them to capture the realities of the classroom as felt by the teacher. They possess skill in arranging observations in such a way that teachers may logically deduct any incongruence between their intentions and their actions. They are skilled in the area of counseling techniques and have the ability to relate warmly with others. They also have the ability to help teachers see meaning in their actions and have skill in helping teachers make curriculum more relevant to the experiences of children. They are skilled in the area of nonverbal observation and know affective assessment techniques that focus on attitude, job satisfaction, self-concept, etc.

Most importantly, they have a high degree of self-understanding which allows them to permit differences in others and to value the uniqueness of others. They understand that behavior is a symptom of some underlying cause and they have the skill, ability, and insight to know that an individual must alter his or her own perception in order for behavioral changes to occur.

Example of a Supervisory Strategy Consistent with Alternative Three

In searching the literature for a strategy consistent with the Alternative Three approach, we had difficulty in identifying a step-by-step approach. Initially, we were perplexed and thought this to be rather odd. It did not take us long, however, to realize that a step-by-step technique or strategy is, by itself, inconsistent with the Alternative Three approach. We did locate a process or series of steps which Abrell has suggested as those in which a supervisor behaving within an Alternative Three framework might consider.

1. Establishing an open, trusting, and collegial relationship. Such a relationship is basic to all meaningful and productive human interaction. Before anything else can occur, the supervisory team must create a climate that reduces tension, fear, anxiety, and withdrawal. Indeed, the climate must encourage an honest exchange of ideas, feelings, preferences, and perceptions so that credibility and trust are continually at work.

2. Identifying needs, aspirations, talents, and goals of both persons and institutions in which the supervisory trusteeship is to take place. Before sound planning can be engaged in, the wishes and talents of those with whom the supervisor is working must be seriously taken into account and utilized. We know that many who are professional educators or aspire to be, value autonomy over dependence, prefer knowledge over ignorance, want activity more than idleness, like much responsibility as opposed to little or no responsibility, and prefer to work in behalf of others rather than against them. If this knowledge is anywhere near correct, then it is important that the existing talents and aspirations of one's co-workers be identified and harnessed to honor such values. Likewise, each institution has its own unique needs and it is the task of the supervisor (with help of his/her working partners) to identify those needs, honoring both personal and institutional needs if achievement and growth are to be realized.

3. Planning what is to be done, how it is to take place, and when it is to occur. Every person is inclined to feel more committed to experiences if he/she has participated in the planning of them. A fundamental component of humanistic supervision is the active involvement of all those participating in the supervisory coalition. The purpose of planning is to turn needs into performance goals, communicate clearly performance expectations, identify barriers to performance, and design strategies for observing, analyzing, and appraising performance progress.

4. Observing the performance by "taking the role" of the performer, the learner, and the supervisor. By "taking the role" of the performer, learner, and supervisor, we mean that one identifies and empathizes with others in the supervisory relationship

and the role expectations of their respective positions. A specific example can be related through the utilization of the college/university supervisor who works with student teachers. When and while the supervisor is observing the performance of a student teacher, he/she can make a much more comprehensive assessment by "taking the role" of the student teacher (how would I feel, think, and act if I were in his/her shoes in this particular situation?); the learners (if I were a student, would I understand and "dig" this instructor?); the cooperating teacher (as a former classroom teacher, how do I see the student teacher's performance?), the college/university supervisor (as one who has much training and expertise, is the student teacher demonstrating those competencies expected of a future classroom teacher?).

If one is successful at role-taking as crudely set forth here, a more comprehensive insight and understanding of performance will indeed take place. This approach to observation must be explained to and accepted by all persons making up the supervisory team. Observation must be frequent, take into account the situation, and be nonthreatening.

5. Analyzing the performance, holding conferences, and sharing appraisal feedback. Because the humanistic supervisor believes that people possess the capacity for self-direction, he/she makes a concentrated effort to help co-workers engage in self-evaluation. Appraising performance is a cooperative and mutual endeavor, with both supervisor and supervisee sharing in comparative analysis and assessment. As participants in the supervisory relationship share feedback, they will have the opportunity to modify wrong impressions, change task strategies, and agree on future expectations and responsibilities.

The role of the supervisor during conferences in which performance is analyzed and shared, is to achieve positive interpersonal relations, share realistic information, and mutually plan solutions to problems. The climate must be supportive, participants must be honest, and the emphasis should be on re-assessment and re-planning as opposed to any sort of grading. Certainly all future planning should again focus on strengths, skills, and talents of the performer who is seeking help and guidance. Throughout the conference, the supervisor plays the role of questioner, facilitator, and resource person.

In his/her efforts to humanize supervision, the humanistic supervisor will have succeeded if all persons in the supervisory alliance emerge from their tasks:

1. Knowing that their skills, talents, resources, and creativity have been utilized significantly in the supervisory partnership;

2. realizing that they have been given wide latitude in self-responsibility, self-management, and decision-making;

3. feeling emotionally enhanced and intellectually richer;

4. emerging more fully as self-actualizing human beings, "as fully human as can possibly be."[21]

Example of a Supervisory Visit to a Classroom

The principal enters the room and is handed a guide as to what will be transpiring while he or she will be in the room. By prearrangement, the principal and teacher have decided that the teacher would make out a plan for what the teacher would like for the principal to observe. In the past, the teacher would have made out a lesson plan occasionally, but today the teacher has decided to ask the principal to look at the aspect of verbal behavior, especially at the nature of the teacher's questions. During the observation, the principal makes some notations and then quietly leaves the room. A conference after school has been prearranged.

When the teacher and the principal meet later in the teacher's room, the teacher initiates the conference by commenting upon some of the questions asked during the activity time. Occasionally the principal asks a question, such as "How would you have phrased the question differently?" The principal may comment, "You think Jean didn't understand that question?" as a summary of the teacher's statements. The conference moves along with the teacher assuming the responsibility for shifts in thought. The principal often paraphrases what the teacher has said in order to facilitate clarification of the teacher's own thinking.

At the end of the conference, the two separate with plans for a visit again in three weeks. The teacher is free to plan for the next visit in any way he or she sees fit.[22]

Strengths of Alternative Three

This approach to supervision, because of increased teacher participation in decision making, may result in high levels of teacher morale. Selection of objectives by teachers themselves may be more meaningful for their individual growth. Individuals in supervisory positions are more likely to be seen by teachers as a source of service and help. When supervisors do not evaluate or "rate," teachers are less threatened and less reluctant to ask for help. Since experimentation is valued and desired, the creative process would be more easily nurtured.

Through this approach, teachers may come to view their supervisors as sources of psychological support. This support results in the improvement of the quality of interpersonal relationships between supervisors and teachers.

This approach to supervision seeks to foster self-evaluation. As teachers move toward this end, they might come to accept increasing responsibility for their own actions.

Weaknesses of Alternative Three

An overemphasis on "people concern" may result in lower levels of teacher production. This approach lacks objectivity and direction and may cause problems for those who desire structure or need to know "where they stand" in comparison with others. Teachers may select those objectives related to professional and personal growth which they are already achieving. Teachers who are incompetent might rate themselves as superior and see no need to change. Supervisors would have little control over such teachers. Finally, it may be that supervisors have not had the therapeutic, nondirective training and background to implement this approach.

THE ALTERNATIVE TWO APPROACH TO SUPERVISION

Conceptualization of Role

Principals behaving in ways consistent with the Alternative Two approach perceive their purpose to be that of improving instruction through a mutual process of staff growth. Supervision is a shared function where people need to grow collectively. Their intentions are directed toward facilitating the linkage among school system goals, individual school goals, teacher goals, and student goals. They are as much task-oriented as people-oriented and seek to make organizational objectives compatible with the needs and objectives of teachers.

   These supervisors seek to establish a permissive and informal atmosphere while at the same time letting teachers know that they will have significant input in their evaluation. Their authority is based on the legitimacy of their position and their competence in both subject matter and interpersonal skills. Their basis for control rests in self-discipline and self-direction. They conceptualize their tasks to be those of goal focus, facilitating adequate communication systems, equalizing power, building morale, nurturing teacher autonomy, and developing a problem-solving capacity. They believe that everyone is a resource to everyone else. In other words, anyone working within the system, at some point in time, may be a "supervisor." Finally, they base their success on the feedback from both teachers and superiors.

Behaviors, Practice, and Methods

The supervisors' behavior with teachers would be both direct and indirect. They would give teachers their own opinions and suggestions and make value judgments. They would also use behavior that accepts and clarifies questions about teaching problems, and they would ask for a teacher's opinions and suggestions. They would convey concern for teacher attitude and feeling and emphasize collaborative problem solving. Their patterns of behavior might remain static with some teachers and changeable with others. Their methods are eclectic and situational. For example, they are aware that helping teachers to write behavioral objectives may be rewarding and facilitating to some, while stifling to others. They select from a wide range of techniques those that they consider to be the most appropriate for the person and the situation.

They may incorporate the techniques associated with group supervision where "the emphasis shifts from supervisor A working to improve the teaching by teacher B, to teachers of reading working to improve the teaching of reading."[23]

While the behaviors associated with the Alternative Two approach emphasize making teachers feel part of the school system and feel important as individuals, supervisors behaving in ways consistent with this approach provide people with *opportunities to experience* the feelings of being both an individual and a part of the organization.

Observation in the classroom would be employed to collect data that are both objective and subjective, cognitive and affective. Their interactions with teachers would be productive and evolve out of a positive interpersonal framework. These supervisors would employ strategies aimed at both process and product evaluation. Their evaluations would be based on both their own and the teachers' analyses of data.

Skills and Understandings

Alternative Two supervisors possess human relations and technical competence. They have conceptual skills and see things in holistic ways. Their skills and understandings include all those that have previously been associated with both Alternative One and Alternative Three approaches. Most importantly, they possess the intuitive skill to know what methods and strategies to use with what individuals or groups of individuals. This skill is based upon their understanding of the broad range of learning and teaching styles.

Example of a Supervisory Strategy Consistent with Alternative Two

Robert Goldhammer has developed a strategy for supervision which captures the essence of Alternative Two. His strategy is called "clinical supervision" and is presented in his book, which is similarly entitled. We have presented a very brief synopsis of his five step approach to supervision which focuses on the teacher in the classroom.[24] We have included some alternative actions within Goldhammer's framework.

Step One: Preobservation Conference

The first step is intended to promote positive supervisor-teacher relationships and to share role responsibilities and expectations. During this conference, teacher goals are mutually agreed upon. A contract is drawn up which identifies the specific objectives to be attacked during the observation and what methods the supervisor will use to collect observational data. Objectives selected for observation are narrow and related to more general teacher goals.

Step Two: Observation

The supervisor observes in the classroom, being concerned only with teacher or student behavior related to the agreed upon specific objectives. A number of observations may be needed to collect data. It might also be the case that observational data may be collected by another teacher, groups of teachers, or the teacher being supervised. (Data related to objectives may, however, be gleaned in ways other than classroom observation.)

Step Three: Data Analysis

The supervisor analyzes the data collected and arranges it in a logical manner. The supervisor then plans how to present this data to the teacher.

Step Four: Post Observation Conference

The supervisor presents his or her analysis of the data and shares personal impressions related to objective attainment. The teacher then has an opportunity to react to this presentation and present his or her interpretation and impressions. Both supervisor and teacher plan a course of action. The teacher identifies or asks for resources which the supervisor may secure.

Step Five: Critique

Independently, the teacher and supervisor critique the process which they have been through. Both are concerned with the questions, "How was I helped? How was I of help? What might I do to improve my performance?" Supervisor and teacher then share their reactions and consider a time for another cycle to begin.

Example of a Supervisory Visit to a Classroom

The supervisor enters the classroom and finds an appropriate position for observation. As prearranged in a planning conference, the supervisor's task today is to observe the general classroom climate using a standardized observation instrument previously selected by the teacher.

During the observation, the supervisor records only the behaviors relevant to classroom climate. When the observation instrument is completed, the supervisor quietly leaves the room, a postobservation conference having been prearranged for later that afternoon.

At the conference, the supervisor presents a profile sheet prepared from the results of the observational instrument. Due to the teacher's need for structure, the supervisor decides to present the data in outline form with specific questions and impressions prepared. The teacher and supervisor discuss the data and plan a course of action based on their conclusions. Later, the supervisor and teacher independently consider how they were of help to one another. After sharing their reactions, they set a time to reinitiate the cycle. They agree to keep the same focus for a follow-up observation.

Strengths of Alternative Two

This approach to supervision allows supervisors freedom in selecting those methods and strategies which they perceive to be the most viable for the individual teacher and situation. Shared responsibility for supervision promotes high levels of teacher morale.[25] Organizational theory literature suggests that when role expectations for an individual within an institution are matched with personality needs, the organization is more likely to achieve its goals and the goals of individuals within the organization. Supervisors implementing a leadership approach which has emphasis on both task production and people concern are more likely to achieve what Argyris has labeled organizational self-actualization.[26]

Weaknesses of Alternative Two

Theoretically, this approach has no major weaknesses. However, an inherent weakness lies in the fact that supervisors may not have had the training and experience needed to implement a variety of supervisory strategies. Also, supervisors' judgments about the possible impact of a certain supervisory technique on teacher behavior may be inaccurate. Finally, since data for evaluation comes in so many forms and so many directions, evaluation may be difficult. Additionally, some staff may feel that it is unfair to supervise and evaluate teachers differently. It might raise the question of favoritism. The interactional supervisor needs to be sensitive to this or it could create a division in staff and lowering of morale.

SUMMARY

This chapter has dealt with the supervision of staff aspect of the supervisory dimension. Three alternative approaches have been presented. There are numerous other supervisory conceptualizations, styles, and approaches which are described in the literature. We suggest that the administrator refer to the reading list which follows for more specific information.

NOTES

1. Thomas J. Sergiovanni and Robert J. Starratt, *Emerging Patterns of Supervision: Human Perspective* (New York: McGraw-Hill, 1971), p. 10.

2. Morris Cogan, *Clinical Supervision* (Boston: Houghton-Mifflin, 1973), p. 9.

3. James R. Marks et al., *Handbook of Educational Supervision: A Guide for the Practitioner* (Boston: Allyn and Bacon, Inc., 1971), p. 2.

4. Ralph L. Mosher et al., *Supervision: The Reluctant Profession* (Boston: Houghton-Mifflin, 1972).

5. William H. Lucio and John D. McNeil, *Supervision: A Synthesis of Thought and Action.* (New York: McGraw-Hill 1962), p. 46.

6. Ben Harris, *Supervisory Behavior in Education*, 2d ed. (Englewood Cliffs, N.J.: Prentice-Hall, Inc., 1975), p. 10-11.

7. Glen G. Eye, and Lanore A. Netzer, *Supervision of Instruction: A Phase of Administration* (New York: Harper & Row, 1965).

8. Kathryn Feyereisen et al., *Supervision and Curriculum Renewal: A System Approach* (New York: Appleton-Century-Crofts, 1970), p. 242.

9. L. Craig Wilson et al., *Sociology of Supervision* (Boston: Allyn and Bacon, Inc., 1969), p. 3.

10. Willian H. Burton and Leo J. Brueckner, *Supervision: A Social Process*, 3d ed. (New York: Appleton-Century-Crofts, 1955), p. 20.

11. Kimball Wiles and John T. Lovell, *Supervision for Better Schools*, 4th ed. (Englewood Cliffs, N.J.: Prentice-Hall, Inc., 1975), p. 37.

12. These questions are adapted from the T-P Leadership Style Inventory in J. William Pfeiffer and John E. Jones, *A Handbook of Structured Experiences for Human Relations Training*, vol. 1 (La Jolla, Calif.: University Associates Press, 1973), pp. 7–8.

13. Arthur Blumberg, *Supervisors and Teachers—A Private Cold War* (Berkeley, Calif.: McCutchan Publishing Co., 1974), p. 68.

14. Ned A. Flanders, *Analyzing Teacher Behavior* (Reading, Mass.: Addison-Wesley, 1970).

15. Louise M. Berman and Mary Lou Usery, *Personalized Supervision: Sources and Insights* (Washington, D.C.: Association for Supervision and Curriculum Development, 1966), p. 38.

16. James Popham, *Criterion Referenced Supervision* (Los Angeles, Calif.: VIMCET Associates).

17. Thomas B. Roberts, "Behavioral Psychology," in *Four Psychologies Applied to Education: Freudian, Behavioral, Humanistic, and Transpersonal*, ed. Thomas B. Roberts (New York: John Wiley and Sons, 1975).

18. Richard B. Smith, "Educational Objectives and the Systematic Improvement of Instruction," in *Four Psychologies Applied to Education*, p. 215.

19. These questions are adapted from the T-P Leadership Inventory in Pfeiffer and Jones, *Structured Experiences*, pp. 7–8.

20. Blumberg, *Supervisors and Teachers*, p. 68.

21. Ronald L. Abrell, "The Humanistic Supervisor Enhances Growth and Improves Instruction," in *Educational Leadership* (Washington, D.C.: Association for Supervision and Curriculum Development, 1974), pp. 212–216.

22. Berman and Usery, *Personalized Supervision*, pp. 41–42.

23. Sergiovanni and Starratt, *Patterns of Supervision*, p. 180.

24. Robert L. Goldhammer, *Clinical Supervision: Special Methods for the Supervision of Teachers* (New York: Holt, Rinehart and Winston, 1969).

25. F. C. Ellenburg, "Factors Affecting Teacher Morale," in *Educational Leadership* (Washington, D.C.: Association for Supervision and Curriculum Development, 1972), pp. 37–42.

26.   Chris Argyris, *Integrating the Individual and the Organization* (New York: John Wiley, 1964).

SUGGESTIONS FOR FURTHER READING

Association for Supervision and Curriculum Development. *Perceiving, Behaving, Becoming*, 1962 Yearbook. Washington, D.C.: Association for Supervision and Curriculum Development, 1970.

Burton, William H., and Brueckner, Leo J. *Supervision: A Social Process*. 3d ed. New York: Appleton-Century-Crofts, 1955.

Cogan, Morris. *Clinical Supervision*. Boston: Houghton-Mifflin, 1973.

Feyereisen, Kathryn; Fiorino, A. John; and Nowak, Arlene T. *Supervision and Curriculum Renewal: A System Approach*. New York: Appleton-Century-Crofts, 1970.

Harris, Ben. *Supervisory Behavior in Education*. 2d ed. Englewood Cliffs, N.J.: Prentice-Hall, Inc., 1975.

Lucio, William H., and McNeil, John D. *Supervision: A Synthesis of Thought and Action*. New York: McGraw-Hill, 1962.

Marks, James R.; Stoops, Emery; and King-Stoops, Joyce. *Handbook of Educational Supervision: A Guide for the Practitioner*. Boston: Allyn and Bacon, Inc., 1971.

Mosher, Ralph L., et al. *Supervision: The Reluctant Profession*. Boston: Houghton-Mifflin, 1972.

Sergiovanni, Thomas J., and Starratt, Robert J. *Emerging Patterns of Supervision: Human Perspective*. New York: McGraw-Hill, 1971.

Wiles, Kimball, and Lovell, John T. *Supervision for Better Schools*. 4th ed. Englewood Cliffs, N.J.: Prentice-Hall, Inc., 1975.

Wilson, L. Craig, et al. *Sociology of Supervision*. Boston: Allyn and Bacon, Inc., 1969.

11

Staff Development

The purpose of this chapter is two-fold: we present a brief discussion and description of the nature of three differing approaches to staff development, and we describe the specific behaviors used in five steps of the staff development process congruent with each approach.

STAFF DEVELOPMENT—ALTERNATIVE ONE

Staff development in an Alternative One school might be concepualized as a process of designing and implementing learning experiences for adults derived from a set of minimally acceptable standards. Staff development programs are based upon the essential teaching and administrative skills and procedures designed to foster teacher and administrator growth guaranteeing skill mastery.

The science of teaching is divided into hierarchical sets of trainable skills and techniques. The subject matter competence required of teachers in different roles provides the basis for the staff development program. The same is conceptualized and developed for the science of administration. For example, the central office administration determines what exact skills an elementary school teacher, a secondary school teacher of each of the disciplines, an assistant principal, and a principal should possess. Again, these skills are based on some minimally acceptable performance standards and criteria and are developed by the central administration or its designate.

All those who work with teachers in the area of skill development have attained a level of skill mastery in systematic procedures which enables them to diagnose teacher weakness. For example, a basic skill for teachers might be the ability to diagnose student skill attainment in language arts. Those responsible for the evaluation of teachers will have developed procedures that allow them to determine the extent of teacher skill in this area. Along with an a priori determination of basic skills related to the teaching of specific content areas, performance criteria are also established. Such criterion-referenced performance is easy to evaluate. The focus of staff development is training to remediate the teaching areas that fall below performance criteria standards based on student achievement. The in-service program would be based upon the central office perception of the need.

For example, through the process of criterion-referenced supervision, observers can indicate that teachers are employing low levels of questioning techniques in their classrooms, after analyzing teacher classroom behavior. Because this is a school-wide goal for all staff (developing higher level questioning strategies in the classroom), an in-service day is planned for teachers which will be directed toward employing higher level questioning strategies in the classroom. The central administration secures a consultant who will address the total staff and present an appropriate one-hour lecture on this topic. After the lecture, teachers will view video tapes depicting other teachers employing these higher level strategies in various classroom settings. Resource material is then provided for teachers to study. Observations are prearranged which indicate that, on a prescribed date, observers will be coming to teacher classrooms with a questioning strategy assessment. They will attempt to determine whether, in fact, teachers have developed their questioning strategies as compared with the strategies they employed before the in-service activity.

Another example might be as follows. The central office staff has observed that teachers do not make appropriate use of audio-visual material, specifically, the overhead projector. An in-service activity is planned for teachers which seeks to provide them with information related to the advantages and disadvantages of using the overhead projector. The objective of the in-service is stated as follows: after participating in the in-service experiences, teachers will be able to state the advantages and disadvantages of using the overhead projector. Upon conclusion of the in-service activity teachers are given a paper and pencil assessment which asks them to list and discuss five advantages and disadvantages of using the overhead projector. These assessments are then evaluated by the central office staff. Teachers who are found not to have completed the task successfully (i.e., they have not listed and discussed five advantages and disadvantages) are eventually recycled through a similar in-service activity. Performance criteria provide the structure for the staff development program.

Dwight Allen presents a description of the three general areas in which these performance criteria need to be developed.

The first general area might be labeled "content knowledge." In whatever situation a teacher is operating, he is communicating through some content area. One of the most difficult tasks facing teacher training at any level is the specification of performance criteria in subject areas. We need to develop a hierarchy of criteria that will serve to distinguish the subject matter competence required to teachers in different roles. What general knowledge should all teachers in a given area demonstrate? What specialization and in-depth knowledge should a teacher in a particular role demonstrate? What should a teacher in a particular professional role be able to do, conceptually, with his knowledge of a content area? What differences in performance related to content areas are required for teachers in schools, college-preparatory versus culturally disadvantaged schools and different professional roles (for example, master teacher versus staff teacher, large group lecturer versus seminar leader)?

A second general area that requires specification of performance criteria might be labelled "behavioral skills." To some extent, at least, the complex act of teaching can be broken down into simpler sets of trainable skills and techniques. These skills should be analyzed in such a manner that good agreement can be obtained regarding a given teacher's success at meeting criteria of performance for such skills.

The final area in which performance criteria are required is undoubtedly the most demanding and quite possibly the most important. We all recognize that effective teaching is more than subject matter plus an active repertory of behavioral presentation skills. The "something more" might best be designated as personalogical skills, although the label "skills" may be misleading. Such amorphous traits as respect for students, spontaneity, empathetic understanding, realness, and acceptance are intended to be included under this heading. Although the terms are notable by their ambiguity, it is clearly crucial that we begin to specify their meanings more precisely, for if we fail to do so, the probability is high that we will continue to leave the development of such highly relevant personalogical traits to pure chance. We are obligated to determine which operationally defined personalogical traits are most appropriate for which instructional situations. In this area perhaps more than the others we are faced with difficult problems in terms of priorities, sequencing the attainment of objectives, and stages of professional growth at which attainment of these goals seems more appropriate. The criteria, however, need to be developed if we wish to demonstrate that teacher training at pre- and in-service levels can have a real and powerful effect on improving and maintaining the professional competency of teachers.[1]

Assessing Staff Development Needs

Staff development needs are determined by the administrative staff or the individual who has been designated with staff development responsibility within a specific school building (in most cases, the principal or subject area supervisor). The process of needs assessment takes place on a regular basis. After basic teacher skills have been identified, structure and procedures are designed which allow evaluators to determine the discrepancy between those minimum acceptable standards of performance and the actual level of practice. These levels of practice are determined through classroom observations, review of personnel records, and some pretesting program.

After these data are collected and collated by those individuals responsible, discrepancy or gap statements are written which reflect the degree of congruence or incongruence between idealized skill levels and actual skill attainment. The administration establishes priorities for these discrepancies. For example, it may be found that teaching skill is lacking in each of the three areas where performance criteria have been written. On the basis of school system goals, these areas of discrepancy are arranged by priority and a staff development program is planned in order of that priority.

Specifying Learning Objectives

The individual or group of individuals from the central administration who have overall responsibility for staff development begin the task of building learning objectives based on the identified areas of skill discrepancy. A number of narrow and specific learning objectives are developed. In other words, when a particular skill is found lacking, a number of learning objectives are specified, which, when accomplished, will result in teachers attaining that particular skill. Again, these learning objectives are performance based and, for the most part, are cognitive in nature. The objectives are stated in terms of "what people engaged in the staff development program should be able to do" when the program is completed.

Designing Learning Activities

After learning objectives for skill attainment have been developed, learning activities are then designed which are congruent with those learning objectives. The administrative or supervisory staff is responsible for learning activity development. Since the majority of learning outcomes are skill oriented and cognitive in nature, the learning activities would be designed with little input by those who will be performing the activities.[2] In other words, activities for staff would be chosen from a prescribed list of skills and designed by superiors. The teachers would receive instruction. According to Harris, those activities which would be low in content control might be lectures, illustrated lectures, demonstrations, and observations.[3] Based on the

Alternative-One approach to staff development, the in-service activities would be packaged and presented to the staff for them to digest and apply to their classrooms.

Selecting Resources for Learning

The administration or supervisory staff would have complete control over the selection of resources needed to implement the staff development program. Answers to the following questions would be sought. What individual(s) will be needed to implement staff development activities? What materials will be needed? Where will the staff development activities take place? What are the appropriate dates for activity presentation? What financial resources will be needed?

Evaluating Learning Activities

Learning activities would be evaluated on the basis of what the participants are able *to do* now as compared with what they were able to do prior to participation in the staff-development activity. Post-testing would take place and judgments regarding skill attainment would be made by the program evaluators rather than staff participants. The evaluation would take place as soon after staff participation as possible. The emphasis would be on the analysis of participant behavior rather than their attitudes, beliefs, or feelings.

STAFF DEVELOPMENT—ALTERNATIVE TWO

Althernative Two depicts staff development as a process of learning and problem solving closely related to continuously evolving (individual) interests and changing (school system) needs. Staff development programs focus on the past, the future, outer reality, and inner reality. The continuity of experience, from the past to the future in terms of purpose and goals, and the ever-present interaction of inner and outer realities are dimensions which structure staff development activities and experience.[4]

The major focus of staff development is to engage staff members in purposeful activities which are a function of individual needs and interests interacting with social reality. Staff development programs consistent with Alternative Two are based on the following principles.

Expression and cultivation of individuality within the organizational structure. Staff development activities are individualized based upon boundaries. Certain skills must be attained, however, the individual not only has many options through which he may attain that skill, he has had a significant part in determining what those skills are.

Learning through experience.   Staff development activities would be experientially based. Staff members would be engaged in an active learning process where they are doing something rather than having something done to them.

Acquiring skills as a means of attaining ends which have vital appeal.   The acquiring of skills needed to function effectively are not perceived as ends in themselves, but rather as a means for the attainment of some outcome which staff members perceive as important to their professional and personal growth.

Making the most of the opportunities of present life.   Staff development would focus on current social issues as they relate to the classroom.

Acquaintance with a changing world. Staff development would include, as a major aspect, experiences concerned with hypothesizing, projecting, and problem solving for the future. Experience that promotes collaborative and resourceful decision making in an ever-changing society would be stressed.

Assessing Staff Development Needs

Assessing staff development needs is a mutual process whereby the administration and staff determine staff development programs in terms of the purpose and goals of the system and the purpose and goals of the individuals who work within that system. Gaps would be identified between the role expectations which the school system has set for varying staff roles and the needs of individuals occupying those roles. This needs assessment process would identify the extent of discrepancy between the two dimensions. After this identification of discrepancy is revealed, priorities are determined based upon the degree of discrepancy. In other words, the area of greatest discrepancy would be priority number one.

Again, the crucial aspect of the needs assessment revolves around the collaborative effort of administration and staff in the determination of staff development needs.

Specifying Learning Objectives

Learning objectives would be determined through a process of consensus seeking after answers to the following questions were determined. Based upon the needs assessment, what does the administrator see as appropriate learning objectives? What does the staff see as appropriate learning objectives? What is the degree of congruence between administrator and staff perception of appropriate learning objectives?

Designing Learning Activities

Activities congruent with the Alternative Two approach would most certainly be problem oriented where participants play an active role. Activities would be so structured that participants would have a high degree of input and control. According to Harris, this high degree of impact would be of demand, multisensory workshops, and much two-way communication.[5]

Selecting Learning Resources

After the administration and staff respresentatives have had an opportunity to become familiar with budget allocations for staff development and the nature of learning objectives and activities, both parties might make lists of human, community, and institutional resources which might be used in implementing learning activities. Once again, determination of these resources would be a result of some consensus-seeking process.

Evaluating Learning Activities

The evaluation of staff development programs and activities would be a two-dimensional and three-part process. The administration and staff would independently seek to collect three kinds of evidence. The first kind of evidence would be related to staff acquisition of new knowledge, skills, or attitudes. In other words, what new information or fact or attitude have staff members acquired as a result of participation in learning activities. The second type of evidence would be concerned with an attitudinal assessment as to how staff members have felt about these learning experiences. The third kind of evidence would be related to behavior in the classroom, has the new knowledge, skill, or attitude resulted in a change of behavior in the classroom?

STAFF DEVELOPMENT—ALTERNATIVE THREE

Staff development in an Alternative-Three school is conceptualized as a process which allows staff members to (1) identify their own objectives concerned with personal and professional growth, (2) collect information concerning strengths and weakness related to those objectives, (3) identify incongruency between objectives and actions, and (4) develop staff development activities which will allow them to lessen the gap between their intentions and their actions. Significant attention is given to teacher attitudes, values, and beliefs. It is assumed that only when staff members assume total responsibility for their own growth will staff development be effective.

Those responsible for staff development hold many of the philosophical assumptions of McGregor's Theory Y Management.[6] The motivation, potential for development, and capacity for assuming responsibility are all present in people. Management (the school administrator) does not need to motivate. It is a responsibility of management to make it possible for people to recognize and develop these human characteristics for themselves.

The essential task of management is to arrange organizational conditions and methods of operation so that people can achieve their own goals best by directing their own efforts toward organizational objectives.[7]

Administrators responsible for staff development see their role as that of facilitator—providing staff with both the time and resources needed to conceptualize their experience and to reach insights that alter their perception of their roles and tasks. Furthermore, they assume that staff development activities should be centered around the objectives in their daily work. They also assume that staff members will become involved and seek out staff development activities according to their needs.

The essence of staff development in an Alternative Three school lies in the staff's determination of their own goals and objectives related to personal and professional growth. Staff development activities are personalized and diversified according to individual need, learning style, relationship with other staff members, need for autonomy, etc. For example, two teachers may identify the improvement of the psychological climate within their classrooms as one of their objectives related to personal growth. From the number of alternatives they have developed, they may choose the experiences which they would like to have in order to give them a greater knowledge, new sensitivity, and awareness of psychological climate. One teacher may choose to read widely on the topic or attend a workshop concerned with improving classroom climate. The other may wish to observe a number of times in teachers' classrooms where a favorable psychological climate seems to exist. The teacher alone would be responsible for evaluating personal accomplishment and the worth of the experience.

Foreign to this concept would be in-service days scheduled for all staff at the same time, with all staff experiencing the same activity. As Rubin has stated, "In a typical faculty, the odds are that different teachers will use dissimilar procedures to pursue the same curricular goals."[8] Staff development is perceived as something the individual does to shape his own behavior and improve himself professionally and personally.

Assessing Staff Development Needs

Staff development needs are assessed on a regular basis by each individual staff member. Each staff member develops a structure and procedure which allows him to collect information about his present self. After analyzing the information, he determines what new pursuits would be of most value.

Specifying Learning Objectives

After deciding on a direction, the individual designs a plan of action which will help him reach his goal. His objectives may cut across the total spectrum of cognitive and affective objectives. He is not limited by any external structure of what he "has to do."

Designing Learning Activities

Based upon the assumption that the individual adult knows under what conditions and in what manner he learns best, the staff member has the freedom to explore alternative routes, even change his plan, to attain his goal. For example, his learning objectives may be best accomplished through activities ranging from straight lecture presentation, role-playing, traveling, or sitting on a mountain meditating.

Selecting Resources for Learning

Individual teachers would submit alternative learning activities to the administrator responsible for the management of staff development programs. Along with the listing of various activities, teachers might also make suggestions as to what activities could be shared with others. In cases where individualized objectives and activities are similar, the administrator might help groups of teachers secure resources which are needed to present some small group staff development activities. However, each individual would still have his own plan.

Evaluating Learning Activities

The responsibility for the evaluation of staff development learning activities lies within each individual staff member. The individual is the source of his own reality and no one can better determine the meaning which learning activities have for him. Only the individual can determine the extent to which he has learned. Learning is only perceived as meaningful when the individual can attach new information to his own experience. Only the individual can know precisely the connection between new and past experience.

SUMMARY

We have presented three alternative approaches to staff development. As explained in chapter 9, certain administrator strategies consistent with a particular approach may not reach some students. It is then legitimate to move to other strategies and practices which are not congruent with the school model. The same may be said of approaches to supervision. What is important is that we first reach teachers where they are and generally move closer to the approaches consistent with our overall purpose. Additional staff development activities are provided in chapter 18, entitled "Climate for Change."

NOTES

1. Dwight W. Allen, "In-Service Teacher Training: A Modest Proposal," in *Improving In-Service Education: Proposals and Procedures for Change,* ed. Louis J. Rubin (Boston: Allyn and Bacon, Inc., 1971), pp. 118–120.

2. Ben Harris and Wailand Bessent, *In-Service Education: A Guide to Better Practice* (Englewood Cliffs, N.J.: Prentice-Hall, Inc., 1969), p. 35.

3. Ibid.

4. *A New Look at Progressive Education,* 1972 Yearbook (Washington, D.C.: Association for Supervision and Curriculum Development, 1972), p. 3.

5. Harris and Bessent, *In-Service Education,* p. 34.

6.   Douglas McGregor, *The Human Side of Enterprise* (New York: McGraw-Hill, 1960).

7.   Douglas McGregor, "The Human Side of Enterprise," in *Leadership and Motivation: Essays of Douglas McGregor*, eds. Bennis and Schien (Cambridge, Mass.: Massachusetts Institute of Technology Press, 1966), p. 5.

8.   Louis J. Rubin, "The Self-Evolving Teacher," in *Improving In-Service Education*, p. 270.

SUGGESTIONS FOR FUTHER READING

Argyris, Chris. *Integrating the Individual and the Organization.* New York: John Wiley and Sons, 1964.

Bishop, Leslie J. *Staff Development and Instructional Improvement: Plans and Procedures.* Boston: Allyn and Bacon, Inc., 1976.

Brainard, Edward. "Individualizing Administrator In-Service Education." *Thrust for Education Leadership* 2 (April 1975):29–33.

Jackson, Phillip W. "Old Dogs and New Tricks: Observations on the Continuing Education of Teachers." In *Improving In-Service Education: Proposals and Procedures for Change,* edited by Louis J. Rubin, pp. 19–36. Boston: Allyn and Bacon, Inc., 1971.

Schmuck, Richard A., and Runkel, Phillip J. *Organizational Training for a School Faculty.* Eugene, Oregon: Center for the Advanced Study of Educational Administration, University of Oregon, 1970.

Section Six

Implementing the Resource
Management Dimension

12

Fiscal Management

If the reader is anticipating a definitive work on all the nuances, strategies, and accounting procedures of school budgets, you will find this chapter hopelessly wanting. At best, we can refer you to some excellent practitioner guides that can fill the void. (See the resource section at end of this chapter.) Instead, we wish to view school budgets from the perspective of the degree of impact that they have. Money connotes power, influence, and prestige in our culture. The statement that our society is materialistic has become a cliché. The ways that monies are used in a school and how those decisions are made have a greater impact on staff morale, school productivity, and the attitudes and learning of our students than what actually is purchased. Simply put, the process of purchasing is of greater impact than what is purchased.

To give an example of this, let us assume that there are two new reading programs on the market. Based on empirical research, reading program A is found to be far superior to reading program B. The first scene goes like this. The Hollymead Elementary School needs to update their reading curriculum with a wholesale program adoption. The principal decides that program A will be purchased. Teachers have no input in this selection and, come fall, are told to stop using all previous reading materials and to use only Reading Program A. The staff begins to grumble and gripe to themselves. They don't like being told what to do and their displeasure at being left out of the decision-making process manifests itself in noncompliance with the reading program. It is easier to displace their anger at the materials than at their superior. The result is a year of half-hearted use of the despised program.

Now let's turn the scene around. The principal gives the staff responsibility of reviewing all new reading programs and coming up with a recommendation for purchase. Various sales representatives give their pitch and the staff narrows their decision down to program A or program B. In a final meeting, they decide that program B is better suited to their ways of teaching and the learning style of most of their students. The principal, with some reservations, goes along with the decision. The teachers are pleased and eager to put this program into operation. The result is a year of full effort to make their decision look good.

Taking the two scenes together, we can see the impact of the process of using money. Although program A is empirically sounder than program B, the staff that wants to use program B probably will have better student results than the staff that is forced to use program A. The teachers' attitude toward the materials will be the most important determinant of their success, not the materials themselves. If I give to you a miracle potion that, with correct application, makes average students brilliant and you resent being told to use it, you might skip steps and slop the potion around. If the hoped for results do not materialize because of this sloppiness, then what good is it? You have to believe in and want it to work before you will take all the necessary steps to apply it properly. Only then will it do any good.

Money is the cement between belief in materials and their actual use. By allowing teachers some control of the school budget, they, in essence, have committed themselves to making their decisions work. Teachers in schools committed to individualization need some control over what they use and must have power in fiscal decisions. Educational leaders must give teachers the degree of control that they wish teachers, in turn, to give their students. Therefore, the degree of control will vary for each of our three alternative school models. This chapter will focus on how school monies would be used to be consistent with each school model. The final section of this chapter will be devoted to providing some time saving and cost efficiency hints as well as some ethical considerations in handling finances.

ALTERNATIVE ONE

Alternative One has a curriculum that is predictable, sequential, and directive. A body of knowledge has been determined as important for students to learn. That body of knowledge has been broken into a hierarchy of smaller skills and packaged for student use. Students move through the same sequence of skills at different rates. The teacher insures that students use materials in a prescribed manner. The teacher controls the scheduling, activities, and materials in order to maximize academic achievement.

This model, which revolves around the teacher as the director of student learning, presupposes a similar role for the principal in regard to his or her staff. The principal facilitates efficiency making decisions and handling most matters in a unilateral way. The teachers' energies are felt to be dissipated from classroom functions if involved heavily in school-wide matters. The teacher is left to teach; the principal takes care of the rest.

The budget is kept centralized by the leader. Since student learning is sequential, it is imperative that all curriculum materials be uniform throughout the school. The same reading system or social studies system must be used by all grades to insure smooth transitions and continuous progress from year to year. For this reason, staff are given the function of making school-wide recommendations for the adoption of programs. Teachers must meet across grade levels and the principal reserves the power to act or not act upon the recommendation. It is believed that only he or she has a total organizational perspective and, thus, must ultimately insure that the programs adopted are in keeping with the needs and abilities of students and staff.

ALTERNATIVE TWO

Alternative Two has a curriculum that is sequential and directive for the three Rs. The other areas of instruction are more open-ended and activity centered. The teacher is, therefore, a jack-of-all-trades, the director of prescribed learning as well as the facilitator of exploration. The principal also must move throughout the spectrum of leadership. The principal does not involve teachers in some issues but keeps them heavily involved in others.

The manner in which school budget allocations are determined clearly demarcates the role of the principal. In purchases of programs for basic skill instruction, the principal must centralize the purchase. The materials selected must be of wholesale use throughout the school. The principal therefore asks for staff recommendations but reserves the right to make the final decision. However, when it comes to decisions on allocations for materials outside of this basic instructional area, he or she encourages the staff to make their own individual assessments. For example, an operating budget for a medium-sized school might be around fifteen thousand dollars for textbooks, consumable materials, and equipment. The principal decides that nine thousand dollars are to go for school-wide adoption or replacement of basic academic program materials. After consulting with the staff, he or she makes the final decision as to what will be purchased. The remaining six thousand dollars may be allocated as teachers see fit. They might decide they need to use the money to restock general art supplies as well as make individual allocations to each teacher for their own individual needs. It is agreed that one thousand dollars will be spent on art supplies, the other five thousand dollars will be divided equally among the teachers to spend as they wish. Via this process, the principal has modeled for the teacher the role they are to play with their students. The principal is a delineator of the boundaries that teachers work within. He or she is the enforcer of certain tasks, e.g., by making expenditures for school programs of basic skills. The principal, as well may be a facilitative colleague in other tasks, e.g., by being only a participant in decision-making concerning classroom materials to be purchased that are not directly related to the basic skill areas.

ALTERNATIVE THREE

Alternative Three has a curriculum that is integrated, exploratory, and open-ended. Students do not learn skills in a structured, sequential, or singular approach in any of the disciplines. Rather, instruction builds on each individual child's interests, development, and style of learning. The teacher allows the child maximum flexibility to pursue his own interests within the broad boundaries of being considerate of others. The teacher stimulates development with probing questions, changing the environment, and serving as a resource to his or her students. The principal, in order to be consistent with this style, must be one who enhances the same autonomy and self-responsibility in teachers. The principal involves staff as full partners in all issues that effect them. He or she participates as an equal member of the staff, working towards consensus of thought as well as helping to clarify alternatives and consequences of various decisions.

The school budget is a tangible issue that effects all members. As such, it is left open to the staff to decide how it is to be implemented. The principal may hold out for certain priorities and make a case for them, but the case is not won unless the group, as a whole, agrees. For example, the use of the fifteen thousand dollar allocation previously mentioned might go like this. Each staff member verbalizes what new purchases he or she perceives would be of benefit to all school members and then states his or her own particular class needs. The staff then decides what the priorities are and allocates accordingly. Perhaps five thousand dollars will be spent on school equipment such as a copy machine, laminating equipment, and filmstrip projectors to be shared by all. Another two thousand dollars might go for general school supplies (paper, paints, rope, etc.). One thousand dollars might be allotted to the principal for discretionary funds. The staff might then decide to disperse the remaining seven thousand dollars by giving a disproportionate amount to the first grade teachers who have many students with special needs and to new teachers who do not have adequate existing materials. Regardless of how the budget specifically works out, the staff makes the decisions through democratic participation.

SCHOOL BUDGET USE

"Now, wait a minute," resounds the unspoken voice of the reader. "There are too many differences in the situations from the preceding discussion on use of budgets (related to school models) to apply in my situation. Here are some of my real circumstances. How do you deal with them?"

Situation 1. "I don't get to decide how to use a lump sum of money. I have to submit a year in advance to the central office a detailed proposed budget that accounts for how each dollar will be spent."

Reply (A). Many schools decide how much money they will need for the following year, write in commercial items and materials that justify the amount to the school board and community, and then when the money is appropriated, spend it in related but perhaps different ways.

Reply (B). If you don't act on Reply (A), then the process of preparing a budget for the following year may be done in the same way proposed for each school model. In other words, the staff can work on formulating the proposal.

Situation 2. "I have no control over the school budget. Materials are selected by the superintendent or curriculum supervisors in the central office. Our school simply receives what *they* order."

Reply (A). If you and your staff have no input or control of the budget, then obviously our previous discussion has little application. Perhaps an Alternative One school could accept this centralization more so than the other two alternatives. However, school systems that do operate in this way might have serious staff morale problems. To disallow the people who are in a changing school and who are most directly affected by school expenditures to have a say is obviously questioning their competence. It indicates scorn and a lack of respect for the people who are vital to the success of the local school.

If this is your situation, we would make two suggestions. First, fight like hell for the decentralization of at least some budget accounts. Don't try to get control over all the line items at once; the general supplies account would be a good start. Secondly, there must be some school monies, no matter how small, that are discretionary. The principal's own administrative account usually contains a few hundred dollars for travel, office expenses, and office equipment. Even on that limited a scale, allow the staff a degree of input that corresponds to your school's goals. We will amplify on this matter later in this chapter under the heading, "Discretionary Funds."

Situation 3. "My staff has never had input or control over the budget; they would go into shock if I turned it over to them. Also, I don't see why the use of budget needs to relate to school curriculum methods, materials, student management, and staff supervision."

Reply (A). You are right. Any dramatic change in habitual procedures will throw people into shock unless they are properly prepared and have had time to work toward the desired amount of involvement. The principal's job, then, is to orient the staff in budgetary procedures, delineate the amount of responsibility that is being given, and then allow staff additional experience by making decisions which involve smaller amounts of money. *We never said that the principal turns over the budget to this teachers.* Alternative Three has the greatest amount of staff control. However, the principal is part of that staff and has as much right as anyone else to push for his or her priorities.

Finally, if the reader does not understand why a principal must give up his dearly held prerogative to unilaterally handle financial decisions, let us reiterate our initial point made in this chapter. The principal is a model for the staff. The way he or she deals with them will have an influence on how teachers, in turn, deal with their students. Since money is esteemed and valued by all, its use in the school is a pivotal indication of the latitude and responsibility expected of staff and, in turn, what will be expected of students.

BUDGETARY HINTS

It would be naïve of us to have the reader "hooked" on the central concept of involving staff in budgetary decisions without supplying some information about implementation. The following should be helpful.

Staff Consensus on Decisions

Whether staff will make a final decision or a recommendation on expenditures, a system for arriving at a consensus is vital. A school leader does not want a battle to take place. Unless consensus is reached, the school runs the risk of group fragmentation created by closed door politics. The principal wants to promote a staff decision or recommendation that everyone can live with. For this reason, it is important for individuals to set their individual priorities within the context of overall school priorities. This might be done in a faculty meeting of approximately thirty staff members in the following way. This procedure is described as taking place in one meeting of two-hours length but it might more realistically take several more sessions. It is important to allow different points of view to be aired fully so that no one feels that the meeting(s) are being railroaded toward a certain end.

Each staff member is asked to come to this meeting with two lists. One list contains those items felt needed to strengthen the overall school program. The other is a list of requests to strengthen the individual staff member's instruction within the classroom. Each expenditure should be attached with a dollar figure. The principal begins the meeting by stating clearly what the end result of this meeting will be—a final decision, a tentative one, or a recommendation for consideration. The principal also specifies the amount of money available.

The staff is then divided into groups of five. Each group is given the responsibility for reaching agreement of overall school purchases needed, listed in priority, and another list of individual needs that cannot be subsumed under the school-wide priorities. Each group should first select a recorder. Each member then presents his or her school list to the group. After each list is read, the group can immediately pick out needs that are common to all individuals. A discussion of individual needs should take place. The group requests are ranked and the list is terminated when the total amount of money available has been accounted for. The recorder is then responsible for presenting the group list in the next part of the meeting.

The next aspect of the meeting consists of having each recorder write his or her list on a chalkboard or large newsprint paper and presenting the group's view. The lists should be clearly visible to all in the room. The principal directs each recorder to read his or her list and to provide appropriate rationale for each item. After each recorder finishes his or her presentation, there is time for other group members to add further detail and for others to ask questions. After each list is presented, the meeting is opened for general discussion. Either the principal or an assigned member can act as the overall school recorder. The principal asks the staff if any items cut across all or most of the group lists. The principal records the common ones on the blackboard including dollar amounts. He or she asks if there are items that are listed differently by groups but could be subsumed under a common heading. He or she then lists those. Now the principal asks if there are any individual group items that have not been recorded on the school list that persons feel are important to include. If there are, a discussion follows; and, if necessary, a vote can be taken as to whether to include it. With the school list on the board, the principal totals the dollar amount of all listed items. If the items are under the total amount of monies available, other suggestions can be taken for adding more items. In all probability, this will not happen and the staff expenditures will be above the total.

The principal now asks the staff to develop a priority ranking. Thirty faculty members active in this particular stage might prove cumbersome. Instead, one individual from each group would form a new group representative of the total school staff. Six members are now working out the priorities in full view of their colleagues. Others may be invited to enter the discussion at the leader's discretion when help is deemed necessary to reach consensus.

This procedure provides a democratic vehicle for soliciting all individual views. Yet, individuals acting as part of a group keep the task focused on collective needs. The final results might be more indicative of a school's philosophy and goals, and will not be unduly influenced by one individual's persuasiveness or dominance.

Purchase orders. The greater the degree of control staff has in making budgetary decisions, the more likely that the number of purchase orders will increase. When expenditures are centralized and made by the principal, it is a relatively easy matter to make orders out to a few large wholesale companies. For some reason, when staff has purchasing power, they shop around and request single items that are only handled by specific, sometimes out-of-the-way companies. (One of us remembers ordering manipulative mathematics materials that had to be retrieved in a warehouse located in the loft of a barn in a remote part of Maine.) Also, when staff have purchasing power, they usually opt to allocate some of the monies equally among each classroom. When each staff member submits his or her own requests, this naturally increases the number of purchase orders.

To save the principal or, more likely, the secretary from being inundated with constant search and retrieval missions, it is best to have the staff take full responsibility for providing all information needed to fill out the official purchase order. In fact, we would suggest mimeographing the exact purchase order forms and having the staff fill in all information needed to process their requested items. Then, the principal or secretary need not search among catalogues for exact prices, shipping costs, catalogue numbers, and addresses. He or she can also gather all the same company purchases on a single form. It is important for record keeping purposes that all official purchase orders go out from the principal's office so that proper accounting procedures can be used to keep budget lines clear and current. This bit of advice may appear trivial to the beginning school administrator, but the experienced person who has spent endless days and nights locating purchase order information, preparing them, and accounting for their delivery, knows that such advice is valuable. Save yourself time and work by asking teachers to give you all the information needed. If the form is brought to you incomplete, send it back requesting the information needed.

Individual teacher allotments.   Since we are discussing how to be efficient in ordering teacher-requested items, special accounting procedures also need to be mentioned. If the staff decides to give each individual an allotment of three hundred dollars per classroom, the principal needs to keep a separate account for each teacher in addition to the regular school account. This is not much additional work provided that teachers have been required to submit completed unofficial purchase orders. Obviously, the principal needs this separate account information to halt the teacher who is overspending. Surprisingly, in our experience, more often teachers do not spend their entire allotment. At one school with over twenty teachers, in three years only two teachers spent all they were allotted. It's ironic how, when the same people did not have separate allotments and the principal made all decisions, they would complain about the lack of money for materials. They would constantly request that their budgets be increased. However, when they were given an allotment to spend as they deemed appropriate, they became very cost conscious. It was as if it were being taken from their own personal savings. To say the least, it is a pleasant reversal to have extra money left over from various unspent teacher accounts. In many systems, money not spent by the end of the fiscal year is permanently lost to the school. As a result, it is a good practice to set a deadline for all individual allotments to be spent at least one month before the fiscal year ends. After that time, remaining money must go into a common pool to be used either at the principal's discretion or based upon the staff's recommendation.

Discretionary funds.   Regardless of the amount of control a staff is given in budgetary matters, we are strong believers that the principal should have some discretionary monies. Most school systems have a line account for administrative expenses. However, we extend discretionary funds to include monies from the textbooks, consumable materials, library supplies, and equipment accounts as well. In Alternative One and Two schools, the principal can simply decide the amount and remove it from staff consideration. In an Alternative Three school, the principal might have to fight to convince the staff of his or her needs. When the school year is in progress, the principal often can see the need to bolster curriculum, provide special materials for a child, or give a troubled teacher a hand with extra supplies. By having such reserve funds, the money can be dispensed quickly.

Line accounts.   In all schools there is a gap between community understanding and teaching realities. The school board, for example, is often more ready to increase the textbook rather than the consumable supplies account. Community people can relate more to a need for more textbooks than to a need for additional art supplies. It is not unheard of for a superintendent to go to the school board asking for increases in textbooks when the need is really for consumables. If the school system is not tied to strict line account budgeting, the approved increase in textbooks might be transferred during the year to consumable goods. Some may object to this practice *but, if there are no legal restrictions* other than staying within the total budget, there is nothing wrong with such switching of accounts. The ability to transfer funds across accounts gives a school greater flexibility in meeting their own needs. What a school requests a year beforehand when submitting a line item budget, will not correspond exactly to the needs when the operating year begins. For these reasons, although we acknowledge that this policy is out of the realm of consideration for some schools, we urge a principal and staff to have as much flexibility with budget accounts as possible.

Other monies.   There are, of course, limits to how school money may be used. For example, personnel cannot be hired from a single school's operating funds without a formal nomination by the superintendent and approval by the school board. Usually capital expenditures are treated in the same manner. This does not necessarily mean, however, that a school is unable to use other readily available monies (not school revenues) to make such expenditures. A school needing a part-time secretary but unable to get school board approval might raise money through P.T.O. fund raising. We know of such cases where secretaries were hired at the minimum wage to work two hours per day (a total cost of nine hundred dollars per year). In another case, a school hired additional playground supervisors at lunchtime by using money from the school's photography fund. Three mothers living near the school were hired to work one-half hour per day at the minimum wage (a total expenditure of six hundred dollars for the year). Admittedly, considerations such as liability insurance have to be checked beforehand. The point is that if a principal looks hard enough, he or she can usually find small sums to be allocated to meet isolated needs. *Monies outside of formal school revenues must be strictly accounted for.* The school administrator is as responsible for these funds as any other. Written checks on these accounts need to be accounted for and should be countersigned.

Ethical considerations.   Money should be spent in order to directly improve the conditions for and the instruction of students. Expenditures for materials, books, audio-visual equipment, field trips, etc. have always been regarded as appropriate. Expenditures for in-service consultants, travel for professional meetings, visits to exemplary schools, and released time, all contribute to the success of a school but often are met with skepticism by the public. At times, a principal is forced into the position of deciding whether to spend authorized money for unauthorized use. For example, if a teacher who is going through an emotional upheaval at home would be better off taking a few days off from school, what should the principal do? The school system has no policy for such absence with pay. They do have a policy for physical illness. What is in the best interest of the school? Should the teacher be forced to legally stay on the job in this case, or should he or she be asked to leave without pay? Perhaps the principal finally decides to have the teacher take a two-day vacation and writes it off as physical illness. The principal feels that this is in the best interest of children, yet he or she also knows that this is not abiding by the letter of school policy.

Obviously, the principal is legally wrong. He or she might face some pointed questions if the truth be known. Principals, supervisors, and administrators all over this country make these "illegal" decisions everyday. The blatant, immoral misuse of funds from the highest offices in America to the local level have heightened the public sensitivity to improprieties. Yet, there is no way that we, as educators, can chastise the principal who uses such funds as described above. The principal may be legally wrong but perhaps morally right. He or she has used funds to improve the conditions of the school. The principal's decision was not based on personal gain and he or she has not cheated the public of their tax dollars. We know others will object to this, but the facts are that if a leader is to lead, he or she may be forced to make ethical decisions. In doing so, the leader must decide whether to follow the letter of the law (school policy) or do what is in the best interest of children. The principal might sacrifice legality for morality. However, extreme caution is recommended and the principal's superiors should always be informed of such discretionary action.

SUGGESTIONS FOR FURTHER READING

Fiscal Management Resource Books

Burrup, Percy E. *Financing Education in a Climate of Change.* 2d ed. Boston: Allyn and Bacon, Inc., 1977.

Candoli, I. Carl; Hack, Walter G; Ray, John R.; and Stollar, Dewey. *School Business Administration: A Planning Approach.* Boston: Allyn and Bacon, Inc., 1977.

Johns, Roe L., and Morphet, Edgar L. *The Economics and Financing of Education: A Systems Approach.* Englewood Cliffs, N.J.: Prentice-Hall, Inc., 1975.

Jordan, K. Forbis. *School Business Administration.* New York: Ronald Press, 1969.

Stoops, Emery; Rafferty, Max; and Johnson, Russel. *Handbook of Educational Administration.* Boston: Allyn and Bacon, Inc., 1975.

13

Environmental Management

After observing many schools and discussing our thoughts with school personnel and colleagues, we felt that there was a need to include a chapter on managing the school environment. As the psychologist Mehrabian wrote:

> Human beings have a Promethean gift amounting to genius for deliberately altering their environments, and to deny or minimize this gift is to be ignorant. But this human genius can be more or less informed, more or less effective in achieving its goals.[1]

It is our intention to show how the environment can facilitate the kinds of learning that a school wishes to promote.

ALTERNATIVE ENVIRONMENTS

Environmental psychology is an emerging field of study. Researchers are beginning to gather information on the effects of the many variables in one's immediate life-space. It is known that light, noise, and visual stimulation have a physiological effect on a person's cardiovascular system. Body temperature rises or decreases according to the degree of exposure to certain stimuli. It is further suggested that the organization of physical space and time have similar effects. That we can shape our environments in different ways, such that we are relaxed, aroused, or put to sleep is not surprising. Just think of how a discotheque is arranged for high arousal—flashing lights, spectrums of color, loud and pulsating noise, changing visual images, and the continuous flow of music. On the other hand, we can think of how a hotel room is set up for low arousal (depending on the hotel), soft colors, dim lights, subdued noises, and minimal visual stimula-

157

tion. The disco is for fleeting, energetic involvement; the hotel room is for sleeping.

The application of such obvious knowledge as it relates to the school environment is often overlooked. We do not consciously consider the variables of color, noise, light, visual stimulation, organization of space, and the use of time, while planning to facilitate desired learning. Possibly we have failed to act because environmental research has focused on physiological relationships more than cognitive ones. More likely it is the result of simply taking the school environment for granted. If the walls need painting and there is some leftover paint in the basement, we decide that we might as well use it. After all, paint is paint. Environmental psychologists are telling us something different. Paint is not just paint; light is not just light; noise is not just noise, etc.

Alternative One

In the Alternative One school, the environment should be arranged so that the student is able to focus on a single variable at a time. Whether it is reading a bulletin board, following a teacher lecture, viewing a filmstrip, or writing in a programmed lesson, all extraneous stimulation should be minimal. What is called for is the student's total absorption in the task at hand. As a result, the school house and classroom should manipulate color, noise, light, visual stimulation, and space and time to promote full student concentration in his or her directed work.

The School Building.   The color scheme of the halls might be a plain gray, green, or brown. Noise is virtually nonexistent. Students need to keep their voices down and walk quietly. The lighting of the building is also subdued. The only visual stimulation is a few widely spaced bulletin boards. Each bulletin board has a particular academic theme such as "Reading Is Fun" or a moral message such as "Considerate Students Become Good Citizens." The halls are kept free of furniture or activities. Any small rooms off the hall are used for specialized instruction (remedial reading, learning disabilities, speech therapy, etc.), or for storage of extra supplies.

Time schedules in this building are precise. Each classroom has assigned amounts of time for instruction. The entire day is segmented according to subject matter (i.e., reading—1½ hours, math—1 hour, language arts—30 minutes, art or music—30 minutes, physical education—30 minutes).

The schedule of time and organization of space is arranged to expedite student travel from one assigned task to the next. This is why school halls are kept clean, quiet, and plain. There is no purpose served by having a lot of noise and interaction during class transitions, students need to move along.

The Classroom.   Color, noise, light, and visual stimulation are also kept at low levels. Most displays around the room are teacher or commercially developed to reinforce previously introduced academic concepts. Time is structured according to school subject areas and strictly adhered to. Furniture is functional with students having assigned desks or tables apart from each other. This minimizes conversation and motion that might interfere with a student doing his or her various assignments. In some rooms, the desks may be arranged traditionally so that all students face the teacher. More often, though, in an individualized Alternative One School, students will be assigned to work on different tasks spaced around the room during one subject period. Some might be working in programmed books, others might be receiving personalized instruction, while others might be working with tapes, filmstrips, or records. Whether the room is traditionally arranged with rows of desks or grouped according to individual assignments, the student is assigned to a particular space. The entire classroom space is used as an academic work area. See Figure 13.1.

Alternative Two

The Alternative Two model attempts to bend both ends toward the middle. The environment has to be organized so as to focus the student's attention on basic skills as well as be organized to encourage exploration and inventiveness. Obviously, it is rather difficult to take the same space and make it simultaneously subdued and active. Unless a school has modular walls that can be moved in and out of the environment, distinctions with respect to space and time allocation need to be made for prescriptive and discovery learning.

The School Building.   The colors of the entrance and halls might be a solid tone of blue or yellow. The lighting is bright and highlights the color of the hall and the displays on the walls. There are many bulletin boards and a variety of themes and messages are evident. They range from the predictable themes of "National Safety Week" and "Multiplication Facts" to "Solve the Riddles" and "Who Are You?" Both the work of teachers and students are displayed. Throughout the building, students are restrained from boisterous talk and action. However, noise which evolves from normal student conversation is acceptable. Time is rigidly scheduled in all classrooms for a part of the day according to subject areas. A visitor walking through the school in the morning might be impressed by the quiet work-like atmosphere.

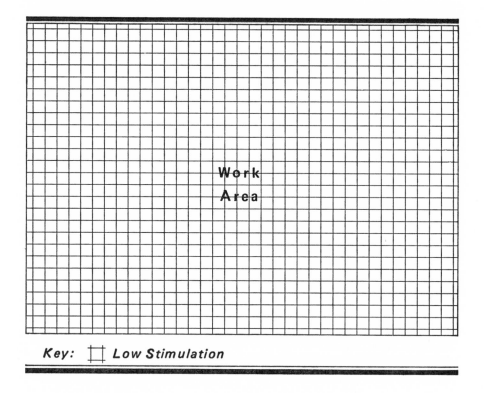

Figure 13.1. *An Alternative One Classroom*

Upon returning to the school in the afternoon, the visitor might experience quite a different atmosphere. Time would be largely interrupted and a wide array of student activity and involvement would be apparent. The noise level would be higher, and much of the physical space of the building would be in use. The halls might be rehearsal places for a play, or a group of students might be measuring the length of the school with erasers. Student traffic would be flowing between room and hall.

Classroom. Since the teacher's role changes from dispenser and supervisor of essential knowledge to that of guider and facilitator of student discovery, the classroom needs to be conducive to both. There should be a large area for attentive learning. This area needs to be devoid of extraneous noise and visual attractions. Students might all face towards the instructional area and thus away from parts of the room that contain glossy pictures, activity centers, aquariums, and other high interest materials. Student carrels, room dividers, and bookshelves might physically separate the work territory from the activity territory. Since time is most commonly scheduled to avoid work and activity periods from coinciding, the teacher need not be concerned with the noise of one area interferring with the other. Rather, the teacher need mainly be concerned with blotting out visual distraction. However, if he or she does decide to have students engage in both types of learning at the same time, the classroom might appear as follows. One half of the room would have individual desks or groups of desks where academic instruction takes place. The other half of the room would consist of tables and materials for manipulative activities and student displays. The academic area would be of low stimulation and the surrounding activity area of opposite intensity. See Figure 13.2.

During activity time, students can use the work area for their group discussions. Since furniture might be arranged or moved out or

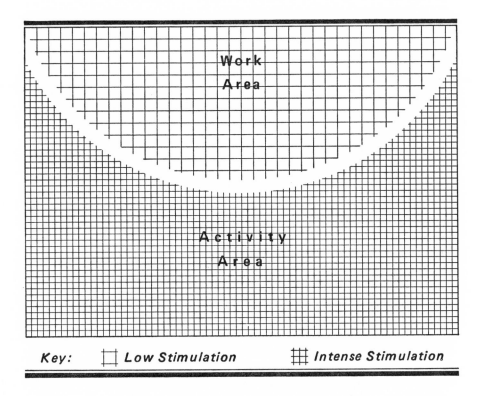

Figure 13.2. *An Alternative Two Classroom*

back depending on the time of day, flexible, movable desks, chairs, and tables in the work area are essential.

Alternative Three

If we can liken the Alternative One environment to a hotel room, then an Alternative Three environment is a hotel's Disco (perhaps an Alternative Two environment is the lobby for sitting, reading, observing, talking, and transacting business). The Alternative Three environment invites children to question, to talk, and to experiment. Environmental variables are chosen for their high arousal value, to encourage a child to be active, to discuss, and to create.

The School Building.   The halls are painted or wallpapered in vivid tones of colors such as red or orange. Visual displays cover the walls. Windows will have homemade curtains. Plants or mobiles are suspended from the ceilings. Tables with an abundance of children's work may greet the visitor at the school's entrance. One cannot walk anywhere in the school without seeing a display that attracts attention. The human noise level throughout the school is high. In the background music may be heard over the school's intercom. Other sounds might be those of manual work; wood being sawed or nails being hammered. The hall is used as more than a passway, but as an overflow area for classroom activities such as plays being rehearsed. Small closet spaces off the halls are also used for children; one might be a carpentry area, another a radio or recording studio, and another a school newspaper office. Light is not only for general illumination, but also to highlight interesting areas. Along with the normal, institutional corridor lights there might also be spotlights shining on art work or standing lamps accentuating table collections. Time schedules do not interrupt student involvement. Other than an official starting, lunch and closing time, the schedule is kept flexible. Some students may even choose to work through their lunch time on particular projects.

The Classroom.   The essential environmental variables of the school building are equally evident in the classroom. The classroom environment facilitates student exploration. The teacher's major function is to be the arranger and rearranger of the child's world to encourage that exploration. Therefore, the room is constantly being rearranged. New materials, displays, and constructions are changed from week to week. Furniture is rearranged, color schemes are revised, and project center themes are replaced.

Color, noise, and lighting are ample. Students schedule their own time, usually with the sole obligation to the teacher that reading

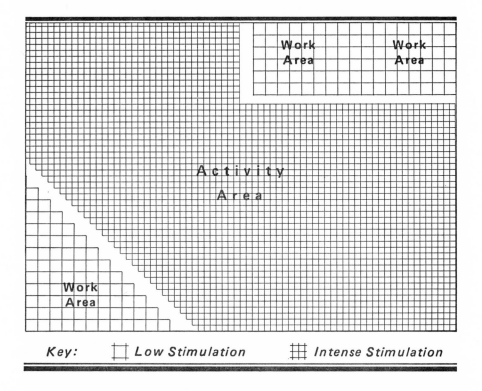

Figure 13.3. *An Alternative Three Classroom.*

and mathematic activities will be completed at some point during the day. Furniture is comfortable and functional. The furniture is physically arranged in the various activity or interest centers throughout the room. Individual desks are not present. Cubbies, tote trays, or shelves serve as student places to put their personal possessions.

Because of the high activity level, most Alternative Three classrooms have space that is isolated from the bustling mainstream. These places serve as retreats for students who wish to be alone or who have work to do that demands quiet concentration. Similarly, the teacher might carve out his or her own mini-environment to hold conferences with individual students. These mini-environments may be found in storage closets, partitioned space (using dividers), or, as one of us has seen, in a cut out refrigerator box. The classroom is arranged for activity, with isolated spaces for quiet work. This room is illustrated in Figure 13.3.

ENVIRONMENT AS REFLECTING
SCHOOL VALUES

To say that an Alternative One school values quiet or that an Alternative Three school values noise is too simplistic and misses the point. Neither one goes to the extreme where absolute silence or resounding volume is desirable. Rather, it is the use of the environmental variables that is indicative of the school's values. Alternative One places emphasis on a quiet environment so students may fully concentrate on their basic task. Alternative Two develops an environment that moves from tranquility to excitement in order to contribute to its ultimate purpose of having students become competent in essential as well as problem-solving skills. Alternative Three creates an environment that is highly arousing in order to contribute to its ultimate purpose of developing self-directed students. The environment is obviously quite important in the achievement of a school's goals for its children. Careful consideration as to color, noise, lighting, visual elements, physical space, and the organization of time is important for promoting learning.

The environment shapes humans, and humans in turn shape it. At all times, each is working on the other. Educators need to determine how to manipulate that environment in ways that contribute to desired student learning. It is ridiculous for a school bent on directive, cognitive skills to have a bombastic, multisensory work area. It is incongruent for a school desiring a balanced content and process learning to have an environment that complements only one to the exclusion of the other. Equally foolish is the school that values discovery to have a "hands off" subdued facility. We are only at the frontier of knowledge concerning what environmental variables do to people. As research provides us with more knowledge about the effects of environmental stimuli, we will be able to develop more exact environments that fit our educational goals. Until then, we must operate on reasonable assumptions and plan accordingly.

ENVIRONMENTAL MANAGEMENT—
SOME LAST THOUGHTS

That the environment can support a school's values, has been made clear. Some facets of the environment, however, cannot be easily changed. The structure of the building, whether it is an open one-level building or an egg-crate with three stories, is a factor that cannot be altered unless money for major construction is expended. Therefore, we have limited our discussion to what *can* be controlled within any building. We used a conventional building in our descriptions (hallways and single classrooms), yet the applications are easily made to a modern, open space building, or a converted warehouse. Other givens in a building are the maintenance areas of heating, plumbing, and electricity. There is reason to suppose that the building temperature, availability of water, and degree of natural light have physiological effects on humans. However, we often are powerless to apply this knowledge. These concerns rest largely in the hands of architects and engineers who plan the facility. Therefore, although important, there is little value in spending much time on these factors.

We have also not discussed the planning of energy conservation or dealing with emergencies. These issues are usually part and parcel of the principal's role. However, these issues are outside the focus of this book in that they do not bear directly upon the instructional process. In the following section, we suggest some books that might help the interested reader to prepare for such matters. Another section provides the reader with additional materials on environmental influences in school settings.

NOTES

1.   Albert Mehrabian, *Public Places and Private Spaces* (New York: Basic Books, Inc., 1976), p. 10.

SUGGESTIONS FOR FURTHER READING

Maintenance of School Buildings

American Association of School Administrators. 1976. *To Recreate a School Building.* Arlington, Va.

Herman, Jerry, and Hirsekorn, Robert. *Administrator's Guide to School Construction, Remodeling, and Maintenance.* West Nyack, N.Y.: Parker Publishing Co., 1975.

Stoops, Emory; Rafferty, Max; and Johnson, Russell. *Handbook of Educational Administration.* Boston: Allyn and Bacon, Inc., 1975.

Environmental Influences in School Settings

Barker, R. G., and Gump, P. V. *Big School, Small School.* Stanford, Calif.: Stanford University Press, 1964.

Birch, Jack W., and Johnstone, Kenneth D. *Designing Schools and Schooling for the Handicapped: A Guide to the Dynamic Instruction of Space, Instructional Materials, Facilities, Educational Objectives and Teaching Method.* Springfield, Ill.: Charles C. Thomas, 1975.

Cohen, M. D. "Recycling Elementary Schools: People, Program, Facilities." *Childhood Education* (1973): 49, 302–306.

Council of Educational Facility Planners. 1971. *Guide for Planning Educational Facilities.* Columbus, Ohio.

Davis, James. *The Principal's Guide to Educational Facilities: Design, Utilization, and Management.* Columbus, Ohio: Merrill Publishing Co., 1973.

Mehrabian, Albert. *Public Places and Private Spaces.* New York: Basic Books, Inc., 1976.

The University of Chicago School Review 4 (1974).

Section Seven

Assessment

14

Assessing the Four Dimensions of Schooling

The purpose of this chapter is to provide the administrator with assessment techniques related to each of the four schooling dimensions. Based upon our experience, we can empathize with the school administrator when we think about all the sophisticated assessment techniques that the experts have recommended for use in the schools. Many of these instruments are difficult to administer and interpret, some may cost too much and require more time than is available. With this in mind, we are presenting techniques that are simple in conception and design and easy to administer and interpret. We do not presuppose that the instruments are *statistically* valid and reliable and should be used for research purposes. The statements selected for assessment are indications of the dimensions as we have previously portrayed them. They are illustrative and in no way meant to be exhaustive. Each of the assessment instruments presented is an outgrowth of the chapter which deals with that dimension. Therefore, definitions of each of the assessment items and questions concerning the items may be answered by referring to the respective chapter.

The assessment instruments should yield data which allows decision makers to determine the extent of congruency within and across each schooling dimension with respect to each of the alternative models. Chapter 15 will focus on procedures that might be used to analyze the data generated by the assessment techniques.

CURRICULUM DIMENSION ASSESSMENT

The following assessment instrument is concerned with the curriculum dimension of schooling. The assessment has two aspects. Subassessment A is directed at assessing general curriculum concerns and encompasses teaching style, method, views of the learner, evaluation, student outcomes, and curriculum planning. Subassessment B is directed at analyzing the specific methods and materials used with students to implement the curriculum design. The responses to each of the questions are reflective of one of the overarching philosophical positions.

Subassessment A—Curriculum

A. The *major* teaching methods in our school are
1. Lecture, followed by individual student assignment
2. Group discussion, seminars
3. Providing students with numerous choices of individual activities

B. Teachers appear to be *most* concerned with students
1. Mastering basic facts and information
2. Acquiring problem solving skills
3. Becoming more aware of themselves

C. Most teachers see their role as
1. Dispensers of fact and knowledge
2. Collaborators of learning
3. Facilitators of a free environment

D. Curriculum emphasis in our school is based upon
1. Subject or discipline orientation
2. Core concerns and flexibile, student-centered activity
3. Individual child preference

E. The major focus of instructional content is on
1. Reading, writing, arithmetic
2. Current events and social problems
3. Free choice

F. Our curriculum is based upon our view of students as
1. Receiving information
2. Experiencing organisms
3. Ultimate choosers of their experiences

H. In general, our curriculum seeks educational output of
1. Students as knowers
2. Students as problem solvers
3. Students as self-actualized individuals

I. Our curriculum is designed to
1. Allow students to "fit" into the existing social order
2. Allow students to "fit" into a changing social order
3. Allow students to make their own reality

J. Curriculum planning is
1. Totally teacher planned

    2. Planned by students and teachers cooperatively
    3. Almost totally student planned

K. How classes are run is determined
    1. Almost entirely by teachers
    2. By teachers and students cooperatively
    3. Almost entirely by students

L. Responsibility for student learning is
    1. Primarily the teacher's
    2. Both student's and teacher's
    3. Primarily the student's

M. Students are evaluated primarily by
    1. Objective examinations
    2. Both formal and informal examinations
    3. No formal examinations

N. Our evaluation of students is
    1. Based on external standards (minimum skill attainment, normal curve)
    2. Based upon student achievement relative to individual potential
    3. Based primarily on student self-evaluation

O. In our school, curriculum objectives related to student learning are primarily
    1. Cognitive
    2. Both cognitive and affective
    3. Affective

P. Learning objectives for students are determined by
    1. The teacher on the basis of pretest
    2. Teacher and student on the basis of pretest and student interest
    3. Students on basis of interest

Q. Our curriculum is
    1. Sequential and standard in all subject areas across all grade levels
    2. Sequential and standard only in the basic skill areas
    3. Nonsequential and nonstandard in all areas of learning.

Subassessment B—Methods and Materials

A. Materials are basically
    1. Directive
    2. Balanced between directive and open-ended
    3. Open-ended

B. One method used over others is
    1. Programmed or sequential packets and centers

      2. Learning centers that are directive and exploratory
      3. Activity or interest centers

C. Students use the materials
      1. In a prescribed manner
      2. In a manner that allows for some individual variations
      3. In any manner that they choose

D. Materials rely heavily on the students'
      1. Language comprehension
      2. Ability to balance language and manipulation
      3. Concrete manipulation

E. Completion of materials results in
      1. Similar products for all students
      2. Individual variations of outcome
      3. No particular outcome

F. Learning centers are developed with
      1. A specific objective in mind
      2. A balance of specific objectives with individual variations
      3. No specific objective in mind

G. Learning packets are
      1. Used extensively
      2. Used moderately
      3. Hardly ever used

H. Activity cards are used
      1. With specific directions as to the activity to be performed
      2. At times to direct activity and at times to raise further questions
      3. To raise questions and interests

I. Learning centers are used
      1. As a supplement to basic instruction
      2. As basic instruction
      3. Only to supplement activity centers

J. Activity centers are used
      1. In a minimal way only when time allows
      2. Equally with learning centers
      3. As the core of learning

K. Spinoff or Experience Approach is used
      1. Almost never
      2. Occasionally
      3. Often

L. Learning contracts are
      1. Teacher developed for students
      2. Mutually developed (teacher and student)
      3. Used only to structure a student who is lost in developing his own projects

M. Simulation or gaming is
   1. Left to interaction
   2. Carefully planned for students to wrestle with real problems
   3. Used only when created and desired by students

N. Students
   1. Do not freely choose their learning activities
   2. Have as many individually chosen activities as teacher chosen
   3. Choose freely most of their learning activities

O. Students use mainly
   1. Programmed books, learning packets, and directive learning centers
   2. Learning centers that are both open and directive
   3. Activity centers, spin off units, probe pals, and open-ended learning centers

STUDENT MANAGEMENT DIMENSION ASSESSMENT

The following assessment instrument is concerned with the student-management dimension of schooling. This assessment tool has three aspects. Subassessment A ascertains staff beliefs concerning the nature of the child's behavior. Subassessment B looks at the teacher approaches to student disruptive behavior. Subassessment C deals with administrator behavior (particularly within the principal's office) as it relates to managing disruptive student behavior.

Subassessment A—A Psychological View of the Child

A. The child
   1. Is conditioned by outside forces
   2. Needs a give-and-take relationship with others
   3. Is intrinsically rational

B. The child
   1. Is shaped by his environment
   2. Has a reciprocal relationship with the environment
   3. Shapes his environment

C. The behavior of the child
   1. Needs to be controlled by adults
   2. Is altered only by mutual agreement
   3. Is best altered by the child himself

D. Children need to
   1. Learn socially acceptable patterns of behavior as determined by adults

   2. Learn what behavior is most appropriate for them in different situations
   3. Maximize their own potential in finding what behavior is of most value to them
E. Assertive behavior is a result of
   1. The reinforcement of inappropriate behavior
   2. A child attempting to find his place with others
   3. An environment which stifles the creative impulse
F. The child is
   1. Inherently impulsive and destructive
   2. Capable of both good and evil
   3. Inherently good
G. The child needs to learn behavior
   1. By conditioning and modeling
   2. Through conflict with outside standards
   3. With a minimum of outside interference.
H. If children were left to themselves
   1. There would be anarchy
   2. There would be confusion at first but they would get around to straightening themselves out
   3. They would respond to such trust with sensitivity and compassion to each other

Subassessment B—Teacher Management of Students

A. Teachers primarily
   1. Do not trust children
   2. Trust them partially
   3. Trust them fully
B. Teachers primarily
   1. Command children
   2. Consult with children before commanding
   3. Ask the child to reflect on his behavior
C. When a child is disruptive, teachers first
   1. Physically intervene or isolate the child
   2. Ask the child what he is doing
   3. Simply glance at the child in a nonthreatening manner
D. Teachers use techniques of
   1. Reinforcement to promote good behavior
   2. Discussion and group meetings
   3. Nonjudgmental statements and helping questions
E. At the beginning of the year, the teacher
   1. Lays down the class rules
   2. Jointly plans class rules
   3. Allows children to make the rules

F. When teachers desire a long-term change in a child's
behavior they
1. Make up a plan for the child
2. Make up a mutually agreed plan with a child that
they enforce
3. Allow the child to make up his own plan

G. Teachers discipline children by
1. Reinforcement, isolation, or deprivation
2. Having other children confront the child and apply
logical consequences
3. Having a conference where the child can relieve the
troubling inner emotions

Subassessment C—Management of Students by the Administrator

A. The principal acts towards students
1. In a stern, authoritarian manner
2. In a businesslike, collaborative manner
3. In an informal, supportive manner

B. Students, when going to the principal's office, feel
1. Intimidated and do not wish to go
2. Serious and somewhat apprehensive
3. Welcomed and willing

C. The principal's office for students connotes a place for
1. Chastisement
2. Acknowledging one's errors and mutually deciding
action
3. Expressing one's feelings

D. The principal usually begins a meeting with a disruptive student by
1. Telling the student what he has done wrong
2. Allowing the misbehavior to be aired and discussed
3. Putting the child at ease

E. During the meeting, the principal
1. Reaffirms school standards and the consequences of
violations
2. Presses for a mutual solution to the problem
3. Attentively listens and acts nonjudgmentally

F. The outcome of a meeting with the principal is
1. An exact principal plan of behavior modification
2. A mutual plan where the student commits himself
and the principal enforces
3. The student arriving at his own possible solutions

G. The amount of talking in a meeting of principal and
misbehaving child is
1. Monopolized by the principal

    2. Shared equally
    3. Monopolized by the student
 H. Common strategies of the principal are
    1. Contingency contracting, reinforcement, and extinction
    2. Probing, clarifying, and forcing a joint resolution
    3. Listening, nonjudgmental statements, and extending questions

SUPERVISORY DIMENSION ASSESSMENT

The following assessment instrument is concerned with the supervisory dimension of schooling. The assessment has two aspects. Subassessment A is directed at assessing the nature of supervision exhibited by the principal. Subassessment B is focused on an assessment of the nature of staff development.

Subassessment A—Supervision of Staff

 A. The principal sees the supervisory role as
    1. Teaching teachers how to teach
    2. Working cooperatively with teachers to improve instruction based upon school system and teacher need
    3. Facilitating teacher personal and professional growth based upon teacher perception of teacher need
 B. The principal's approach to supervision is
    1. Standard for all teachers
    2. Individualized for each teacher
    3. Based upon teacher perception
 C. The principal
    1. Determines teacher objectives related to improvement of instruction.
    2. Works cooperatively with teachers in determining goals for the improvement of instruction
    3. Allows complete freedom for teachers to set their own goals for the improvement of instruction
 D. The principal encourages the use of uniform procedures
    1. Most of the time
    2. Occasionally
    3. Almost never

E. The principal allows teachers complete freedom in their work
   1. Almost never
   2. Occasionally
   3. Almost always

F. The principal states objectives for instructional improvement in precise performance terms
   1. Almost always
   2. Occasionally
   3. Almost never

G. The principal
   1. Evaluates and rates teaching
   2. Provides a structure which allows for cooperative evaluation
   3. Provides teachers with data to evaluate their own teaching

H. The principal decides what should be done and how it should be done
   1. Almost always
   2. Occasionally
   3. Almost never

I. The principal pushes for increased production
   1. Almost always
   2. Occasionally
   3. Almost never

J. The principal sees as a primary objective
   1. The efficient operation of the organization
   2. Maintaining an organization in which learning and accomplishment can jointly take place
   3. To help members of the organization find themselves and become more aware of who they are

K. The principal sees the most important element in judging a person's performance as
   1. Technical skill and ability
   2. Cooperation with peers
   3. Success in meeting goals which the person has set

L. The principal would perceive which ideal to be *most* important?
   1. Making sure that all members have a solid foundation of knowledge and skills that will help them become effective and productive
   2. Helping people learn to work effectively in groups, to use the resources of the group, and to understand their relationships with one another as people
   3. Helping people become responsible for their own education and effectiveness and take the first step toward realizing their potential

M. The principal has a very definite idea as to what constitutes the behavior of an effective teacher *and attempts to help teachers demonstrate those behaviors.*
   1. Almost always
   2. Occasionally
   3. Almost never

N. The principal's major concern is
   1. Task production
   2. Task and teachers
   3. Teachers

O. In conferences with teachers, the principal is
   1. Telling, giving opinions
   2. Giving judgments, listening to teacher judgment, planning together future action, and suggesting that teachers behave in certain ways
   3. Listening, asking opinions, reflecting the teachers' ideas

P. The principal perceives which goal to be most important?
   1. School system goals
   2. School goals and teacher needs
   3. Meeting teacher needs and goals

Q. The principal provides service and help to teachers
   1. When the principal perceives they need it
   2. When cooperatively they decide it is needed and wanted
   3. When teachers ask for it

R. The principal seeks to motivate teachers through the use of
   1. External variables
   2. External and internal variables
   3. Internal variables

Subassessment B—Staff Development

A. In our school system, staff development (in-service) is perceived by teachers as
   1. A program for teachers, designed by the administration, for the purposes of facilitating personal and professional growth of teachers in terms of school system need
   2. A program for teachers, designed cooperatively by the administration and teachers, for the purpose of meeting school system and teacher needs
   3. A program for teachers, designed by teachers, for the purpose of meeting individual teacher needs

B. Staff development program needs are assessed by
    1. Administrators and supervisors
    2. Administrators, supervisors, and teachers, coopera-
       tively
    3. Teachers

C. Learning objectives of the staff development program
    are designed by
    1. Administrators and supervisors
    2. Administrators, supervisors, and teachers, coopera-
       tively
    3. Teachers

D. Learning activities to attain learning objectives are
    designed by
    1. Administrators and supervisors
    2. Administrators, supervisors, and teachers, coopera-
       tively
    3. Teachers

E. Participation of teachers in staff development programs
    is
    1. Mandated for all teachers
    2. Decided cooperatively by teachers, administrators,
       and supervisors
    3. Optional for each teacher

F. Resources needed to implement the learning activities of
    staff development programs are identified by
    1. Administrators and supervisors
    2. Administrators, supervisors, and teachers, coopera-
       tively
    3. Teachers

G. The entire staff development program is evaluated by
    1. Administrators and supervisors
    2. Administrators, supervisors, and teachers, coopera-
       tively
    3. Teachers

H. Staff development learning activities are evaluated by
    1. Administrators and supervisors
    2. Administrators, supervisors, and teachers, coopera-
       tively
    3. Teachers

I. The extent of the accomplishment of learning objec-
    tives is evaluated by
    1. Administrators and supervisors
    2. Administrators, supervisors, and teachers, coopera-
       tively
    3. Teachers

J. Generally speaking, the purpose of staff development programs is to facilitate
    1. Teacher acquisition of technical skills
    2. Problem-solving skills
    3. Teacher self-actualization and inner-direction

K. Which of the following methods of instruction are most predominant in in-service programs?
    1. Lecture, illustrated lectures, demonstrations
    2. Individualized instruction based upon participant selection
    3. Discussion, seminars, projects, role playing

L. Individuals who present learning activities for inservice programs are perceived usually as
    1. Fact oriented—knowledgeable about scientific and technical data
    2. Individuals who can present meaningful problems with skill
    3. Individuals who are both teachers and learners—who provide a free environment

RESOURCE MANAGEMENT
DIMENSION ASSESSMENT

The following assessment instrument is concerned with the resource management dimension of schooling. This dimension has two aspects. Subassessment A focuses on fiscal management as it relates to the role of the staff, principal, and procedures for deciding upon allocation of funds. Subassessment B is directed at environmental management as it relates to the variables of space, time, noise, color, physical structure, and the level of stimulation in the overall school facility and the classroom.

Subassessment A—Fiscal Management

A. The principal's role in decisions affecting school expenditures is
    1. Total
    2. Partial
    3. Only as an equal member of the staff

B. The staff's role in decisions affecting school expenditures is
    1. Providing input in helping the principal make the final decision

      2. Final in some areas and advisory in others
      3. Final in all areas
C. The principal
      1. Wants to protect teachers from having extra tasks that detract from their teaching responsibilities
      2. Wants staff to make the decisions on how to spend money for materials that are not part of a standardized curriculum
      3. Wants staff to make decisions on all money matters that have an effect on student learning
D. The budget is
      1. Centralized
      2. A combination of centralization and decentralization
      3. Decentralized
E. Money is spent
      1. Totally to support standard instructional programs in all subject areas throughout the school
      2. Partially to support standard instructional programs in basic subject areas and partially for nonstandardized materials appropriate for individual teachers and students
      3. Totally to support nonstandarized materials in all areas of learning
F. Money decisions are made based on the rationale that need can only be determined by the
      1. Principal, who has a total view of school needs
      2. Principal, who has the best perspective in some instructional areas, together with the staff, who have the best perspective in other areas
      3. The people in the classroom, who know what is really needed
G. Decisions are arrived at by
      1. Privilege of position
      2. Privilege of position and consensus
      3. Consensus

Subassessment B—Environmental Management

A. School halls are
      1. Plain and uniform
      2. Plain but with occasional eye-catching display
      3. Full of eye capturing displays
B. The purpose of the school space is to
      1. Move students efficiently from one place to the next
      2. Allow students to interact with each other at appropriate times
      3. Foster continuous interaction and involvement

C. The inner building is decorated in
  1. Subdued pale colors
  2. Strong bold colors
  3. A variety of bright and flashy colors

D. Bulletin boards are
  1. Prepared or supervised by teachers and have a theme of reinforcing learning, academic content, and standard valuing
  2. Both prepared or supervised by teachers and initiated by students with conventional as well as unique themes
  3. Initiated and developed by students with unique themes that invite further exploration

E. Noise is
  1. Suppressed
  2. Acceptable at certain times
  3. Acceptable at all times

F. The students work area is
  1. Kept free of distraction
  2. Varied with minimal distraction at instructional periods and high stimulation during activity periods
  3. Highly stimulating and changing from day to day

G. The environment is of
  1. Low arousal in order that students might attend to specific learning tasks
  2. Varied (low arousal and high arousal) at different times of the day or different places in the room
  3. Highly arousing to promote student spontaneity and exploration

H. The schedule of the day is
  1. Divided into subject areas to which students are assigned
  2. Divided equally into segmented time, for basic instruction, as well as continuous time, for student projects
  3. Largely uninterrupted in order for students to work as long as they wish

I. Furniture is
  1. Spaced apart for students to work alone and in the location of their assigned subject
  2. Flexibile, can be arranged in cloisters and as separate spaces depending upon the type of instruction
  3. Clustered to encourage student interaction and questions

J. Physical space is used
  1. Mostly for academic instruction
  2. Equally for academic and exploratory learning
  3. Mostly for exploratory learning

CONCLUSION

In this chapter, we have provided four assessment instruments which will generate data concerning school beliefs and practices. The next chapter will show how such information can be interpreted and serve as a springboard for action.

The instruments which have been presented are by no means exhaustive or definitive. What is unique is the fact that our instruments in each of the areas are related to one another and to the dimensions as we have presented them.

15

Checking for Consistency

The purpose of this chapter is to present some recommended procedures for analyzing the data generated by the assessment instruments. The objectives of the assessment are threefold. The first objective is to determine the degree of consistency *within each* of the four dimensions. In other words, are the alternative model beliefs or practices varied within each dimension, or is there some degree of consistency. Second, how consistent is *each* dimension with the alternative model selected. For example, if Alternative One has been adopted by the school, are beliefs and practices consistent with that approach within each dimension. Thirdly, what is the extent of consistency *across* each dimension as it relates to the alternative model selected.

SCORING PROCEDURES FOR ALL
ASSESSMENT INSTRUMENTS

Each of the assessment instruments ask a number of questions related to a dimension of schooling. Responses to each question are keyed to one of the three alternative models. All number one (1) responses in each assessment instrument are reflective of beliefs or practices consistent with Alternative One, which is based upon the educational philosophy of essentialism. All number two (2) responses are indicative of beliefs or practices consistent with Alternative Two, which is based upon the educational philosophy of experimentalism. All number three (3) responses are related to Alternative Three, which is based upon the educational philosophy of existentialism. Although many individuals, such as outside consultants, groups of teachers, community residents, and students, might respond to the assessment instruments, we would recommend that initially only the principal go through the assessment instruments. (We will discuss later how other individuals could be involved.)

185

Assessing Consistency within Each Dimension

This assessment will allow the administrator to determine the extent of consistency within each dimension. It also might be noted that this phase of the assessment may be used in developing a school philosophy (refer to chapter 3). After completing each of the assessment instruments, the principal should transfer each response to the tally sheets related to each dimension. The tally sheets can be found in Appendix C.

After transferring the responses to each tally sheet, the number and percentage of responses in each of the categories should be determined. Figure 15.1 is an illustration of a tally sheet where responses have been indicated and summarized.

As can be observed in Figure 15.1, fifty-three percent of the responses are consistent with Alternative One, thirty-five percent are consistent with Alternative Two, and eleven percent are consistent with Alternative Three. The consistency score within this dimension would be the highest percentage of the three response categories or, as illustrated, +53. It is important to note that this consistency is *within the category* and not the consistency with the alternative model selected. In other words, it may be that there is consistency within a particular dimension but not with the model adopted. An internal consistency score should be ascertained for each dimension.

Consistency within Each Dimension Related to Alternative Model Selected

The same data may now be used to determine the consistency between the alternative model *selected* and each dimension. Let's assume that Alternative Two is adopted by the school. We would determine the consistency score between Alternative Two and the particular dimension by ascertaining the percentage of responses for Alternative Two within that dimension. For example, refer to Figure 15.1. If Alternative Two were adopted, the consistency score between the resource-management dimension and Alternative Two would be +35.

Consistency across All Dimensions with Alternative Model Selected

Once again, the data gleaned from the first assessment process can be used to determine an overall dimension consistency. In order to determine overall consistency, we would first determine the percent-

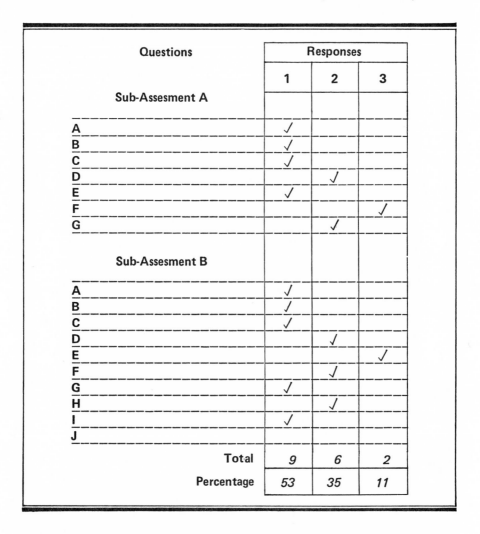

Questions	Responses		
	1	2	3
Sub-Assesment A			
A	✓		
B	✓		
C	✓		
D		✓	
E	✓		
F			✓
G		✓	
Sub-Assesment B			
A	✓		
B	✓		
C	✓		
D		✓	
E			✓
F		✓	
G	✓		
H		✓	
I	✓		
J			
Total	9	6	2
Percentage	53	35	11

Figure 15.1. *The Resource-Management Dimension Tally Sheet*

age of responses in each dimension as related to the model selected. For example, let's assume that we have adopted Alternative Two. We analyze each dimension with respect to the percentage of responses in Alternative Two and find the curriculum dimension to have a forty percent response, the supervision dimension to have a sixty percent response, the student-management dimension to have a thirty percent response, and the resource-management dimension to have a fifty-three percent response. Add these percentages and the sum is 198.

Dimension	Percentage Response in Alternative Two
1. Curriculum	40
2. Student Management	45
3. Supervision	60
4. Resource Management	53
Total	198

Consistency Score
198 ÷ 4 = 49.5

Figure 15.2. *The Overall Consistency Score*

Divide 198 by 4 to determine the consistency score across all dimensions. The consistency score would be 49.5.

PLOTTING AND INTERPRETING YOUR SCHOOL'S CONSISTENCY

After determining the three consistency scores, an administrator might attempt to graphically depict where the school is at. This will provide information in a concrete, observable form for all those who are concerned with implementing a more consistent educational program. However, before we discuss plotting the school's consistency, we should discuss what the consistency scores might mean and what the administrator's focus might be in terms of action.

Arriving at one-hundred percent consistency might very well be impossible. However, we do believe the schools should, in fact, strive for the highest level of consistency possible. When a consistency score is below 50, this should be an indicator that the school's focus and emphasis be reexamined. In other words, let's look at internal consistency within a dimension. A consistency score of less than fifty percent is indicative of the fact that more than one-half of the aspects within the dimension are inconsistent with one another. The administrator's initial focus might be to alter the practices or beliefs within a dimension. The same can be said of consistency scores related to each dimension in terms of the alternative model selected. Any time the consistency score is below fifty percent, a red flag should be waved!

One method of graphically depicting the school's consistency might be as illustrated in Figure 15.3 (using Alternative Two as the desired model).

OTHER PROCEDURES FOR
ASSESSMENT

We have suggested that the principal initially respond to each of the assessment instruments. Obviously, there are a number of other procedures that might be incorporated. We have listed ways in which others can collect assessment information:

1. Have an outside person observe school practices, speak with administrators, teachers, students, and community members with respect to each of the four dimensions.

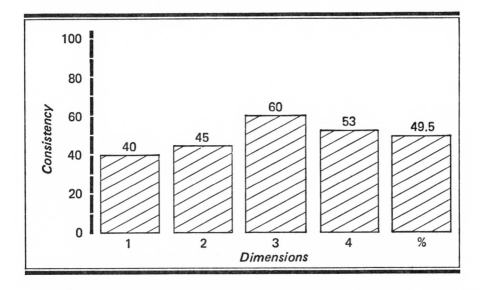

Figure 15.3. *A Consistency Graph*

Have the consultant then respond to the assessment items.

2. Examine the congruence between consultant and principal perceptions.

3. Have a representative group of teachers respond to the assessment package.

4. Examine discrepancies which might exist between teacher and principal perceptions.

5. Have a representative sample of community members respond and check the congruence between their responses and principal or teacher responses.

6. Alter the questions somewhat and examine upper-level student perceptions.

7. Examine the discrepancy between student and teacher perceptions.

Discrepancies of perception may be of value to the principal and serve as springboards for staff-development activities. For example, if teachers assess student management as reflecting an alternative different from that in the principal's assessment, there is now an area of discrepancy to discuss, to become better informed about, and a focus for altering practices to conform with the desired alternative.

SUMMARY

In this chapter, we have explained how to score and interpret the assessment instruments. The principal will generate a score for each dimension. He or she can then look for (a) consistency within each dimension, (b) consistency with the desired alternative model within each dimension, and (c) overall school consistency. We have suggested ways to gather information from others and what a principal might do when discrepancy is found. The following list refers the reader to other assessment approaches or instruments.

SUGGESTIONS FOR FURTHER READING

Assessment References

Beegle, Charles W., and Brandt, Richard M., eds. *Observational Methods in the Classroom*. Washington, D.C.: Association for Supervision and Curriculum Development, 1973.

Beegle, Charles W., and Edelfelt, Roy A., eds. *Staff Development: Staff Liberation*. Washington, D.C.: Association for Supervision and Curriculum Development, 1977.

Borich, Gary D., and Madden, Susan K. *Evaluating Classroom Instruction: A Source Book of Instruments*. Reading, Mass.: Addison-Wesley, 1977.

English, Fenwick W., and Kaufman, Roger A., eds. *Needs Assessment: A Focus for Curriculum Development*. Washington, D.C.: Association for Supervision and Curriculum Development, 1975.

Fitzgerald, Thomas P., and Clark, Richard. "Process Evaluation for Inservice Training." *Reading Improvement* 13(1976): 194–98.

Gronlund, Norman E. *Determining Accountability for Classroom Instruction*. New York: Macmillan, 1974.

Hyman, Ronald T. *School Administrators' Handbook of Teacher Supervision and Evaluation Methods*. Englewood Cliffs, N.J.: Prentice-Hall, 1974.

Ingersoll, Gary M. "Assessing Inservice Training Needs through Teacher Performance." *Journal of Teacher Education* 27(1976): 168–73.

Lake, Dale; Miles, Mathew; and Earle, Ralph Jr., eds. *Measuring Human Behavior: Tools for the Assessment of Social Functioning*. New York: Teachers College Press, 1973.

Means, Donald. "Evaluating Inservice Education Programs." *Education* 93 (1973): 292–94.

Pfeiffer, J. William, and Heslin, Richard. *Instrumentation in Human Relations Training*. Iowa: University Associates Press, 1973.

Walberg, Herbert J., ed. *Evaluating Educational Performance*. Berkeley, Calif.: McCutcheon Publishing Co., 1974.

Section Eight

Schools within Schools

16

Schools within Schools – A Rationale

Why must a school be committed to one alternative educational model? Why not have all three within the same building? We have written this text based upon our assumption that for a school to be effective, it must be consistent across all of the schooling dimensions. We have chastised schools that have no commitment to a particular philosophy and, instead, have practices that vary from person to person. The result is nothing—what Silberman refers to as the mindlessness of schools. Our critics might argue that the school which embraces one alternative model is restrictive to its students. They might say that though the school's goals and objectives will be realized, what about the creative child who will be forced through the structure of an Alternative One school, the disoriented child who will become further disorganized in an Alternative Three school, or the child who needs a full concentration in one or the other (basics or exploration) and who instead will get neither in the Alternative Two school. What is to become of these children?

Our critics have raised a most relevant question and one that must be answered fully. There are several ways that we will reply; but to begin with, we want to first state that we agree with our critics. They are not critics after all but allies in our quest for effective schools. Ideally, schools should have all three alternative models for their students, from entry to exit. However, this is a most ambitious change for a school to undergo. In a short time, to move from no comprehensive model to three, is unrealistic. It is better to begin with one, get it working correctly before starting another. The ultimate goal of having all three is admirable and something to work towards. In the next chapter, we will describe how a school might do just this. For now, we wish to return to the question of restrictive education when only one model is present.

THE ADVANTAGES OF HAVING ONE
MODEL

Obviously, the most significant advantage of one model is that a school might better accomplish what it sets out to do. If the school and community decide that they wish to promote a certain type of learning, by throwing all their resources and energy towards this goal, they will most likely succeed. By focusing on an overall priority, the school can reverse the trend of declining achievement scores, lack of human creativity, or the stifling of multitalented individuals. Instead of the nebulous "do everything-and-accomplish-nothing" mentality of schools today, schools can make a difference.

Would one child, who is out of step with the school's purposes, be hurt? Perhaps, but less so than if he or she was in a school that had no consistent practice. Why? Because the teacher in an effective school can more readily identify the student and provide individual variation. We will explain.

Out-of-step children who are in schools that lack consistency are not easily detected. Why are they out-of-step? A highly dependent child who needs instruction that is organized and sequenced may do fine with middle-of-the-road Ms. B in grade one. He is no problem. However, in grade two, with free spirit Ms. H., he falls to pieces. She works with him patiently until at last he begins to control and organize himself. In grade three, he moves to teacher Mr. T., who is a throwback to the 1800s. He tells the child when to do everything; when to inhale and exhale. All of the child's progress in self-learning erodes. By the next year, he is with Ms. Z., another free spirit, and again he falls apart.

What is the desired learning for this student? Is the child's tendency to work within the structure to be encouraged or should he instead be asked to become the creator of his own structure? In an inconsistent school, each year the teacher has to pick up the pieces of the child left from the year before and begin all over again to achieve what he or she wishes. One year's development is negated by the next. The outcome is too often a confused, noneffective learner. At least if a school has a consistent model, then a diagnosis can be made upon a child's entry into school. The student is in or out of step with the desired type of learning. If out-of-step, the staff can then do one of two things:

1. They can develop a program to help the child get in step (i.e., giving the dependent child a less structured experience), or

2. They can determine that the child's style, although

deviant from the mainstream, is acceptable and thus to be given special considerations.

This decision can then be carried out and revised from year to year.

This leads to our next point. A consistent school can still have variations within itself. In other words an Alternative One, Two, or Three school does not have to force all children to learn in their prescribed way. For example, a child who lacks rudimentary knowledge of essential skills might be given an all day intensive sequential, academic program in an Alternative Two or Three school. A child who has interests beyond the conventional subject areas might be allowed to devote considerable time to an individual project in an Alternative One or Two school. As square blocks will not fit into round holes, there will always be some students who do not thrive in a particular model. It is only humane that the school be flexible enough to accommodate their different learning styles. The school must also accept that, for these children, the desired school goals will not be fully met—for most, yes, but for some, no. Which brings us to the issue of trade-off.

We have mentioned that ideally, a school should be composed of three distinct, alternative models to best meet the needs of all children. Yet, if for the immediate, this is not realistic, what is the trade-off of having one school model for all children instead of having none at all? Admittedly, as we have explained, one model does not meet the needs and uniqueness of each child. That each model is one of individualized learning helps, but it still does not cover all of the individual styles of learners. It is safe to believe that not all children will develop to their fullest. But what is the recourse?

Some might argue that by not having a model, and allowing each teacher to do their own thing, "children will be beneficially exposed to many different classrooms and individual development will be enhanced." Such reasoning supposes that each teacher and administrator has the enthusiasm and flexibility to continually alter his or her style for every child. Let's face it, this nonmodel approach is exactly what we have in most school's today. We do not hear many (if any) supportive arguments on how this unthinking eclecticism has been proven successful. Without goals and objectives, we are at a loss to know how to measure its success. Rather, it is the schools which have thoughtful direction that are documenting success. Therefore, the trade-off is either maintaining the no-model school with negligible impact on student success, or a single-model school with powerful impact on most students (success is easily determined when a school's purpose is clear), but with the chance of failing some. (Others might still argue that maybe schools should not have any impact at all. This is a higher question raised by Illich and others. As public school educators we have to believe in powerful schools or why do what we do?) As we see it, one model is better than none. However, we cannot easily dismiss the children who are still not reached, and, therefore, must explore the use of three models at once as the best of all solutions.

THE RATIONALE FOR SCHOOLS
WITHIN SCHOOLS

Schools are geographic accidents. There is no ultimate reason why one school had to be built in its designated place while others were built a few blocks or miles away. They could have been built in different spots or built together. The more mundane considerations such as economics, transportation, availability of land, and central population are the basis for each school's location. Therefore, it is only a geographic accident that a child goes to one school and not another. He or she happens to live across an arbitrary district line and, therefore, attends a designated school. Taking accidents one step further, it is only arbitrary that the child attends a school that has one particular alternative model (or none at all). So, we can see the role that chance has played in bringing together the position of a school building, a child, and a curriculum model. By and large, it is a matter of luck that a child attends a certain school and receives a certain type of instruction.

One of the tenets of individualized instruction is that children are different. They learn at different rates and in different ways. Why must a child be excluded from different alternative learning because of a geographical coincidence? If children do indeed learn in different ways, then why shouldn't there be environments within district boundaries that capitalize on their various ways of knowing? It is too important an issue to leave to luck!

To be blunt, public schools are gargantuan monopolies. Any child who lives within the boundaries, unless economically privileged, is literally and legally forced to attend a particular school. That school can be the best or the worst in the land. It can be a pleasant oasis or a degrading pit. It makes no difference. Children still have to attend. The school's existence is assured by its captive audience and its required subsidy. It does not need to change one iota to be assured of its continuation. Some experiments such as the Voucher System and Performance Contracting have been sponsored by the federal government to instill competition and shake up this listless monopoly of schools, but the trend remains the same. Now what remains a tragedy is that no matter how high or low the quality of the school, a child who learns differently from the way he is taught is at a disadvantage.

There has been much outrage from reform-minded parents, educators, and concerned lay persons about the traditional school. Parents who want an individualized program for their children are often met with a stonewall of resistance. The school principal simply explains that this is the way the school is. The parent might sulk or carry on his or her fight elsewhere. However, if the parent remains unsatisfied, he or she still has no recourse but to send his or her child to the despised school. A moral question might be asked: "Should each parent have the right to choose the type of education for his or her child?" The question is largely hypothetical since there are no provisions in most schools for matching education to a child's style or allowing parents to choose. Even schools that have undergone dramatic changes and moved from traditional, all-class, self-contained instruction to open-space, individualized team teaching, have not provided an option. They have simply moved from *one* old way of instruction to *one* new way of instruction.

What happens as a result? The school and the school leader are in a "no-win" situation. The school that remains traditional is attacked by progressive parents who wish a different program for their children. The school that moves into an individualized model is attacked by conservative parents who wish a different program for their children. We need not document this occurrence; you, as a reader, can readily identify local schools who have or are causing such a problem. How does one satisfy the objections of parents and match education to children? We have already explained the comprehensive use of a single-alternative model that meets the majority of parent and community needs and has a built-in flexibility of providing individual programs for out-of-step children (and/or parents). An ideal solution is to have all three models, or three small schools, within one school. This way a child can be in the most suitable learning environment for himself and the most desirable situation for parents, all in the same building.

Let us go on a bit more about the political ramifications of providing no choices for children and parents. Much of the controversy and roadblocks thrown in the way of a changing school can be traced to a vocal minority of parents. They do not want the change for their children, they are satisfied with the status quo. However, when the school changes, the only way they can win the battle for their children is to knock out the encroaching change and return to the old way for *all* children. This is clearly a case of the minority imposing their belief on the majority. They often can triumph. They are upset, they organize, and they raise havoc. The majority of parents who are satisfied do not have the frenzied energy of the opposition. If and when they rally, it is often too late. The schools are already swirling in publicity, images are tarnished, and the response by the school is to retreat until the storm subsides. By providing an alternative-education model for the minority, as well as providing other school models, the opposition is diffused. Parents need not be alarmed about the proposed change. If they object they then still have a suitable school model for their own child. It not only makes sense politically, but more importantly, in today's age of ideological and cultural pluralism, it makes sense educationally.

To be more specific, a school which is undergoing a major Alternative One (predictable curriculum) change and will stress essential instruction might be wise to develop a smaller Alternative Three model which will stress spontaneity and informality. Therefore, the parents who would fight the Alternative One model for their child can have an Alternative Three model instead. Eventually, the school might develop an Alternative-Two model as well. Not only can the school manipulate the variables of models of instruction, but also the grouping of students and staffing arrangements. A school with as few as six classrooms can easily have two models, a school of ten or more can have all three. But more on this later.

If we were to rank the routes of change going from least to most desirable, we would see increasing advantages in this order:

1. No model school. Another possibility that we should mention is the no model school which has a few teachers who wish to have a comprehensive educational program that departs from the rest of the school. As few as two classroom teachers can implement an alternative-model program for grades K through six and still not upset the regular classroom program to any large extent. The educational leader in a particular school, where faculty and community resist all change, might support such an endeavor by the few willing teachers in order to act as a catalyst for beginning to move the school towards some manner of individualized instruction.
2. One alternative model school.
3. One alternative model school with individual variations for out-of-step children.
4. Two alternative models (two schools within a school).
5. Three alternative models (three schools within a school).

SUMMARY

In summary, we are saying that any school that has one fixed way of instruction is providing little option for those children and parents who might desire a different type of education. The fact remains the same. Whether a school is a conclave of traditionalism or of progressivism, there is no flexibility within the program; it is an institutional monopoly forced upon children. It is better, in our opinion, to have an individualized, alternative school model that has the capacity for varying its instruction for those students who need a different program. It is ideal to have all the different, comprehensive alternative models from entry to exit within the same school. In any case, having at least one individualized school model is better than no model at all. In the next chapter, we will demonstrate how all three of our delineated alternative models might be implemented within the same school.

17

Schools within Schools— A Case Study for Realists

This case study is based in part upon the program entitled "Alternatives for Children" which took place at the Hilltop and Chandler Elementary Schools in Somersworth, New Hampshire. This program was selected by the New Hampshire Council for Better Schools for its Major Achievement Award in 1974.

Twenty organized parents stormed the school-board meeting in protest against the local elementary school's adoption of the British Primary multiage, activity-centered concept for next fall. They voiced their disapproval and submitted a signed petition sta ing the following: "Children do not need less discipline, less drill, and less work on basics, but more. The proposed innovation would be a disaster for our children. They will not be prepared for secondary schools, colleges, or jobs. We want our children taught, graded, and made to learn." The petition carried nearly fifty signatures. The chairman of the school board listened to the complaints, received the petition, and stated that the decision had not yet been finalized and their input would be taken into consideration. The superintendent added that the teachers, principal, and himself would rethink their plans and come back with detailed information about school changes at the next board meeting.

The following morning the principal and superintendent met. They reviewed the reasoning behind a drastic change in the first place. All evidence of student success was dismal; attendance was increasingly low, achievement scores continued to drop, student attitudes toward school were poor (evidenced by the increasing numbers of students found vandalizing), and teacher morale was low (high turnover rate, constant bickering about students and among each other). The decision had been made to adopt the British Primary Model because it was highly exciting and involving for children. In reality, the administration felt that anything would be an improvement over the current educational situation. The school lacked direction, the teachers used the same old textbooks and continued to lecture to all students at the same time. Individualization was certainly part of the answer and the British Primary manner of individualization appeared to be the most appealing (Alternative Model Three).

Consultants from England were already contracted to conduct summer workshops for the teachers. New materials and furniture had been ordered and would be arriving shortly. During the previous year the staff had met several times with the principal and superintendent before accepting the change. Many of the faculty members were somewhat skeptical; however, they agreed because of the subtle pressure they were feeling from the administration. On the other hand, there was a small group of teachers, five out of nineteen, who were thrilled at the prospect. In fact, they had been trying out many of the British Primary ideas before they really knew what they were doing. Now they were excited about receiving some formal training.

The decision facing the superintendent and principal was centered around what they might do about parent opposition. The parents, who were visibly upset, constituted at most, only ten percent of the parents. It could be concluded that the remainder of parents were either supportive or apathetic toward the change. Yet, these parents were not only politically organized, but they also appeared genuinely concerned about their children's education. It did not appear likely that they could be convinced to change their minds.

After lengthy meetings held every few days over the next two weeks, the superintendent and principal agreed to go back to the staff for their input. Although many had doubts about being part of such an innovation, they had remained professional and kept their criticism within the school. Now that the issue was "out in the community" perhaps they had some ideas to help solve the present dilemma.

The entire staff and principal held an in-depth session to get all opinions out in the open. Prior to this meeting, the principal had talked with each teacher informally and asked him or her to prepare individual position papers. After nearly three hours of discussion, the staff and principal came to an agreement on a proposed solution that would seek to implement the original plan and meet parent and teacher concerns.

It was agreed that the opposing parents had raised some valid points. Pushing aside the hostility and antagonism, the school critics were correct. Their contention that the school, in shifting to one direction only, was prohibiting their children from receiving the educational program they desired was accurate. Perhaps the old plan had not met the needs of some children and parents. However, was not the new plan equally discriminating? The opposing parents' most valid argument centered around the issue that their children were being raised in homes which stressed values and beliefs antithetical to the values and beliefs that provided the basis for this new school program. They were convinced that such a radically different approach would turn their kids upside down. Their kids would become victims of change. The teachers agreed. They knew those children could not function effectively in this new school environment. Perhaps their school should create different environments for different children. It was easier to agree with the statement than to transpose a conceptualization into specific educational models. However, a decision had been reached. The superintendent reported at the next board meeting to the anxiously waiting parents (now over three hundred in number). He stated that the wishes of all parents would be accommodated. The school would not develop the British Primary model to the exclusion of all others. This model would be developed in the future, but parents would have an option, in fact, a veto over the school's placement of the child. They were assured that their child would not be in a place which they felt undesirable. The only concession parents would have to make to the school was that they would allow all instruction to be individualized. Whether teacher-structured or child-initiated, all classrooms would have children working at their own ability levels.

The principal then reported that the full details and logistics would still need to be worked out. The program would be explained at the final parent-teacher meeting in May and letters of explanation would go home to all parents. In the meantime, he and the staff would have to plan how to operate different educational models, suitably placing over five hundred students in grades K through six, into nineteen classrooms, and matching teacher style with desired educational environments.

Parents were flabbergasted. Not only had a group of opposing parents been heard, but the professionals actually had acted upon their criticisms. Even more amazing was that the parents who had supported the new concept also left the meeting knowing that their hoped-for change would materialize. At least in theory everyone had won. Now the task was to put the concept into operation. What follows is a description of how that was done.

SELECTING ALTERNATIVES

The first task before assigning classrooms, teachers, and students was to decide what philosophical purposes were commonly held by which groups of teachers. Since the Alternative Three philosophy of promoting the inherent potential of individual decision making and exploration had already been identified and enthusiastically supported by some teachers, one identifiable model was apparent. Most of the other teachers had initially balked at the Alternative Three approach—they simply did not possess the unbridled optimism in a child's capacity to govern himself. Instead they felt that learning should be structured for a child, that the child needs to be taught in an orderly manner. Since their classrooms had reflected this order (in scheduling, types of activities, and instructional style), they readily identified an individualized mode of instruction which could fit their already established operations. Therefore, Alternative One was chosen. Some teachers leaned towards Alternative Two but it was decided that, for at least the first year, a teacher needed to implement one of the two models before possibly collapsing them into a third.

DEFINING THE MODEL

Now that Alternative One and Alternative Three were selected, teachers needed to define their models in terms of goals and objectives, methods and activities, classroom organization, classroom appearance, student grouping, and student management. With a common definition, teachers could follow agreed-upon procedures and insure continuity for children from first grade through six. Furthermore, parents would have a clear understanding of what their choices were.

We have already devoted much time to the description of the multidimensional consistencies of Alternatives One and Three and do not need to repeat them in detail here. Each model was described in written form and then sent home to parents. We present a form which allows for a more detailed explanation of the two alternatives.

Alternative One

Philosophy.   There is age old wisdom that is essential to the evolution of our civilization. It is the school's role to insure that children will learn that knowledge. The purpose of education is to insure that children will have the basic skills to cope in later life.

Major Goals.   The child will be able to

1. Attain optimum proficiency in the basic skills of listening, observing, speaking, reading, writing, and mathematics
2. Gain skill in logical and critical thinking

3. Have knowledge of the world's societies, particularly his or her own

Selected Objectives. The student will

1. Score, in a Reading Proficiency test, on a minimum fifth-grade level before exiting from school
2. Score, in a Mathematics Proficiency test, on a minimum fifth-grade level before exiting from school
3. Be able to write an essay of three hundred words with ninety percent accuracy of spelling, grammar, and sentence structure by the sixth grade

Curriculum. The child will have an individualized instructional program. He or she will master skills in a sequential order based on his or her own rate of development. The teacher will individually evaluate, diagnose, and prescribe instruction. Instruction will be divided into the subject areas of language, reading, arithmetic, science, social studies, art, music, and physical education.

Methods and Materials. The student will use standard basic skill text books as the core of instruction. Learning centers, learning packets, and teacher contract units will be assigned as supplemental activities.

Environment and Schedule. The classroom will be quiet. Students will have assigned work places and there will be a minimum of movement. The child will have a schedule to follow and will be expected to finish all assigned work before having any "free time."

Management of Students. Children will at all times respect the authority of adults. Classroom rules and manners will be enforced strictly. A child who misbehaves will be dealt with in a direct manner. Any severe disruptions will be handled by isolating and/or suspending the child from school.

Alternative Three

Philosophy. The child is the center of his own reality. The human person is by nature inquisitive and ever expanding. The purpose of education is to release that creative potential within the child.

Major Goals. The child will

1. Exercise free choice

2. Understand self and own relationship to other people
3. Develop own capabilities, interests, and talents

Selected Objectives: The child will

1. Schedule himself
2. Select his own learning materials
3. Decide with whom to work

Curriculum. The curriculum is determined by the student. The teacher will continuously provide varying materials to allow a child many choices. The student will learn in his or her own way by choosing those activities suited to personal interests.

Methods and Materials. The student will have many activity centers where materials are grouped according to a theme. There will be numerous manipulative objects. Children will have the opportunity to bring in projects from home if they so desire. Daily meetings will be held in class for students to explore their own feelings and values.

Environment and Schedule. The classroom will be full of materials. Student work will be displayed on all walls. Movement and verbal interaction will be encouraged. The child will schedule his or her own time and work for as long as he or she desires on an activity. The child will be responsible for doing a reading and mathematic acitivity before the end of each day.

Management of Students. Every child must determine what behavior is most appropriate. Therefore, he or she will be allowed to form his or her own rules and standards as long as they do not transgress on another student's right to do likewise. When disruptions occur, the teacher will allow the child to talk out problems and propose solutions.

CLASSROOM ASSIGNMENTS

The placement of each teacher had to be made with the following considerations.

First, there were 503 students and nineteen classrooms. The following year's projected enrollment was grades one through four, eighty students at each level; grades five and six, ninety students at each level.

Second, there were four first-grade teachers and three teachers for each of the remaining grades. Categorized in another way, there were ten primary teachers for grades one through three (one position was to be vacant) and nine intermediate teachers for grades four through six (two positions were to be vacant). Of those returning teachers all had indicated that they wished to stay with the same-aged children.

Third, there were five teachers who wished to definitely work in Alternative Three, eight who were definite about Alternative One, and three who were undecided. Three positions were vacant.

Fourth, the breakdown by grade looked like this:

Alternative Three Definite

Grade	Teachers
1st	2
2nd	1
3rd	0
4th	2
5th	0
6th	0

Alternative One Definite

Grade	Teachers
1st	0
2nd	1
3rd	2
4th	0
5th	2
6th	3

Undecided or Vacant

Grade	Teachers
1st	1 (und.), 1 (vac.)
2nd	1 (und.)
3rd	1 (und.)
4th	1 (und.), 2 (vac.)
5th	1 (und.)
6th	0

Fifth, there had to be enough classrooms to accommodate children from grades one through six in each model.

Sixth, an estimation had to be made as to how many parents would strongly prefer one model over another and how many children would benefit from a particular model. By surveying each teacher, the following figures were determined.

Parent Preferred or of Definite Benefit to the Child

	Alternative 1	Alternative 3	Uncertain
1st grade	15	15	50
2nd grade	12	7	62
3rd grade	18	12	51
4th grade	16	10	55
5th grade	22	7	61
6th grade	15	11	64

With this information, action could be taken on classroom assignments.

Action One: Based on the figures, the Alternative Three program would be allotted six classrooms, six teachers, enrolling 168 students (20–1st; 27–2nd; 27–3rd; 27–4th; 30–5th; 30–6th).

Action Two: The Alternative One program would be allotted thirteen classrooms, thirteen teachers, enrolling 335 students (53–1st; 54–2nd; 54–3rd; 54–4th; 60–5th; 60–6th).

Action Three: The five teachers who wanted to teach in Alternative Three and the eight teachers who wanted Alternative One would be assigned accordingly. The three undecided teachers were placed in Alternative One. One of the fourth grade teacher vacancies would be filled as an Alternative One position. The other two vacancies would be filled with persons who could function well in Alternative Three.

Action Four: All teachers in Alternative Three would have multiaged classrooms composed of two grade levels. This was done to balance out the standard class ratios of 20 to 1 in the first grade, and 30 to 1 in fifth and sixth grades. In this way no Alternative One classroom would have more students than normal.

Action Five: One sixth-grade teacher would have to switch to a fourth-grade classroom. This would create a balance of two Alternative One classrooms at each grade level.

All three sixth grade teachers had initially requested Alternative One. The choice was for one of them to switch grade levels or remain at the same age range in an Alternative Three classroom.

It boiled down to what was most important, grade level or alternative. One teacher chose to switch to the fourth grade.

DISTRIBUTION OF STUDENTS

The distribution of students to classrooms could now be determined. The principal worked the figures out in a way to insure that (1) teachers received their preference, (2) students who needed a particular model would receive it, and (3) classroom size would remain the same across each grade.

The classroom distributions were made as follows:

Alternative One

Number of Teachers	Grade Levels	Number of Students	Ratio per Teacher
2	1st and 2nd combined	10 first graders and 13 or 14 second graders	23 or 24:1
2	3rd and 4th combined	13 or 14 third graders 14 or 13 fourth graders	27:1
2	5th and 6th combined	15 fifth graders 15 sixth graders	30:7

It was a simple mathematical procedure of breaking down the total number of students at each grade level into the number of available classes. For example, a total of eighty students in first grade needed to be distributed into three combination grade (first and second) classrooms. Therefore, twenty students were placed in each self-contained room and ten into each of the two combination classes.

CRITERIA FOR PLACEMENT OF
INDIVIDUAL STUDENTS

With the paperwork done to insure that such a plan could materialize, the principal and staff had to wrestle with the thorny question of how to specifically assign each child. The school has been committed to allowing parents the right to veto their placement and the procedure for that still had to be decided upon. First, criteria were needed to place a child in one model instead of the other. When faculty had responded to the principal's survey of which of their current students needed to be in a particular model, each teacher had used their own criteria. The fear growing among the staff was that one model would become a dumping ground for all of the problem children. The Alternative One teachers feared that they would receive all the students who had little self-control and needed to be watched. The Alternative Three teachers were equally afraid that children would be assigned to their classrooms because they were slow learners. Both groups of teachers felt that unless they could work out objective criteria to insure heterogeneously grouped classes then some teachers would shoulder an unfair burden. If one model received most of the difficult children then that model's teachers would be severely handicapped and that alternative approach could not be fairly evaluated.

The staff decided to place all children according to learning style and not academic or social considerations. In other words, those children who learned best in a quiet environment when time and materials were organized for them, would be placed in Alternative One classrooms. Those children who were active learners by nature were placed in Alternative Three classrooms. Most teachers could readily identify these two types of students. Some children learned best with an established routine, other children found such a routine oppressive. In neither case was misbehavior or academic ability a criteria for placement. There were as many bright and well-behaved children who learned in a regulated way as there were children who best learned in an active way. The same was true for low-ability and/or disruptive children.

Using "learning style" as the criterion for placement made it relatively easy to assign one-third to one-half of all students. However, teachers found that many children seemed capable of functioning well in either type environment. These children were randomly placed in both classrooms.

Every teacher was thus assured that all classrooms would

1. be heterogeneously grouped with children of all academic and social levels;

2. contain children who had a particular mode of learning; and

3. contain children of flexible modes of learning.

Those teachers in Alternative Three classrooms were additionally assured that their multiaged classrooms of two-grade-levels each were to be heterogeneous in ability. For example, a first and second grade combination classroom would not be composed of advanced first graders and slow second graders. Children from each grade level would exhibit the spectrum of abilities from slow to advanced first graders and from slow to advanced second graders. Also lower grade children would remain with the teacher for two years. First grade children in a first-second combination would continue with the same teacher in second grade.

PROCEDURE FOR ASSIGNING INDIVIDUAL STUDENTS

Teachers were asked to attend a meeting for the purpose of placing their current students into next year's classroom. They were to bring a list consisting of each student's name and a brief description of his or her learning style and any extra information pertinent to placement (behavior, any disabilities, close friends, students not to be grouped together, parent preferences, etc.).

The principal told the staff that at this meeting they would place all of the children who needed a particular alternative. He would later use their descriptions to place the remaining students. The meeting would be conducted in two stages. The current first-grade teachers would meet with the next year's second-grade teachers and, keeping to the already established criteria, they would place students. The third grade teachers would meet with fourth; and fifth grade teachers would meet with sixth. The group's task would not be complete until all teachers were satisfied. The next stage would be fourth-grade teachers meeting with fifth, second-grade teachers meeting with third; and first-grade teachers by themselves. First-grade teachers would place incoming youngsters according to preschool screening information which had been conducted earlier.

At the conclusion of the meeting, the principal received the partial roster of each classroom for the next year and a list by grade levels of students still not assigned. The principal then completed the rosters within a week and returned them to teachers. Tentative classroom rosters were not finalized until after parent input. The teachers had the remainder of the school year to familiarize them-selves with their incoming children and to begin to make plans.

Teachers were satisfied since they had participated in the placement procedure and knew in advance who their students would be.

The staff was asked to keep their lists confidential. Parents would not be notified of student assignments until the end of the school year. However, since parents could exercise a veto on their child's placement the principal needed to know what placement individual parents preferred.

The Parent Veto—
How It Was Explained

Parents were invited to the last Parent-Teachers Organization meeting in May where the new program entitled "Alternatives for Children" was to be discussed. At this meeting, the principal and staff described the program. The two alternative models were described. The number of classrooms and teachers for each model, how students were placed, and the heterogeneity of each classroom were explained. The principal made particular mention of how children had been carefully placed according to professional judgment of their individual styles of learning. Any parent who wished to provide the school with further information as to where they thought their child should be placed could contact the school and put their opinion in writing. If there was no difference between the parent's choice and the schools' professional judgment, then no problem existed.

However, if the parent made a choice which differed from the school's, the principal or designated staff members would arrange a conference with the parent. At that time the principal would explain the basis for the school placement and the parent could explain his or her thoughts. If the parent still wanted the child placed in an environment that differed from the staff's professional judgment, the school would comply with one condition. The parent would have to sign a statement that he or she was going counter to the school's professional judgment.

Parent Veto Form

    I _____ have asked that my child _____ be removed from Alternative ____ and put in Alternative ____. I realize that this request goes against the _____ _____ school's professional judgment.

_____

Parent's Signature   Date

The child would then be placed as the parent desired.

The Parent Veto—Rationale

In beginning a new program, a school staff has enough to contend with in developing the alternative model without fighting off parent criticism at the same time. If a parent was so dissatisfied with their child's placement that he or she was willing to go through the procedure of contacting the office, attending a conference, and then signing a form, then the school would accommodate the parent's desires. To place that child in a classroom where the parent was not satisfied, no matter how sound the original staff decision was, would be asking for later trouble. The parent's negative attitude would obviously have impact on the child and create tension with the teacher. Perhaps later the parent might see that his or her judgment was not best. The staff might also determine that the parent's decision was correct. By giving parents their choice, the staff would have one less obstacle to contend with in implementing their program.

The Parent Veto—What Happened?

For a school to give parents the power to decide might seem mind boggling to the school leader when one contemplates parents pounding on doors, paperwork piling up, and continuous revisions in student placement. However, this is not what occurred. First of all, parent's had to register their opinion by the last day of school. After that, placements were finalized. Secondly, a parent had to be extremely committed to go through this process and counter the school's judgment. Thirdly, the parent had to live with his or her decision and could not blame anyone else for its possible failure. It is a large responsibility for a parent to assume. In the school system where this procedure was employed, only nineteen parents out of five hundred initially contacted the school to make their preference known. Of those nineteen, ten were told that their children were already placed as the parent desired. The other nine used their option and had their children placed in a different alternative. It was surprising how such a dramatic school undertaking had such a positive impact on parent relations. A mere nineteen phone calls, ten office conferences, and ten placement alternations was certainly tolerable, particularly when the principal knew he would have parent support during a year of change. The following year, the number of parent requests were even less.

To be frank, parents may holler and complain about their child's school but when it comes down to taking the responsibility and effort to act, the majority will back down. Very few parents have the confidence in themselves to think that they can make a better judgment than the educator. The responsibility usually remains where it should—with the professional staff.

This does not mean that a child improperly placed should remain in a particular classroom come hell or highwater. What it does mean is that a staff needs to continually assess the needs and learning style of children to insure placement of students in the most suitable environments.

Of course, not all schools that implement such a procedure will have as few parents using their veto as the one school cited. Some schools will have more; some, less. However, in most places, the number of parents will be less than anticipated and the parent support for new school directions will far outweigh any temporary inconveniences.

EVOLUTION OF ALTERNATIVES

The school cited had gone almost an entire year with Alternatives One and Three. It was soon approaching the time to begin planning for the following year. The staff, principal, and superintendent began asking each other some questions:

> How many classrooms of each Alternative for next year?
>
> What about another Alternative?
>
> What about making the Alternatives even more distinct from each other by varying staffing patterns and student grouping?

The answers to these questions evolved into a more comprehensive program of alternatives for children. The first year had been successful, especially as viewed by the parents. A survey indicated that over ninety-one percent of all parents were more than satisfied with their child's education. The previous year, before the change, a similar survey showed only sixty percent satisfied. Teacher perception of school climate was positive, student attendance had risen dramatically, and student achievement on standardized tests was slightly up.

In contemplating the future, the staff saw the need to increase the number of alternatives. The single model was relegated to the dead-file heap. Some teachers who had originally been uncertain as to which alternative to work in and others, who felt that neither Alternative One nor Alternative Three were suited to their style, opted for initiating an Alternative Two model.

Based on parent support and teacher preference, the plan for next year was altered. The Alternative Three model increased in size from six to nine classrooms. The Alternative One model decreased from thirteen to six classrooms (one at each grade level). The new Alternative Two model was comprised of six classrooms. Teacher assignment, student placement, and balancing size was accomplished based upon the procedures of the previous year. More classrooms had to be multiaged to keep class size equitable. Parent veto stayed in effect. Three alternative models covering the spectrum of educational practices were now available for students.

DEVELOPING OPTIONS

To conclude this case study, we need to mention one more development. Over a three-year period, the schools within schools concept was expanded to include distinct student grouping and staffing patterns. Alternative One remained self-contained, with one teacher, and one grade level of students. Alternative Three remained self-contained, with one teacher, and multiaged, with two grade levels combined. Alternative Two developed into team teaching, (two teachers) with the wall between classrooms partially removed, and multiaged, with two grade levels.

With these different options of self-containment versus open space, one teacher versus two, single-age grouping versus multiaged grouping, a child could be placed according to his or her style of learning but also according to other variables as well. For example, Susan is to begin school next year. She is a shy, passive child. She is also bright, but likes to work in a quiet atmosphere and complains often about noise or disruption. She is an only child who does not play well with children her own age. She likes to be with kids older than herself. Her mother has indicated that she does not want her in an Alternative Three classroom. The first grade staff of teachers can now take all this information, look at the options available and place her in the most suitable environment. They reached their decision by this thought process.

1. Liking quiet and few disruptions, she might be better in an Alternative One classroom. However, Alternative Two would provide more project time to encourage social activity and, perhaps, help her overcome her shyness.

2. She does not play much with others. Alternative Two would provide more social interaction and she likes to be with older children. A multiaged classroom of grades one and two would provide her with older companions.

3. She is an only child. Perhaps having two teachers
would help her be less dependent on one adult.

It now appears that she should be in a team teaching, multiaged
classroom, which has a balance of quiet, scheduled work time and
project time for social interaction. Therefore, Alternative Two is the
choice.

As you can see, there might be factors other than learning style
that need to be assessed before placing a child. The bully kid who
works best with a consistent schedule might cognitively be better in
Alternative One, but socially be better off in Alternative Two or Three
where he will be one of the younger students in a multiaged
classroom. If he starts pushing his weight around, the older children
will start pusing him back and maybe that's exactly what he needs.
Therefore, social consideration might outweigh academic concerns. If
all alternatives had the same student grouping and staffing patterns,
let's say all self-contained and single-aged, then some variables that
might be important would be useless to consider.

The point we are trying to make is that the more alternative
instructional models and options available, the greater the probability
that a school will provide a successful placement for each student.
Automobile manufacturers determined this fact a long time ago. A
consumer can pick out one of several basic models and then have the
choice of numerous options to tailor the vehicle for his needs. The
same rationale holds true for schools. The only difference is that a
school needs to get at least one model, or perhaps two, running
properly before even thinking about further variations.

CONCLUSION

This chapter presented a case study of one school's attempt to
implement "schools within schools." Their procedures do not correspond exactly with the multidimensional development of each alternative model as described in this book. For example, *initial placement theoretically should be based upon parent, teacher, and student
selection of goals and objectives reflective of a certain educational
philosophy.* However, there is enough substance to give the reader a
reality base for implementing such a program.

Section Nine

Important Internal Considerations about the Changing School

18

Climate for Change

As mentioned previously, the *physical* environment that exists within a school is not a crucial factor. A school's readiness for learning and change (student or teacher/administrator) appears to be independent of such factors as walls, floor coverings, and heating and cooling systems. This readiness is found to be dependent largely upon the nature of the school as a social system—its degree of psychological health. Many researchers have documented that the psychological environment of a school has more to do with its success than do things such as the school's structure (physically and organizationally) or the quantity of resources.

Specifically, a learning environment is centered around how people perceive their relationships with each other and how well they see themselves fitting into the scheme of things. It also includes their perception of the behavior of their leader.

It is our belief that any school that seeks any kind of change must deal with the organizational or psychological climate which permeates that school. We believe what many other researchers have found to exist. No comprehensive change is possible if the climate is closed. "The very nature of a closed climate makes the conditions for change impossible."[1]

More specifically, Hughes has found that psychological climate has also distinguished innovative from noninnovative schools.[2] Essentially, we are suggesting that an initial procedure in institutionalizing any meaningful change is the assessment of psychological climate and subsequently the initiation of staff development activities to remediate aspects of the climate that may not be conducive to change. Bateman and others have found that the climate of a school can be altered through the implementation of appropriate in-service activities.[3]

There are a number of climate assessments that the administrator may wish to become familiar with, and a reference list is suggested at the end of this chapter which includes a brief description of some assessment instruments related to school climate and where they may be obtained. We would now like to focus on one approach to assessing school climate.

USING A CLIMATE ASSESSMENT

Halpin and Croft have developed an instrument designed to assess the organizational climate of elementary schools. The instrument, titled The Organizational Climate Description Questionnaire (O.C.D.Q.), was developed by the authors while working through a grant from the United States office of Education, and was first published in 1966 in Halpin's *Theory and Research in Administration* (the theoretical rationale and procedural descriptions of the instrument's development may be found in this reference).[4] The sixty-four items of the questionnaire are brief statements of situations involving the interpersonal behavior of teachers and principals. The respondent (teacher) is asked to decide in each instance how typical the described behavior is of his or her principal, fellow teachers, and the school in general. The respondent answers each item through the use of a four-point scale: 1—rarely occurs; 2—sometimes occurs; 3—often occurs; and 4—very frequently occurs. Each of the items are assigned to one of the eight subtests; four are related to characteristics of the group (teacher's behavior) and four are related to characteristics of the leader (principal's behavior). The definitions which follow are summaries of a more detailed analysis provided by Halpin and Croft.

Teacher's Behavior

   I. *Disengagement* refers to the teachers' tendency to be "not with it." This characterizes a group which is merely going through the motions. The group is "out of gear" with respect to the task at hand.
  II. *Hindrance* refers to the teachers' feeling that the "principal burdens them with routine duties ... and other requirements that impede the teaching-learning process...." Teachers perceive the principal as hindering rather than facilitating their teaching.
 III. *Esprit* refers to morale. The teachers feel that their social needs are being satisfied and they are enjoying a sense of accomplishment in their job.
  IV. *Intimacy* refers to the teachers' enjoyment of friendly social relations with each other. "This dimension describes a social need satisfaction...."

Principal's Behavior

   V. *Aloofness* refers to the behavior by the principal which is characterized as formal and impersonal. Such an individual "goes by the book" and prefers to be guided by rules and policies rather than to deal with the teachers in an informal face-to-face situation.

VI. *Production Emphasis* refers to the behavior of the principal which is characterized as formal and impersonal. He is highly directive and plays the role of a "strawboss." His communication tends to go in one direction only and he is insensitive to feedback from the staff.

VII. *Thrust* refers to behavior of the principal which is typically an effort to "move the organization." Such behavior is not marked by close supervision. He sets personal examples and asks of teachers only that which he willingly does himself.

VIII. *Consideration* refers to that behavior by the principal which is characterized by an inclination to treat the teachers "humanly," to try to do a little something for them in human terms.[5]

The eight subtest scores permit a measure of the openness and restrictiveness of a school's climate. The openness of the organizational climate is determined by high scores on the subtests of Esprit and Thrust, and a low score on Disengagement. The restrictiveness of the organizational climate is determined by low scores on Esprit and Thrust, and by a high score on Disengagement.[6]

The authors have identified six distinguishable climates, each represented by a different combination of scores on each of the eight subtests, which can be graphically depicted. Vignettes also were developed, describing each of the climates.

The following are the graphic depictions and vignettes of the two extreme climates.

Open Climate

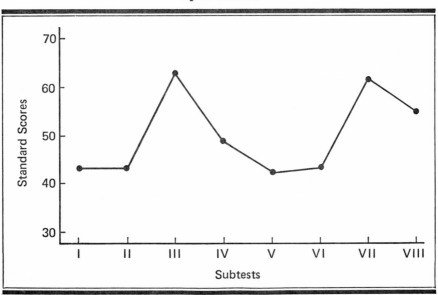

The open climate depicts a situation in which the members enjoy extremely high esprit. The teachers work well together . . . they are not burdened by mountains of busywork or by routine reports; the principal's policies facilitate the teachers' accomplishment of their tasks. . . . The teachers obtain considerable job satisfaction. . . .

The behavior of the principal represents an appropriate integration between his own personality and the role he is required to play as principal. Not only does he set an example by working hard himself, . . . he can . . . criticize, . . help, . . show compassion, provide leadership for the staff.[7]

Closed Climate

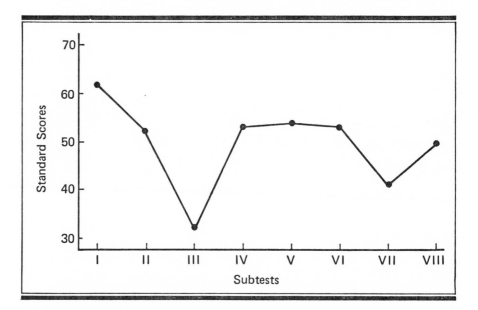

The closed climate marks a situation in which the group members obtain little satisfaction in respect to either task achievement or social needs. In short, the principal is ineffective in directing the activities of the teachers. At the same time, he is not inclined to look out for their personal welfare.

The teachers are disengaged and do not work well together. . . . Esprit is at a nadir, reflecting low job satisfaction in respect to both job satisfaction and social-needs satisfaction. . . .

The principal is highly aloof and impersonal in controlling the activities of the teachers. . . . This climate characterizes an organization for which the best prescription is radical surgery.[8]

After administering the O.C.D.Q. to all teachers in the school, the principal might analyze the data collected by comparing each of the actual subtest scores with each subtest score for the open climate. In other words, the degree of congruency between the ideal (open) climate and the actual climate can be determined. Staff Development activities can then be designed and implemented which are directed at altering subtest variables contributing to the restrictiveness of the climate.

A Case Study Using the O.C.D.Q.

One of our doctoral students, a former principal, analyzed the organizational climate of an elementary school and found that the subtest variables of hindrance and consideration were other than open as compared with the open climate profile.[9] After examining the specific items in each of the two subtests (i.e., what did teachers see that caused high degrees of hindrance and what did they see that the principal was doing to be ranked low on consideration), meetings were held with both the teachers and principal to consider in-service activities which might correct the problems of hindrance and consideration. The following is an example of one staff's attempt to improve the psychological climate:

1. Three committees of teachers were established immediately: (a) *a paperwork committee*, (b) *a curriculum committee*, and (c) *an evaluation committee.*

The *paperwork committee* had the responsibility for studying the streamlining of the paperwork in the school. This committee was to establish a checklist for each paper request so that each request met the criteria of legitimate work for teachers. Also, this committee was assigned the task of developing ways of having teachers informed as to the importance of accurate records. Finally, the paperwork committee agreed to investigate the possibility of bringing parent volunteers into the school to assume many routine noninstructional duties. In general, this committee was to consider ways to remove an apparent burden of too many noninstructional duties.

The *curriculum committee* had the responsibility for developing a needs assessment ... of students and parents. Also, this committee was to examine the various competencies of the faculty members in order to match them appropriately with student needs. Following these studies, the curriculum committee agreed to make recommendations relative to the allocation of human and material resources at the school.

The *evaluation committee* had responsibilities that were both formative and summative. In the category of formative evaluation, this committee agreed to monitor the work of the other two committees to certify that they were working toward their objectives. Also, this committee was assigned the task of looking at the job descriptions of *principal, curriculum specialist, classroom teacher, itinerant teacher, counselor, visiting teacher, school psychologist, teacher's aide, secretary,* and *custodian* in order to make sure that all duties were delineated clearly and that everyone on the staff understood the responsibilities of all others on the staff. Finally, the evaluation committee agreed to evaluate the work and to make recommendations for the establishment of permanent school committees for the following year.

2. The faculty requested that certain activities take place at the next meeting:

(a) The faculty requested that someone be present at the next meeting to explain the process of setting objectives and evaluating whether or not objectives had been achieved successfully. This presentation would be given to the entire faculty.

(b) The curriculum committee requested that following the next plenary meeting of the faculty, that someone present suggestions regarding the execution of a needs assessment for students.

(c) The paperwork committee requested that following the next plenary meeting of the faculty, that someone present suggestions on the utilization of parent volunteers.

(d) The evaluation committee requested that following the next plenary meeting of the faculty, that someone present an explanation of how to carry out both formative and summative evaluations. Also, this committee requested that copies of appropriate job descriptions be made available to them at the occasion of the next meeting.

3. It was agreed that the committees would present their plans for operation on a subsequent specified date.

4. It was agreed that every professional staff member should be on a committee. Seven teachers volunteered for the evaluation committee, seven teachers volunteered for the curriculum committee, and six teachers plus the principal volunteered for the paperwork committee.

A meeting was held with the principal in order to consider possible activities that would be directed toward the subtest consideration. The following conclusions were reached during this meeting:

1. The principal agreed to attempt to compliment each teacher at least once each week on a personal or professional matter.

2. The principal agreed to visit the work areas after school at least once each week to offer assistance to the teachers on their work.

3. The principal agreed to encourage teachers, in faculty meetings, to seek his assistance on professional and personal matters.

4. The principal agreed to spend two hours each week with teachers in an informal setting (either before or after school or during the instructional break) during which time he agreed to talk with teachers about matters not having to do with teaching.

5. The principal agreed to monitor his contact with teachers through the use of a checklist to be completed on a weekly basis.

6. The principal expressed concern about his perception that social cliques were evident in the school among teachers and that certain teachers were excluded consistently from many informal activities. As a result, he was supplied with a copy of a book entitled *The Faculty Team* by Gerald H. Moeller and David J. Mahan (Chicago: Science Research Associates, Inc., 1971). In this

			Principal's Contact Sheet *Week of* _____					
	Contacts initiated by principal	Contacts initiated by teachers		Question	Complaint	Friendly Conversation	Compliment
Monday							
Tuesday							
Wednesday							
Thursday							
Friday							

book the authors offer suggestions to principals that were designed to help remedy such problems.

7. The principal was supplied with the following books in which designated pages could serve as springboards to further actions on the part of the principal: Gross, Neal and Robert E. Herriott, *Staff Leadership in Public Schools: A Sociological Inquiry* (New York: John Wiley and Sons, Inc., 1965), pp. 51–58.

Lane, Willard R., Ronald G. Corwin, and William G. Monahan. *Foundations of Educational Administration: A Behavioral Analysis* (New York: The Macmillan Company, 1971), pp. 325–381.

Sergiovanni, Thomas J., and Robert J. Starratt. *Emerging Patterns of Supervision: Human Perspectives.* (New York: McGraw-Hill Book Company, 1971).

Wiles, Kimball. *Supervision for Better Schools* (Englewood Cliffs, New Jersey: Prentice-Hall, 1955), pp. 1–110.

One week later, a second meeting of the faculty was held. On that occasion a presentation was made to the entire faculty on the subject, "The Process of Setting and Evaluating Objectives." The following text was used as the basis for the presentation: *Effective Teaching Strategies with the Behavioral Outcomes Approach* by Muriel Gerhard (West Nyack, New York: Parker Publishing Company, 1971), pp. 159–186, 239–244.

The next day a presentation was made to the curriculum committee on the subject, "Developing a Needs Assessment Based upon Student Needs and Interests." The following text was used as the basis for the presentation: *Assessment Techniques: An Introduction.* Barrie Hudson, editor (London: Methuen Educational Ltd., 1973), pp. 157–190.

The following week a consultant from a local university made a presentation to the paperwork committee on the subject, "Utilization of Parent Volunteers." The following texts served as the basis for that presentation: (1) *Partners in Urban Education* by Barbara Thompson Howell (Morristown, New Jersey: Silver-Burdett, 1972), pp. 1–57; (2) *Practical School Volunteer and Teacher-Aide Programs* by Benjamin DaSilva and Richard Lucas (West Nyack, New York: Parker Publishing Company, 1974), pp. 15–48, 149–161.

The next day a consultant from the State Department of Education made a presentation to the evaluation committee on the subject, "How to Execute Formative and Summative Evaluations." The following text was used as the basis for the presentation: *Principles of Educational Measurement and Evaluation* by Gilbert Sax (Belmont, California: Wadsworth Publishing Company, 1974), pp. 554–571.

The next week a meeting was held with the entire faculty. Each committee reported, in turn, to the faculty specific plans for operation for the remainder of the school year. An agreement was reached that in one month's time, all committees would report again on the progress being made and that the committee should continue to serve permanently. It was agreed that it would be beneficial to the instructional program of the school if these committees continued to monitor the factors that tended to add to or reduce *hindrance* in the school's operation.

The committees continued to meet throughout the school year. The only change that was made to the original plan was that the teachers devised a scheme for rotating membership on each committee. The arrangement was such that each member of the staff was able to serve on each committee by the end of the school year. Each teacher was able, therefore, to confront the issues faced by each of the committees. Many other consultants were brought in and many other resources were utilized beyond those that were involved in the in-service training period. Although several auxiliary projects could be described as "spin-off" activities, the three committees initially established became permanent fixtures in the school's organization.[10]

After the in-service was completed, the O.C.D.Q. was again administered. It was found that through the in-service program, directed at altering two of the subtest variables which initially were found to be less than open, the climate of the school became more psychologically open and hence increased the school's chances for higher levels of any change implementation.[11]

SUMMARY

It is our belief that an open psychological climate is a major condition which must be addressed before meaningful change can occur. We have presented one procedure for collecting information related to school psychological climate and presented ways in which one school leader has used that information. Any change strategy will meet with greater levels of implementation when initial efforts focus not on the specific change intended, but the readiness for that change.

Description of Other Assessments Related to Organizational Climate Analysis

1. *The Group Dimensions Description Questionnaire* by John K. Hemphill measures thirteen dimensions which, according to Hemphill, characterize groups. An overall view of organizational climate may be ascertained from an analysis of each of the dimensions. The instrument can be obtained from the Educational Testing Service, Princeton, New Jersey 08540.

2. *The Organizational Climate Index* by George G. Stern and Carl R. Steinhoff assesses individual needs and organizational or environmental demands. Psychological climate may be inferred by the degree of discrepancy found between each of the two dimensions. The instrument can be found in Stern's *People in Context*, published by John Wiley in 1970.

3. The Organization Description Questionnaire by Robert J. House and John R. Riggo assesses nineteen dimensions of organizational climate. It can be obtained from Dr. Robert J. House, University of Toronto, 246 Bloor Street West, Toronto, Ontario, Canada.

4. *The Organizational Health Survey* by P. T. Kehoe and W. J. Reddin assesses eight dimensions of organizational climate. The test can be obtained by writing Organizational Tests Ltd., P.O. Box 324, Fredericton, N.B. Canada.

5. *The Organizational Climate Index* by Rensis Likert assesses the extent to which schools are perceived as characterized by four distinct climates. The instrument can be found in Likert's book, *The Human Organization*, published by the McGraw-Hill Book Company in 1967.

NOTES

1. E. Dale Doak, "Organizational Climate: Prelude to Change," *Educational Leadership* 27 (January 1970): 368.

2. L. W. Hughes, "Organizational Climate: Another Dimension to the Process of Innovation?" *Educational Administration Quarterly* 4 (1968): 16–28.

3. C. Frederick Bateman, "The Effect of Selected In-Service Activities Upon the Organizational Climate of an Elementary School" (Ed.D. diss., University of Virginia, 1976).

4. Andrew W. Halpin, *Theory and Research in Administration* (New York: Macmillan, 1966).

5. Ibid., pp. 150–51.

6. Ibid.

7. Ibid., pp. 174–75.

8. Ibid., pp. 180–81.

9. Bateman, "The Effect of In-Service Activities."

10. Ibid., pp. 70–81.

11. Ibid., pp. 102–104.

SUGGESTIONS FOR FURTHER READING

Anderson, Donald P. *Organizational Climate of Elementary Schools.* Minneapolis: Educational Research and Development Council of the Twin Cities Metropolitan Area, Inc., 1964.

Cass, James. "Environment of Creative Teachers." *Saturday Review World* 1 (April 1974): 51.

Coughlan, R. J. "Job Satisfaction in Relatively Closed and Open Schools." *Educational Administration Quarterly* 7 (Spring 1971): 56.

Doak, E. Dale. "Organizational Climate: Prelude to Change." *Educational Leadership* 27 (January 1970): 368.

Halpin, Andrew W. *Theory and Research in Administration.* New York: Macmillian, 1966.

————. *Administrative Theory in Education.* Chicago: Midwest Administration Center, University of Chicago, 1958.

————. "Change and Organizational Climate." *Ontario Journal of Educational Research* 8 (Spring 1966): 235.

Halpin, Andrew W., and Croft, Donald B. *The Organizational Climate of Schools.* Washington, D.C.: United States Office of Education, 1962.

Hand, Herbert H.; Richards, Max D.; and Slocum, John W. Jr. "Organizational Climate and the Effectiveness of Human Relations Training Program." *Academy of Management Journal,* 16 (June 1973): 190.

Helsel, A. Ray; Aurbach, Herbert A.; and Willower, Donald J. "Teacher Perceptions of Organizational Climate and Expectations of Successful Change." *Journal of Experimental Education* 38 (Winter 1969): 39.

Holst, A. W. "Educational Climate: A Prime Responsibility of the School Administrator." *Clearinghouse* 48 (November 1973): 168.

Howard, Eugene R. "School Climate Improvement." *Thrust for Educational Leadership* 3 (January 1974): 10.

Likert, Rensis. *New Patterns of Management.* New York: McGraw-Hill, 1961.

Owens, Robert G. *Organizational Behavior in Schools.* Englewood Cliffs, N.J.: Prentice-Hall, Inc., 1970.

Steinhoff, Carl R. *Organizational Climate in a Public School System,* USOE Cooperative Research Program Contract No. OE-4-225, Project No. 5-083. Syracuse University, 1965.

Wertheimer, P. A. "School Climate and Student Learning." *Phi Delta Kappan* 52 (May 1971): 530.

Wiggins, Thomas W. "Comparative Investigations of Principal Behavior and School Climate." *Journal of Educational Research* 66 (November 1972): 105.

19

Staffing: Group Solutions to Individual Problems

A favorite song one of our daughters sings on the way home from school goes something like this.

> Teacher don't wop little Buford
> Teacher don't pound on his head
> Teacher don't wop little Buford
> I think we should shoot him instead!

(The song's origin is unknown, and we must admit substituting the word Teacher for Mama.)

Very few of us have not held similar thoughts about particular students. It is a natural (and healthy) way of temporarily relieving frustration. This dark humor is characteristic of almost all good natured, well-intentioned teachers and administrators. It is usually the person who is prone to being physical with students who would never mention or admit to such thoughts.

This chapter centers around the fact that we do get terribly frustrated in dealing with a particular child who is difficult to handle. We feel helpless and grope for ways to keep our own sanity. We leave school exhausted, we constantly talk about him, dream about him, and get up in the morning with a not-too-keen appetite for facing another day. We would like to ask for help in successfully interacting with this child but are reluctant since we think this might be taken as a sign of incompetence. However, as we near the end of our rope, we begin to think that this child is beyond hope and should be referred to specialized personnel. Perhaps, he will be diagnosed by the guidance counselor or psychologist as severely disturbed and sent to a "special" school or at the very least, receive counseling.

Now, between us, the typical experience of referring a child for a psychological work-up goes like this. The teacher has to fill out a multitude of forms and keep extensive notes on the child's daily behavior. After processing these papers through the proper channels and receiving (hopefully with success) the parent's permission for an evaluation, there is a wait to see if the child is deemed serious enough to be tested. Finally, if all goes well, six weeks to three months later, the psychologist finally has the child examined. The report gets back to the school in a few weeks that, at last, confirms the teacher's suspicions. The child is diagnosed as emotionally disturbed, or learning disabled, or slightly brain-damaged. So, after half a year, we now know that the child is a bona fide, certified, classroom problem (we scratch our heads realizing that we knew this all along, only now it is officially documented). Admittedly, more schools now have services for such children but more common is the case that after the official diagnosis, all help ceases. In effect, this entire process is for naught. Usually there is no more room in the L.D. Center, special education or emotionally disturbed class, or perhaps these classes do not even exist. These children, according to many school and state board policies, are required to remain mainstreamed in the regular class. It is not our intention to criticize child services that are underfinanced and understaffed. It is simply to point out the reality to teachers and administrators. If a student is with a class and school at the beginning of the year regardless of how his behavior deteriorates, he will most likely still be there at the end of the year.

It is proposed that a technique, called "staffing," be implemented based upon the assumption that the child is here to stay. (We are indebted to Dr. Geneva Puffer-Woodruff, former Head of the E.P.D.A. program and Director of Pupil Personnel Services in Somersworth, New Hampshire and now Assistant Superintendent in Massachusetts, for introducing us to this concept.) The solution to helping the child is not looked for outside of, but rather within, the present resources, finances, and staffing pattern of the school. It is a simple, direct technique that may be used successfully by teachers and administrators regardless of their present approach to schooling.

STAFFING—WHAT IS IT?

Staffing is a process whereby one teacher explains to his or her colleagues the difficulty experienced with a particular child. The group then works together with the teacher to come up with various plans of action to improve the student and teacher situation. The outcome of a staffing is a clear commitment on the part of the teacher to carry out concrete actions which are part of a selected plan and to report the results back to the group. It is a technique a school staff can implement to help themselves and their students by drawing upon their own resources.

HOW DOES STAFFING WORK?

Time. A meeting time is set aside once every two weeks. The session lasts no more than sixty minutes. The time schedule is adhered to religiously. Making the dates the first and third Tuesday afternoon of each month alleviates having to constantly check the calendar from day-to-day. A routine is established whereby participants can schedule other appointments around these days. The meeting should begin fifteen minutes after school and stop after exactly one hour. This one-hour time limit is important and should be explained to all staff. In this way, all participants know the exact amount of time they have obligated themselves for. If a meeting is still going on at the sixty minute mark, it should be stopped and left incomplete unless *all* members agree to continue on.

The necessity of such detail can be explained in terms of task accomplishment and credibility. There is nothing that stifles one's willingness to participate more than to have the feeling of being taking advantage of. Meetings should have a clear beginning and end. To sit through a meeting that is nebulously scheduled, to be anxiously waiting to carry out one's responsibilities at home, and then to have a meeting drag on will certainly create negative attitudes. Teachers, like most people, are not overjoyed to meet after school, after the usual busy day. Equally distasteful is to schedule a clear sixty-minute session and then to continue past the designated hour.

Mr. Quiet is too shy to get up and leave, but his wife is waiting for him to go visit friends. Before leaving for school this morning, he told her that he would be home at 4:30 sharp. We need not go on about Mr. Quiet's feelings as 4:30 becomes 4:45. The next time a sixty-minute meeting is scheduled, one can imagine the skepticism that Mr. Quiet will have. The credibility of the meeting arranger, usually the principal or supervisor, will be quite suspect.

One more point before leaving the issue. Keeping the staffing meeting for sixty minutes is not only based on a concern for the teacher's time and a leader's credibility. When time constraints are known in advance, *the task usually gets accomplished.* Discussion does not wander, time is not wasted. The goal is clear. Everyone works to meet that deadline. Naturally, one must provide ample time to reach sound group decisions but in our experience, sixty minutes is quite adequate for the goal of staffing. Participants leave the meeting with the satisfaction of accomplishment and the knowledge that their time has been well spent. This feeling insures renewed enthusiasm for the next meeting, two weeks from that day.

Participants. Staffings should be entirely voluntary. They should include those staff members who have a concern for the plight of other teachers as well as students. These sessions are solely to help people. Their purpose is not for teachers to impress the administration, to put in official "browny" points, or to gab, complain, or intellectualize. The purpose is *to do* something about a difficult problem. Participants who do not partake in such a session of their own free will detract from this aim. This is not to say that those who do not attend are uncaring people and should be categorized accordingly. Many have other obligations and simply have to make a choice as to their own priorities. It is hard to mentally chastise Ms. Community Helper who does not attend a staffing in order to collect money for the Multiple Sclerosis Foundation. Another much more mundane reason for making the meeting voluntary is the fact that in many school systems, the meetings simply cannot be made compulsory. As part of many negotiated teacher contracts, classroom teachers are required to attend few designated after school sessions.

An interesting phenomenon which occurred in one school that used these staffing meetings should be cited. At first, only five or six teachers out of about twenty, regularly attended. Others began to wonder what was going on and dropped in. Perhaps they felt that it made good political sense to make an appearance from time to time. But when they actually saw that a teacher in trouble was being helped with his or her student, the "chip trading" principle came into being. It goes something like this:

> *Given:* I have or will have a child with whom I don't know how to deal.
> *Observation:* Teachers are receiving help from others in coming up with a plan to deal with children whom they have having difficulty with.
> *Conclusion:* If I help others by attending and contributing to the staffings, then when my turn comes to be helped I will be clear of debt in accepting such help. By collecting moral chips through service to others, one is entitled to cash them in (conscience free) when one needs help.

After two months, staffings increased in attendance to about ten or twelve staff members. At this point, after the majority were in attendance everyone began to show up. Unspoken social coercion must have had something to do with this dramatic upsurge in attendance. It seems that if the majority of the staff is involved in what is such an obviously well-intentioned, cooperative enterprise, then what does that do to the minority who are not participating? This coercion was not part of a contrived scheme to force people to volunteer. It simply happened. The only exception to voluntary attendance should be the principal, the educational leader. After all, if you do not view the helping of a student or teacher as a top priority, then there is little probability that your staff will.

No one in the school should be excluded from attending. There are no hidden agendas, nor should the meeting be perceived as a confidential meeting of a few making decisions for others. If one has an interest to help or is merely curious, he or she is welcome. Of course, when focusing on a particular child, persons who are most familiar and have contact with that child should be at the meeting. This might include the child's former teachers, such auxiliary staff as the physical education or art/music instructor, and of course, the guidance counselor. Such nonprofessional staff as school secretary, custodian, bus driver, or cafeteria workers could also be asked to attend if they have particular knowledge or contact with the youngster. In order to protect the child and with the recent legislation of the Family Rights and Privacy Act, it must be noted that all discussion should be unrecorded and pledged as strictly confidential, not to be shared with persons outside of the school.

The key participant is the teacher who has the problem child. He or she will come to the principal and will volunteer for the staffing to be done on the student at the next meeting. This usually happens when the teacher is at the end of the rope. When he or she comes to the principal or supervisor and says, "I have tried everything. I do not know what else to do. This kid is absolutely driving me nuts. It is either me or him. I need help," the leader then suggests that the next staffing be focused on the situation. In the meantime, the teacher is able to survive with the hope that somehow, something is going to transpire at the next meeting to help. The principal or supervisor then contacts those persons who are vitally involved in this particular situation, and asks them if they would care to come. When the meeting is about to begin, the seating arrangement might look like this. The Needing-Help Teacher (to be referred to in the remainder of the chapter as the N-H teacher) sits at the head of a conference table. Dispersed around the table will be others intimately involved with the case as well as the staff members who are concerned with simply providing a different perspective and helping a colleague. The leader is seated among the others.

Group Size. The optimum group size is six to ten people. This number facilitates the verbal involvement of each person as well as for cross-examination and fertilization of ideas. A group much larger than ten, unless unusually cohesive, often fragments with disconcerting effects occurring such as side discussions, quiet withdrawal and "performed" speeches to impress others. In a large school, it is best to subdivide staff into optimum size groups. This can be done in several ways. One meeting can have two or three staffings going on at the same time. Each N-H teacher can briefly explain his or her situation, and teachers can then decide in which case they might be able to offer the most aid. Another manner of keeping group size at the optimum level is to run staffings according to grade units. For example, primary teachers (K through 2nd), intermediate teachers (3rd through 5th), and middle grade teachers (6th through 8th) could meet. There should be representation of at least three age levels at each meeting. The perspectives and alternative plans of action appear to multiply with increased heterogeneity. In fact, some of the most successful staffings (conducted when we were acting consultants to schools) have been with grade level spans of kindergarten through eighth grade. An N-H teacher of second graders was amazed at the practical solution given by an eighth grade social studies teacher. At times, persons who have different experiences and preparation than our own can give us a suggestion completely outside our realm of previous comprehension that might just work.

The Agenda. The agenda is framed around one central word, *focus*. The leader should write the agenda for the staffing on a chalkboard in clear sight of all participants. It might look like this:

Agenda for Staffing

	Topic	Speaker	Time Allotment
1.	Overview of the situation	Needing Help Teacher	5 minutes
2.	Response to each item of staffing form	Needing Help Teacher	10 minutes
3.	Questions to gather additional information	Participants	10 minutes
4a.	Recording solutions	Participants	3 minutes
b.	Round the table solutions	Participants	5 minutes
5a.	Record commitment of action plan	Needing Help Teacher	2 minutes
b.	Verbal commitment of action plan	Needing Help Teacher	5 minutes
		Total:	40 minutes

(An ongoing staffing meeting would begin with a fifteen minute report from the previous N-H teacher. The forty-minute staffing would then take place. At its conclusion there is a five-minute buffer time for any miscellaneous discussion or information for the next staffing.) The leader then passes out the staffing form and goes over the five steps, continually emphasizing the need to follow the agenda explicitly and focusing only on the topic at hand.

STAFFING FORM

Subject: Data for Staffing on a Child

I. Social

1. What is the child's social interaction? With whom does he/she play? Work?
2. Under what circumstances does he/she interact best? with adults? with peers?
3. How does he/she respond to adult assistance?

II. Academic

1. What are the child's best subjects?
2. What are the child's interests?
3. How long can the child stay with a task?
4. Is he/she able to concentrate on an assignment? What assignment, for what length of time?
5. Is he/she able to finish an assignment?
6. What are the child's learning strengths? Is he/she motivated? persevering?
7. What are the child's learning weaknesses?
8. At what point does the child's learning break down?
   a. Time of day?
   b. During a lesson?
   c. Under special circumstances?
      (1) Near a student
      (2) Particular assignment
      (3) Writing answers
      (4) Placement in the room
9. What is the child's learning style? Is it visual, auditory, tactile, or what combination of these modalities?
10. What can the student do unaided?
11. What can the student do with assistance?

III. Emotional

1. How does the child cope with stress situations?
2. How does the child respond to being corrected?
3. What have you found to be a successful means of interacting with this child?
4. What kinds of avoidance behavior does the child demonstrate?

IV. Physical

1. Is the child active? sluggish?
2. How is the child coordinated?
3. Does the child demonstrate difficulty in fine motor coordination such as penmanship?

NOTES:

Step 1: Overview

The N-H teacher introduces the situation to the group. He or she describes in general what has been going on between the student and teacher. The teacher discusses what major incidents have occurred and what has been tried. He or she might also describe some characteristics of the child. *Only the "Needing-Help" teacher is allowed to talk.* The others may take notes on their staffing form. *No other sheets of paper are to be used.*

Step 2: Response to Each Item of Staffing Form

The N-H Teacher now moves from a general description of the situation to a specific analysis of the many aspects of the child. The form serves the purpose of prodding the teacher to look at the whole child and not just the irritating characteristics. It also serves to provide the participants with maximum information in minimal time. The teacher must go through the entire form, section by section, answering each question. With a time limit of ten minutes, he or she must give direct concise answers. Again, *only the "Needing-Help" teacher is allowed to talk.* The participants may take notes on their staffing form.

Step 3: Questions to Gather Additional Information

After fifteen minutes of listening, it is now time for the group to become verbal participants. They are to use the ten minutes to ask any questions that will give them additional information that may have been missed. They may also cross-examine the N-H teacher as to what he or she has previously tried with the student. Questions must be concerned with asking and probing, not presenting solutions in disguise. For example, statements such as "Have you ever tried this, it might work?" or "I think that you might do this, what do you think?" or "Last year, I had the same type of case and I did such and such, do you think you could do that?" are *not* allowable. There will be time for these in step four. This ten minutes is to gather as much knowledge as possible before attempting solutions. The N-H teacher *may only respond directly to a question and may not initiate any further discussion.*

Step 4a: Recording Solutions

All dialogue ceases and each participant writes down two or three possible actions that the teacher might take or a solution that he or she could personally help with. The participant is urged to be a free thinker and to write down any idea, regardless of how "hairbrained" it may sound. (Step 4a is an addition to former staffing procedures. We felt it necessary to have people write down their ideas before openly disclosing them. We found that by writing them down, when their turn came in the round-the-table time, they were less apt to modify, change, or omit ideas. Some people would become overly influenced by what other persons had previously said and, therefore, changed ideas to fit the previous theme.) *The N-H does not respond during these three minutes.*

Step 4b: Round-the-Table Solutions

Each participant shares his or her written ideas and actions that the Needing-Help teacher might attempt. The participant might also include some possible ways that he or she might help (e.g., lending instructional materials or books, taking the student for a period each day, releasing older students to work with the younger, relieving the teacher from recess duty, etc.). No discussion takes place. Each person has approximately thirty seconds to make points and then to give up the floor to the next person. The N-H teacher records all of the ideas on his or her staffing form, listens attentively and refrains from comments such as "Oh, I tried that once" or "That won't work because. . . ." Instead, the teacher is mentally processing what ideas might work and how they can be modified to fit the situation.

Step 5a: Record Commitment of Action Plan

The N-H teacher records on the staffing form what he or she is going to do now as part of a plan to help the child and alleviate the situation. The teacher writes down the long range plan and the one or two specific, concrete actions that will be taken beginning on the following school day and completed within two weeks (for the next meeting). *The group remains silent for these two minutes.*

Step 5b: Verbal Commitment of Action Plan

The N-H teacher now has the opportunity to explain what he or she has been able to gather from the group. If desired, the teacher might also explain why some ideas were rejected. He or she delineates the actions to be taken to improve the current situation. Each action is specified in terms of (1) What is to be done? (2) When will it happen? (3) How it is to be accomplished? (4) Who will do it and with what help? and (5) What will be the determination or criteria of success? No more than two or three specific actions should be undertaken. To hope for the miracle of complete eradication of a difficult problem within two weeks is absurd. However, we are concerned with some detected improvement resulting from concrete action that might be indicative of a direction to continue or pursue. The N-H teacher then makes a pledge to implement this plan and report back to the group in two weeks.

Throughout this meeting, one person, usually the leader, has the additional task of being the clockwatcher, the focuser, and the collector. The leader keeps to the time schedule. He or she stops the group after each alloted segment regardless of the degree of completeness. When discussions go astray, the leader points out the rules and the purpose of the segment and asks the group to refocus. This is of vital importance. If discussion goes astray or beyond limits, the overall goal of the staffing, i.e., to reach a committed plan of action, will not be reached. Finally, the leader serves the function of collecting and destroying all staffing forms and reminding participants of the confidentiality of the information that they now possess.

Before continuing, we wish to address the aspect of confidentiality. Transcripts or notes should not be kept beyond the meeting and it is probably not wise to use any staffing information as part of a child's permanent file. No mention has been made as to parent, or legal-guardian involvement. Remember, the purpose of a staffing is to determine what the school personnel can do to help a child. Staffing *should not* result in a plan referring a child to an outside agency or suspension from school. It also should *not* result in a plan that requires parent treatment at home. It is a school situation, to be handled by the school, and not to be parceled out to others.

Our position is that parents should be informed of a staffing that is going to take place and be *invited* to attend. No requirement is made. If the parent comes, fine; if not, then so be it. However, parents have the right to know what the staff is doing about their child and to have the opportunity for input and perhaps veto. It is a well-used statement by teachers and administrators that "parents whom we wish to see about their child's behavior never come in, and those whom we have no reason to see are the ones that do come." It is the same in our experience of inviting parents to staffings. However, even if most choose not to attend, they still should not be denied the right to have that choice.

WHAT HAPPENS AS A RESULT OF STAFFING?

Upon conclusion of the meeting, everyone involved has a new sense of confidence. Not only has the distressed teacher been helped but the other participants often have been able to take an idea or suggestion away that has application for improving their own work with one or several students. There is a sense of camaraderie. Through this group problem, official lines of command have been relaxed. Whether it is the principal, the schoolmarm with twenty-five years of experience, or the neophyte teacher, each has been listened to as an individual with a contribution to make. It is the value of the idea rather than the status of the person speaking that matters. There is a feeling of collective power, that as a group they have the ability to master their professional problems. And lastly, there is a new respect for each other as professionals. Professionals are persons that have been highly trained, who measure alternative actions and consequences before making decisions.

For the educational leader there arises a question to be answered. How often is it that a school problem is deflected to outside agencies because it is deemed insoluble? For example, school reading scores are declining. The solutions to this problem are always outside our immediate realm; there is need for more reading specialists, more money for instructional materials, or better parental involvement with their preschoolers. These are all plausible explanations and may be rational. However, to put it bluntly, this type of reasoning does not get the immediate job done. It is highly unlikely that schools, particularly with today's monetary crises, are going to spend additional monies to fund more reading specialists, increase supplies, and begin a comprehensive early-childhood, parent-training program. Basically, to place the blame outside of the existing structure, school staff, and budget, although perhaps true, leads to a defeatist and "copping-out" attitude. In effect, we are saying, "Don't expect us to improve on this reading program until we receive additional funds for. . . ." We assume that by now the reader is mumbling hotly under his or her breath that these ivory-tower authors are just like the school board and public, expecting the school to be responsible for everything wrong in our society, and then, without adequate support or solutions, condemning public school people when they do not deliver results. This is not our point. Basically, the issue is that if there is a need for improvement in your school, then realistically, either you or your staff have to tackle the problem with your existing resources or nothing is going to be done.

To bring this matter home on a more personal basis, let's look at what transpires in the principal's office or at staff meetings. You know that Ms. Goofoff has been neglecting her recess duties. You confront her with the observation that she has been late for playground duty every day this week. She says that this is true but it is because of all the extra classwork that she has to do. "What we need," she says, "is a full-time teacher aide in my class or a full-time playground supervisor to relieve all teachers of this duty." You know (and hopefully she does too) that the school board has just approved a no-growth budget for next year and such a request is impossible. Now what is really transpiring is that Ms. Goofoff is protecting herself by attacking conditions outside of herself. She may be perfectly right, but that is not going to help when tomorrow's playground duty comes around. If the situation is to improve, Ms. Goofoff has to be out there on time.

Without belaboring the point, the same kind of reasoning often occurs when a teacher has difficulty with a child. The blame is put on inadequate auxiliary help, the lack of special services and classes, negligent parents, or poor administrative support. What staffing has done is placed the problem in the context where it must be solved. The members of the school are thus becoming a self-sufficient unit who need not cry on anyone's shoulder.

There are several other benefits of the staffing procedure:

1. *Promotes emotional health.* When teachers (or administrators) become frustrated with a particular child, they lose objectivity. The responsibility for this child seems to be bearing down on their shoulders. You can often observe the changed physical reactions of the despairing teacher: glum facial expressions, sloped shoulders, no lilt to the voice, and mournful eyes on the verge of tears. A staffing lets this teacher know that others have had and are experiencing similar feelings. A staffing also lets the teacher know that others care about him or her, and are willing to give support in thought and action. Often, after such a staffing, teachers will make a point during the following days to seek this teacher out for friendly conversation and a "how goes it" discussion.

2. *Coordinates staff actions in working with a child.* A staffing gives direction to all of those involved with the child. This knowledge

sensitizes the staff so that they may deal with the youngster if something comes up in the hall, cafeteria, or elsewhere. It also helps the principal in determining an approach to take with the child if sent to him or her. For example, a staffing has let people know that Johnny goes into severe temper tantrums when he is criticized in front of others, and, therefore, the best course of action would be to pull Johnny aside and use a quiet, nondirective approach when he misbehaves. The teacher will then use this approach for the next two weeks. The staff will also carry out this approach if they have to discipline Johnny. It only makes sense. If a plan is to be tried, it is best to have consistent treatment. Think of all the time and conscious effort Johnny's teacher might take to treat him nonthreateningly only to have it all wasted when Johnny blows skyhigh after being jerked out of line and scolded harshly by an unknowing colleague. In our own experiences in school, we know that it is crucial for all adults to act consistently, especially with oversensitive and aggressive children.

3. *A plan for a child gives future direction.* A plan developed for a child provides a conscious exploration of what works and what does not. Instead of the daily, haphazard, and reactionary way of dealing with misbehavior, a plan enables the teacher to document what aspects of the plan worked. If nothing about the plan was successful, then at least there is an empirical basis for moving on to a different treatment. Over time, this reasonable process of trial and error will enable one to eventually focus on what actually works.

4. *Commitment to action produces answers.* The pledge that the Needing-Help teacher takes to implement his or her plan of action and to report back to the group provides some sense of closure. Unlike other meetings where issues are left unresolved (usually to be thought about and discussed further) this one has a concrete ending. Having the teacher contract to report back to colleagues in two weeks forces implementation. Well-intentioned persons often make grandiose schemes. However, the day-to-day maintenance tasks of the classroom somehow swallow up the time and the scheme is shelved until after Christmas and then spring break, until finally the year is over. The staffing procedure makes the teacher accountable for his or her plan. The teacher must face a group of peers who have committed their own time in order to help. There is much self-imposed pressure to carry out the task when one must face an expectant group.

Some Other Ways to Use a Staffing

As one toys with a strategy and then implements it successfully, the mind becomes locked into applying the scheme in other ways. A staffing need not be solely used for student behavioral concerns. It can be used for diagnosing academic weaknesses and planning individualized instructional programs as well. The composition of the group theoretically includes more learning specialists, but the regular classroom staff should not degrade their own capabilities and should not fear tackling such a task themselves. The staffing form itself might need some modification (even for its intended purpose, a staff might wish to make revisions). Another interesting use of the staffing procedure was implemented by educators in a small mining town when they focused on professionally related personal problems of teachers. For example, a teacher might have difficulty in organizing his after-school time efficiently enough to accomplish both school work and home responsibilities. Using the staffing procedure, he describes his plight in step one, and steps two and three are combined for a twenty-minute question-and-answer period. The remaining sequence is used with a commitment to action and report back. Staff members would need a greater degree of intimacy and trust to be comfortable in staffing on problems that include emotional and private concerns that are affecting the teaching process. In summary, there is no one way to use this procedure. (If you think of some other applications we would like to know.)

A Disclaimer—It Might Not Work

The procedure of staffing, how it works, and what will happen have all been discussed in the affirmative. In fact, if we substituted the word "miracle waters" for staffing, you might think that this was an old western medicine show exalting the be-all therapeutic cures of a fabulous drug. Authors have a tendency to highlight the positive about their approaches and conveniently ignore the negative. We admit to being guilty of this. To rectify this guilt, we now wish to make some disclaimers.

Even if you and your staff have followed our process exactly, you still might not come up with the solution for a teacher and a child. Children have what we call the "squirm factor." (We got the idea of the squirm effect when watching a psychologist who claimed to have a fool-proof method of communicating to young children. He sat down with his brief case, took out his puppets and began to talk. To his dismay the youngsters kept squirming, getting up, walking behind him, and playing with the latch of his brief case, totally ignoring the puppets.)

It seems as though no matter how solid our analysis and logical our plan, somehow children never exactly fit into our program. They have the annoying habit of not sitting still and doing as we have planned. Instead, they constantly surprise us by behaving in ways that were unpredictable. This is both the frustration and beauty of working with children. The child, the class, and the school are never the way that we would ideally like. There is always more that should be done. When we have one situation close to our satisfaction, something else pops up that demands our attention. This is the challenge of teaching. Students are so individually different that we are never sure of what to expect from day to day. We value this individuality. It is what makes education so exciting and at times so terribly demanding.

With the above in mind, let us look at what might go wrong with a staffing. First, no one may come to the staffing. If that happens then it is a strong indication that the staff is pulling apart from each other. The staff does not have a purpose and direction. You need to go back to the blueprinting stage of this book. Secondly, the staffing may come about but the discussion does not stay focused. This would indicate the lack of a respected group enforcer or it might mean that the person in charge of this function is not assertive enough or bright enough to know when the dialogue is moving away. In this case, the group needs to go over the ground rules again and might choose a new enforcer that they will listen to. If there is no respected enforcer available, there is no reason for proceeding with the staffing. Thirdly, the Needing-Help teacher might decide at the commitment stage that nothing new has been offered and, therefore, sees no obligation to verbalize any action. If this happens, then the leader of the group should ask the teacher to make a commitment to retry some previous actions. The teacher must leave with a plan. If the teacher refuses then (this is easy to say), he or she should never have wasted the group's time in the first place. Prior to the staffing, each Needing-Help teacher (and all participants) should know that one makes a commitment when one asks for a staffing on a situation. Fourth, after the initial euphoria of "getting the job done," the N-H teacher may go back in the classroom, try a few things, and meet utter failure and despair. This is a real possibility and the teacher should come right back and present this information at the next staffing. With this additional information of failure given to the group, step two may be skipped and the staffing can proceed from step three on. You might wonder what happens to the teacher until the next staffing? Unless the leader deems it an emergency and wishes to call an immediate voluntary staffing for that day, the teacher, principal, and counselor will have to come up with some stop-gap method. This is, of course, what is typically done when a school does not have a staffing procedure. It is quite probable that, with a particularly disruptive or unsettling student, staffings on that one child might take place throughout the entire year. As to when is it time to stop with a particular student, the staffing group may make that decision for themselves as they run out of solutions. One final observation that pertains to the negative elements of a staffing—teachers will always have problems with kids. There is a "pop-up discipline phenomenon" that works in every class and school. No matter how many of the top priority problem students have been helped, there is a new group that immediately "pops up." It is never ending, perhaps because behavior affects us so relatively. George does not seem so bad. After all he only sticks thumbtacks on chairs while Leroy hits people with a baseball bat. Now when Leroy ceases, George's thumbtacks become inexcusable. We can only attempt to minimize behavior problems. We can never eliminate them.

Examples of Plans of Action Derived From Staffings

The reader is probably wondering what actions actually come about via a staffing. Are there strokes of brilliance that have never occurred to people before? In a few cases, the answer is yes, sometimes a Needing-Help teacher will hear an idea that another person has tried that will hit like a thunderbolt. In most cases, however, the answer is no. The N-H teacher will hear ideas that he or she has been exposed to or even tried before. Sometimes they will have been forgotten or not used with the particular child of concern. At other times, the ideas might reinforce what the teacher was wishing and attempting to do all along.

It is with some reluctance that we present some examples of action plans that were successfully used. We do not want to limit you or your staffs vision by having your thinking restricted to these lines of practice. Rather view them as an outgrowth of the thinking of particular people in their own particular environment. Some might be applicable, but please do not superimpose these on your situation. If they do come out in similar ways, they will be a creation of your staffs thinking in helping an individual teacher with a single child.

Examples

1. *Problem.* Teacher cannot handle Sonny when he throws a temper tantrum. If she takes him out into the hall, or isolates him, he runs away. She cannot keep chasing him all around the school and leave the class unsupervised.

Plan. The teacher across the hall, who had Sonny last year, asked the N-H teacher to send a student to her when Sonny goes out of control. She will come across and bring him to her room until he settles down and is ready to go back.

2. *Problem.* The N-H teacher explains that Regina has a low opinion of herself. She is withdrawn, passive, and almost nonverbal with the teacher and her classmates.

Plan. The upper grade teachers volunteer to send two of their girl students, who live near Regina, out with her on the playground for half an hour each day. There job is to befriend Regina and to organize games with her that will attract some of her classmates.

3. *Problem.* Jamuel, although capable, never gets his work done. He is always daydreaming. As a result, he has to keep working during the free-time period. The N-H teacher says that nothing seems to motivate him and she is always having to get on him to hurry up.

Plan. The teacher will survey Jamuel, his friends, and his parents to see what he enjoys doing and then use that as an incentive for him to finish his work. She discovers that he is constantly playing table hockey at home. She borrows a table hockey game and includes it in free time for Jamuel to use when he finishes his assignments.

4. *Problem.* Anthony is a very active, defiant child. The N-H teacher explains that as long as she remains calm, she can keep up with Anthony and keep his energy directed towards constructive pursuits. However, after a while he gets to her, particulary at the end of the day and by Thursday and Friday, she is ready to explode.

Plan. Other teachers volunteer on a rotating basis to switch classes with the N-H teacher for a half-hour, midafternoon every day. The change of classrooms, different-age students, and curriculum content might be a welcome change of pace for all of them. On Fridays, the kindergarten teacher who has a full-time aide, says that her aide can work in the N-H teacher's classroom in the morning. Some upper-class teachers also volunteer to send some of their more responsible students to tutor Tony for fifteen minutes each day, thus giving N-H teacher another daily break.

5. *Problem.* Patricia is incapable of doing any of the work that the other second graders do. All pencil and paper work are out of her grasp. She gets easily frustrated and then begins to lash out at others. The N-H teacher acknowledges that she needs more of a manipulative, concrete instructional program but she cannot develop an all-day program for Patricia because of her lack of knowledge, materials, and time.

Plan. The kindergarten and first-grade teachers volunteer to supply the N-H teacher with some of their materials, games, and learning centers. They also ask that Patricia come to their class during her regular reading and arithmetic periods to receive instruction in those areas with their students. The other times of the day (music, art, physical education, health, social studies, etc.) she works with her regular classmates.

Some other typical plans have called for precise changes in teacher behaviors or procedures and recording the change for two weeks. This is using the scientific method to ascertain causal effects for the behavior and thus enables the teacher to make a determination of continuation or cessation of such behavior. Some teacher plans for behavior or procedural changes have been as follows: giving reinforcement with a ratio of three positive to one negative; talking only quietly when disciplining; talking sternly with rapid commands when disciplining; isolating a child from the group after only one previous warning; not waiting for a tardy child; rewarding specific work accomplishment via tokens; meeting with a student on a personal basis outside of school. This list could go on and on but the basic treatment is always to do something different.

Variations in Plans According to the Three Alternative Models

Discussed in the preceding chapters has been the relationship among school goals, curriculum development, instructional methods, and student management. How do staffings fit with the various models of predictability, unpredictability, and a combination of the two? A staffing is of relevant use to each model. What is different is in the direction of each derived plan of action. The staff in an Alternative One school, for example, would be free to come up with an individual plan of action derived from Alternative Two or Alternative Three. However, in using Alternative Two or Three practices, it is knowingly and with the intent of eventually moving toward ways more consistent with Alternative One. Each staffing plan, regardless of the alternative school model, is developed to fit the immediate situation.

20

Extra Help—
Proceed with Caution

The new principal meets with his staff on the first day on the job. He is young, just out of the classroom, and imbued with the idea of what a school should really be. He addresses his staff in a nervous but expectant manner on what he personally believes about education and where he would like to see the school go over the next three years. One of his central points is that a school belongs to the community and that the door to any classroom should always be open to parents. To underscore this point, he tells the staff that tomorrow a notice will go out inviting parents to come and volunteer their time in the school. All that parents will need to do is contact their child's teacher, tell them when they will arrive, and they then can begin to volunteer. The neophyte principal, knowing that in the past the school has had no volunteer program and parents could only vist by making an appointment that needed clearance with the school office, feels that this change will create a greater understanding and a more open relationship between the school's staff and the community. At the end of the principal's discourse, he asks the teachers if they have any questions or concerns. When none are forthcoming, the meeting ends, the notice goes out to the parents and the new era is about to begin.

Regardless of how lofty the ideal, the principal had made a huge blunder that will create much conflict and pain, and could actually reverse the desired outcome of an open, understanding relationship between the community and school. The school had until now been left alone by the public. The students seemed to be doing reasonably well, discipline was thought to be strong, and the children appeared happy. Parents had a respect for the institution and had voiced no objections about being excluded from its operation. The belief that parents' held was that the school professionals knew what they were doing. "Teachers do not come and participate in my work, why should I, as a parent, feel slighted if I do not participate in theirs?"

251

So what happened with the new era? The principal opened the school to parents. Most parents did not come, but some did volunteer. The teaching staff had not voiced any objections when the principal made his original announcement, but now, after a few weeks, teachers were voicing opposition. Parents were coming in and trying to discipline students. They were challenging teachers about allowing children to work on the floor, letting students play "games" during school time, and letting the classrooms get so "noisy" and "messy." The principal assured each teacher who was experiencing such difficulties that this was part of the process of establishing more positive relationships.

Unfortunately he was wrong. This had become a process of disintegrating public confidence rather than improving relationships. Within the next few weeks parents and teachers began to respond to each other as adversaries. Teachers planned their schedules so that only the most sedate, neat activities would transpire during the parent-volunteers presence. Parents were asked to leave the class-room immediately after their scheduled time. The teachers became "too busy" to have any discussions and parents were asked to make arrangements to meet with them "some other time."

Teachers who were conversing with each other in the hall would suddenly cease all discussion when spotting an approaching volunteer. A cold silence would ensue until the parent was out of hearing range.

Parents reacted to the teachers' cold shoulder by taking their complaints elsewhere. The new principal was besieged by phone calls and visits from volunteer parents about the intolerable conditions in the various rooms. Volunteer parents discussed their complaints downtown, at the grocery store, post office, and beauty parlor. Finally, after five weeks of this "new era of openness," after complaints continued to pile up from parents and teachers about each other, the principal halted the volunteer program. He used a convenient excuse that after the approaching vacation the school would be engaged in many curriculum projects and the staff would have no time to give to the volunteers. He added that the volunteer program eventually would be reorganized to fit those project needs and that parents would be contacted again after such projects were completed. The message that went out to parents was a tactful way of saying, "Thank you for your help; it did not work. We may try later. Don't call us, we'll call you."

Parents cut through the subtleties, knowing full well that they were being barred from the school. What they had seen in the school as volunteers had shocked them. They were not perpared to accept this "new, modern education." Now that the principal had closed the door, they took their concerns to the school board, the superintendent, the newspapers, and the local radio's morning talk show. A full scale attack was mounted against the teachers and the principal. In only a few weeks, dramatic reversal had occurred. The new principal's intent was to open the school to the community. The opposite occurred.

This seems quite an unlikely story; pure fiction. Not at all. One of us was that neophyte principal and has the scars to prove it. Surely, other school leaders have experienced similar occurrences. This story is not being told to persuade leaders to avoid parents or other auxiliary personnel. Instead it is a lesson to be learned from. It is an example of why planning is so necessary. The leader and staff must first determine the need for auxiliary help, then which group of outside persons to use, and finally, how to prepare, educate, and train such personnel. We will take each group of persons who might serve as extra help and discuss plans for how they might be used. (These groups are not exhaustive of groups which might help school personnel.)

GROUP ONE: PARENT VOLUNTEERS

Since we have begun this chapter with a nightmarish story of the erroneous use of parents, it is best to begin here with a discussion of some appropriate ways to use parents in a school. Parents are understandably the most sensitive group to deal with. Due to their concern for the welfare of their children, the money that they pay every year in taxes, and their prior experiences as students, they have a personal, vested interest in what goes on. This personal interest can be used constructively to improve the school program. If handled insensitively, using parents has the potential for destructive impact. Every parent wants the best for his or her child. Not every parent is sufficiently educated or aware of changes which have been made in schools that are in the best interests of children. A parent does not bat an eyelash upon shopping in today's supermarkets. How different are these stores from the "Mom-and-Pop" grocery stores of twenty years ago? The changes in retail selling of such goods has taken place over a period of time, but the consumer, shopping daily, has kept intimately informed. There is little debate that supermarkets today, with their garish displays, wide selections, comfort, convenience, and economic pricings are a definite improvement from the old days (how many people still shop in small grocery stores?). Yet, the same consumer is, as a parent, shocked when he or she returns to a school after a twenty-year absence. He or she remembers schools as sitting in rows, passively receiving all class instruction, and reciting only when called upon. The evolving concepts of individualized instruction, flexible grouping, comfortable environments, and active student involvement are as foreign to the parent as walking into a supermarket would be after a twenty-year absence from the planet. Not only would the perception be startling, it would cause confusion and a threat to one's notion of what is "supposed to be." The parent, in the same manner, is an alien from education. He or she has not had direct contact with the evolving changes in education and, therefore, cannot be expected to grasp immediately how such changes are improvements (we are assuming throughout this discourse that we indeed can validate such changes as improvements). Therefore, the key to any parent involvement program is the gradual assimilation of new concepts (of how schools have changed) over a period of time. This orientation is essential if parents are to work *with* and not *against* the school.

Recruiting Parent Volunteers.

To begin a program, a notice should go out to parents specifying that a parent volunteer program is being considered. The letter should explain the kinds of volunteer work needed (individual tutoring, making materials, clerical tasks, field trip supervision, etc.). It should also explain that a four-to-six-week training program, involving meeting one afternoon per week, will be required before actual volunteering begins. Parents should sign and return the letter if they are interested in becoming a part of such a program.

The principal and staff, upon receiving completed forms, will then have a reasonable idea as to the amount of interest in the program. By mandating a training program, the school can be sure that proper preparation of each parent will take place, as well as knowing that the volunteer has made a serious commitment. The principal and staff, having agreed upon the dates and topics for each training session, then follow up with a second notice to all those parents who have completed and returned the first form. This notice contains the details of the training program. Parents who are still interested and can attend at those specified times are asked to sign up by returning the second notice. Placement of parents in particular classrooms with certain teachers is not made until after the training program.

Training Program

The particulars are best left to the staff and leader to work out. However, a generalized schedule might include some of the following:

Session One. Introduction by the principal of the school's philosophy and goals and an explanation of some of the differences in "contemporary" schools. This session ends with a social tea to acquaint parents with teachers.

Session Two. A walking tour of the classrooms, lead by the principal or staff, followed by a question and answer period. The first tour should be after school so that parents can concentrate on room arrangements, class schedules, materials available, and teacher record keeping without being distracted by students.

Session Three. A walking tour of the classrooms with students present, again led by principal or staff with a question and answer session to follow.

Session Four. Instructional training in working with individual children or small groups. It is best for classroom teachers to lead this session. They can show how their materials are to be used with students. (This instructional training might be extended over several sessions.)

Session Five. Presentation of firm guidelines for volunteers. This is a crucial meeting prior to the actual placement of volunteers in classrooms. The principal and staff should make it clear verbally and in writing exactly what is expected of the parents. The point being stressed is that, as a volunteer, the parent needs to act in a professional manner. All information learned about children is treated with the strictest of confidence. Any concerns that arise should be handled as a school matter, first to be aired with the classroom teacher, then if necessary with the school principal. *School matters are not to be discussed downtown.* All time arrangements made with the assigned teacher should be faithfully kept. The teacher should be notified the day before if an absence will occur. There may be other guidelines that the staff wishes to include. This list of guidelines should be given to the parents at the conclusion of the meeting. At the bottom of the sheet should be a statement that reads somewhat like this:

I __(name)__ understand the guidelines for being a parent volunteer and wish to participate in the program.

Before this meeting ends, parents should fill out a slip of paper giving their first three choices for grade placement, teacher, and type of work.

One might think that this detailed accounting smacks of paranoia. However, parents are not being viewed as enemies. Anyone who enters a new environment feels more secure when knowing what the parameters are. The person then has a choice to enter or not. It is unfair to allow a person to enter an organization without such guidelines and then later to criticize the person for not acting in an appropriate manner. Parents do not learn what schools expect of them through osmosis.

Session Six.   The principal should have compiled similar preference information from teachers and then, either by himself or with the staff, match the volunteers and willing teachers. It is usually best not to place a parent with his or her child's teacher. Although there are exceptions, such a situation is too distracting for all involved. The primary purpose of this session is to announce placements and provide time for the individual teacher and parent to go over arrangements (scheduling, type of work to be done, and any extra information pertinent to beginning in a particular classroom). At the close of this session, it might be well to recognize parents' participation in the training program with a social get-together and to hand out certificates of achievement.

Volunteers are at last ready to function. Periodic, ongoing meetings to "touch bases" with all involved and to gather additional information related to future training needs is advisable. Also, to insure that the placement of parents with teachers does not become troublesome, it is wise to make the initial placement on a two-week trial basis. If all parties are doing well, then the arrangement becomes permanent. If trouble arises, then the principal has an escape hatch to make rearrangements without creating a major issue.

To do all of the above might sound like a lot of work. Some readers might say that they already have well-informed parents, others might claim to have an ongoing, successful volunteer program. For those persons, do not tamper with success. Keep doing what you are doing. However, for those of you who wish to begin, to expand, or to adjust your present parent-volunteer program, we feel that the time spent in providing a comprehensive training program will pay off in less time being spent dealing with conflict caused by misunderstandings.

In the aftermath of Watergate and the emergence of Sunshine laws, we must admit to being uneasy with how the reader might interpret our emphasis on the details of planning a program and having parent volunteers (and other auxiliary personnel) keep their concerns about teachers and classrooms within the school. Let us explain our personal convictions. We feel that schools are indeed open institutions belonging to all the people. We do not think that schools can legally or morally close themselves to criticism. Criticism and conflict, to the extent that it spurs improvement, is vital to schools. However, criticism and conflict is not the concern of parent volunteers. If parents are volunteering to help children, which is the ultimate aim of volunteerism, then that should be where their energies are directed. If a parent has a criticism to make then channels are open within the school. First, the parent goes to the teacher; secondly, to the principal. If after these meetings, the issue is unresolved, the parent should be encouraged to talk to the superintendent and, if still unsatisfied, then to the school board. If these encounters do not lead to a satisfactory conclusion, *then and only then* does a parent have the right to "take it to the street." In this manner, petitions, marches, and public meetings of protest are all acceptable to us. What is unacceptable is a parent who has an ax to grind and signs up to volunteer without any inclination of helping children, and instead has only the intent of "gathering the goods." A rigorous training program and recruitment procedure may possibly counter the negative attitudes of some people and is a tough commitment in time and involvement for negative persons who are not sure of their intentions.

One more thought is needed to clarify possible misinterpretation. A school that is closed to criticism would hardly encourage a parent volunteer program in the first place. We assume a school that takes the time to plan and train parents will also take the time to listen to them, and if the concerns are valid, then to make the necessary adjustments.

GROUP TWO: UNIVERSITY STUDENTS ENROLLED IN REGULAR CLASSES

If a school is fortunate enough to be situated near a university or college, there exists the potential for tremendous help. Most of us are fairly aware of the possible uses of undergraduate student teachers and graduate (Master's degree) school interns. The use of this group usually involves some official exchange of forms and monetary compensation. We will discuss the use of this group later on in this chapter. But for now we wish to highlight three other university populations that are much more easily available with little or no paperwork or money involved.

Undergraduate Education Majors

Many universities are requiring that a field-based component become part of their undergraduate training programs. Students, from the first semester of their freshman year to their last semester of student teaching are being placed in schools. They spend from three to six hours per week in a classroom. Concurrently, they take related education method or seminar courses at the university and are given assignments related to working with children. When the school and teacher accept such a student, it is usually with an implied agreement to be flexible, The university student is expected to fit into the overall routine of the classroom and to carry out teacher assignments; yet the teacher is also expected to accommodate the student in carrying out his or her university assignments. Universities prefer to place a cluster of students in a single school. Students can thus travel together and share common experiences. At most universities, there is a tendency to place students first at schools which want them. University personnel do not feel comfortable with having to "sales pitch" their students into a school. They often have more students to place than places immediately available. If a school is interested in securing such help, often all that is needed is for the principal to call the chairperson of the Education Department (Early Childhood, Elementary Education, Middle School Education, Special Education, etc.). The chairperson ought to be able to fill in the general details of the program and connect the caller with the supervisor of the field-based program.

In our experience with field-based undergraduate students (from both perspectives of school principals and as university supervisors), we feel that these college students are a definite plus. They possess rudimentary skills in working with children, have tremendous enthusiasm, and often develop a rapport with particular children that a regular teacher may not. On the other hand, we must note that there might be a few "clunkers" in the group who do not show up when expected, simply go through the motions when present, and deal insensitively with children. For the sake of your school children, future children, and the college student, you are doing the university a favor by bringing such a person to their attention before he or she gets any closer to student teaching and graduation.

Undergraduate and Graduate Students in Related Fields

Aside from formal, field-based programs, there are many individual courses offered at colleges and universities which include a laboratory or research project. A course in Learning Disabilities might require the students to use certain materials with children, or a child psychology course might require observations and interactions with individual children. There are courses in business management that require an organizational study or cost analysis project. What we are getting at is that there are often particular courses in which competent university students might fulfill their requirements besides meeting a particular need in your school. To hire consultants to fulfill such a service would cost more than most public schools could afford. However, such a service done by college students and supervised by a well-qualified professor is almost the equivalent of getting the consulting service for free.

For example, at times we felt a great need for a comprehensive preschool screening of our incoming kindergarten children. We wanted to look at many areas of development; perception, hearing, coordination, articulation, emotional stability, cognitive skills, etc. To hire a team of specialists for a three-day period would cost an unthinkable amount. Instead, we looked through the local university's course offerings, and contacted instructors of courses in the areas of tests and measurement, nursing, speech and hearing, etc. They were more than willing to have their students receive such practical experience. In many cases they even supplied the necessary materials and equipment.

On another occasion, we wanted an evaluation of a new curriculum model. Again, instead of going to private research consultants, we went to the instructor of a graduate course in Advanced Educational Research Design. She took it from there. Her students designed the study, collected the data, did all the analysis, and sent back an understandable, concise report. Doctoral students doing their dissertations are another source of research resources at minimal cost and effort. It might well be worth the time of a principal and staff, when needing outside service, to thumb through the description of course offerings at the nearby university. If a course description and its requirements come close to matching your local need, call the instructor directly and discuss the possibilities.

Now we will let you in on a closely guarded university secret. When professors come up for tenure and promotion at their college, the reviewing committee always looks at the category of *community service*. Do not feel defensive in discussing your needs and asking for a gratis service, you probably will be helping to provide security for an aspiring assistant professor.

GROUP THREE: UNIVERSITY STUDENTS ENROLLED IN STUDENT TEACHING OR TEACHING INTERNSHIP

Since student teachers and interns usually spend daily and extended periods of time within a classroom and school, we feel that it is necessary to discuss their selection, training, and use separately from other auxiliary personnel. In most cases, student teachers finish their undergraduate education with a final semester of full-time involvement in the classroom. A semester runs about fifteen weeks with the student progressing from responsibilities typical of an aide, to that of a team teacher, to eventually becoming the teacher in charge. Each university and public school devises their own schedules for student teaching progression. They range from the student taking over the entire class from the first day of the semester, to the student teacher going no further than one week of full responsibility. Many Master's Degree programs in teaching (M.A.T.'s) have a one-year internship requirement. The graduate student teaches for the full year. Since they already have more experience than the undergraduate, they can quickly assume responsibilities for large groups of students. In some localities, master degree students are paid a stipend by the public school and are contracted as regular employees. It must be fairly obvious that student teachers and Master's Degree Interns can have a substantial impact on the children, the staff, and the community. With that impact in mind, we think that a school needs to be careful about the selection and placement of such personnel.

Since university students and school staff will have to make a commitment to each other for a great amount of time, they should have the opportunity to choose with whom they will work. It is understood that such a democratic selection is highly improbable in large, centralized school districts and universities. Yet, we wish to make our case for such and then outline a program that might be used, at least in part by any school.

> Oakview school has a strong individualized program with a heavy emphasis on programmed, computer assisted instruction (Alternative One). The central office has placed three master degree interns (M.A.T.'s) to work at Oakview. The principal and staff have decided that they can use the most help at the sixth-grade level in reading and arithmetic. The three sixth-grade teachers are firm, directive instructors who are looking forward to the extra hands that the M.A.T.'s will provide.
>
> Sue Jordan, Ashlyn Eckelberger, and Dana Velvet are young women beginning the intership aspect of the Masters of Arts in teaching. They have read, thought about, and practiced a philosophy of liberal openness. They believe strongly in an education consisting of activity, exploration, and creativity (Alternative Three) for children. They are very excited about trying out their ideas and have spent the summer gathering materials for the coming year.
>
> The day before school opens, Sue, Ashlyn, and Dana eagerly arrive at Oakview. They meet the principal and teachers, and are given a tour of the school. After the tour, the teachers sit down with them. They listen to what their responsibilities will be, and the more they listen, the more uncomfortable they become.
>
> After one week of school, the sixth grade teachers become concerned. They have tried so hard to help the M.A.T.'s but they seem so reluctant to check the childrens' work, to administer the programmed tests, and to keep the class orderly. The M.A.T.'s in turn have become glum, despondent, and uneasy.

What good is this arrangement? Both teachers and interns have the best of intents, but they are working in an untenable situation. The M.A.T.'s have few recourses. They can try to convince the teachers and the school of the rightness of their approach, or they can resign themselves to a year of conforming to procedures that they disagree with, or they can go underground and try to subvert the system by promoting their ideas with the children clandestinely. What about the sixth grade teachers? What can they do? They can try to persuade the M.A.T.'s of the rightness of their approach, they can use their power to knuckle the M.A.T.'s under, or they can give in and let the M.A.T.'s "do their thing." None of these paths, if chosen by the teachers or M.A.T.'s is going to help a school which is clear in its purpose and direction.

We are not telling you, the educational leader, anything new by stating that such incompatible M.A.T. or student teaching assignments happen frequently. In a school that has little direction or consistency, to expose children to another incongruent situation merely compounds the existing ineffectiveness of the school. In a school that has purpose, such an arrangement is prone to failure. Following is an outline of steps that can help to avoid such occurrences. (The label "intern" could be used synonymously for student teachers or M.A.T.'s)

Placement of Interns

Preliminary Step.   Interns visit several schools. The public school district usually has little control of how many schools an intern visits before selecting or being assigned to a particular school. It is ideal for interns to first visit schools of divergent practices. The university student can then make a preliminary assessment of which school would be most suitable to his or her preferred style of teaching. If this is not the procedure in one's own location, then the educational leader can still provide for optimal placement in one's own school by proceeding with these steps.

Step One.   Ask for classroom teachers to volunteer as potential cooperating teachers for interns. The principal can simply meet with the staff or pass out a memo to find out which teachers would like to have an intern. There is no commitment at this point beyond agreeing to allow interns to visit their classrooms.

Step Two.   Have interns rotate to designated classrooms. After the principal has met with the interns and gone over the philosophy and practices of the school, a schedule is drawn up for each intern to spend one full day in each classroom. This schedule, depending on the number of classrooms, should be kept within two weeks.

Step Three. Have interns and teachers make up a confidential preference list. After the rotation is completed, the principal asks for each teacher and intern to indicate, by a priority listing, whom they could work with most comfortably. At this point if an intern or teacher decides that they do not want to participate in the program, they indicate so on the form. For the teacher the matter is then dropped, the intern will need to make arrangements with another school. For those who do indicate preferences, the principal in private can make matches that correspond closely to individual choices. When there is no correspondence, the principal needs to meet with those involved individuals and plan jointly some other arrangement.

Step Four. Internship begins. Now that both parties (intern and teachers) have had major input into the selection of working mates, they can begin the internship with a fuller understanding of each other and the shared responsibility for making their decision work.

This four-step approach provides for "ownership" of placement by intern and cooperating teacher. Much of the success of an intern's participation in a classroom or, in fact, any team-teaching arrangement is how well they can relate to the teacher, adult to adult. If they are comfortable with each other, can express their opinions openly, and have mutual respect, then the internship begins with a high probability of success. Both teacher and intern will work towards making that probability a reality.

Education of Interns

We need not go on in great lengths about the education of student teachers or M.A.T.'s. They have received a considerable amount of education prior to the internship. The university also continues with seminars and workshops during the teaching period. However, there are a few special considerations that the leader of the school should take into account. We all know that university instruction does not always correspond with the real world of the school. It becomes the concern of both the leader and the staff to let the intern know the realities of the local situation so that they become an integral part of the school community. The leader needs to orient interns in the philosophy, practices, procedures, and regulations of the institution. He or she also needs to clearly delineate the morals and values of the community and the expectations that the community has for education and educators. Two areas of involvement that can become troublesome for interns are student management and dealing with parents. The principal and staff need to make the intern's role clear as to their responsibilities. For example, upon a chance meeting with a parent, should an intern discuss George's behavior, or should this be left to the regular teachers? In the midst of a student fight, the intern pulls the combatants apart and says, "Stop!" What is he or she to do when an angry youngster yells back, "You can't tell me what to do, you're not my teacher!"

The greatest education that the intern will receive is in the day-to-day involvement as a staff member. The intern should become involved in all of the extraneous functions of being a teacher, from collecting lunch money, to recess duty, to P.T.O. functions. One final suggestion: if the university does provide quality seminars and workshops for interns, it does no harm to ask the university to conduct the session at the school, after working hours. By doing so, your staff and you might be able to attend and receive the free benefit of some normally costly in-service. When interns and cooperating teachers attend together, they often can come out of such workshops and immediately plan how to use the new knowledge in their classrooms.

Discussion

Student teachers and M.A.T.'s can be of immeasurable worth to a school. Not only do you get extra hands in the classroom but you also receive knowledgeable, fairly experienced heads to go along with the appendages. Interns often come with a fresh perspective and the "latest" in methods. They can serve as a resource to responsive teachers. Many interns are anxious to build, through education, a new, more caring world. This is an admirable vision to keep recharged and alive in our schools. Of course, you also have to put up with some strokes of innocence. We remember the young, visionary intern who wanted to pack eighteen of her students into a Volkswagon Van, at a "teachable" moment, and travel forty miles to climb a mountain. After much discussion, we convinced her (we think) that such prerequisites as prior notice, gathering parent permission slips, and adherence to the legal limits on human cargo were essential even if spontaneity had to suffer. Since then, she and most other interns that we have worked with have gone on to become fine classroom teachers. Admittedly, there might be a few poor interns in a university program, but if you use the suggested placement steps (or some other screening device), your changes of getting them are minimized.

PEER TUTORS

Existing within one's own school is a source of help for the classroom teacher in the form of older, more advanced students. Peer tutoring has become a growing phenomenon.[1] Many schools have initiated their own programs and considerable federal and state monies have been made available. The advantage of using students to help students is that first, they are always available, and second, the helping relationship is educationally sound for both tutors and tutees. In fact, empirical studies have shown greater academic gains by the tutor than the students being tutored. This phenomenon supports the assumption that if an individual is to teach a subject then he or she is motivated to learn something about it. This concept is applied by having an older student, let's say a sixth grader, who is a poor reader, tutor a first grader in beginning reading skills. The responsibility of helping a younger child might motivate the older student to learn some of the basic skills which he or she may be having difficulty with. Therefore, both parties benefit.

Peer tutoring can be used across different age groups of students. A teacher can (and many do) have the more able students play educational games, check work, and go over reinforcement activities with less able students within the same classroom. On a larger scale, students in upper grade levels can be scheduled into younger-grade-level classrooms daily. Additionally, a school that has a good working relationship with its senior schools can receive help by establishing a program whereby high-school students (or middle-school) may work with elementary students. Logistics can be a problem but many secondary students attend schools that permit them to drive their own cars. In fact, some innovative high schools have given course credit for such participation and have made peer tutoring a part of a regular course (e.g., home economics, psychology, physical education, industrial arts).

Training of Tutors

To be candid, beginning such a program across schools can become quite bothersome. A designated adult on the high-school level needs to work out schedules, course credit, and keep track of attendance. At the elementary end, another adult needs to prepare for and instruct the high-school students in the use of materials. Peer tutoring kept within a single school can be done on a less formal basis with the classroom teacher taking a few minutes to go over the daily assignments for the tutors.

Some teachers have been heard to remark that the time spent training the tutors is not worth the help rendered. Research generally disputes this. However, if a staff feels negatively about peer tutoring, then school-wide programs should not be initiated. Perhaps a few interested primary teachers could meet with a few interested intermediate teachers and work out an informal program. If it works, others will eventually wish to try it.

If you and your school have such a program in existence, then you can perhaps affirm what we are about to say. Peer tutoring is of great help to the older underachieving tutor but should not be done at the expense of younger students. It is not a good idea to use tutors who are poor behavior models for younger children. Older students, at times, like to impress children with their knowledge of matters outside of schooling. When screening tutors, care should be taken so that young children can have older students whom they can learn from both academically and socially.

COMMUNITY PERSONNEL

An untapped resource for a school exists among local agencies and organizations in the community. Agencies have contact with persons who have the time and are interested in working for the school. Some agencies such as Community Action (out of the Office of Economic Opportunity) have programs in which persons unemployed may be retained as paraprofessionals and are paid by federal funds to work in schools. Most, if not all, expenses are incurred by the federal government. Most educators are aware of such poverty programs as Vista and Teacher Corps that provide trained personnel to schools located in low income areas. Groups and associations which provide help on a volunteer basis are the Big Brother Associations, Service Clubs, Volunteer Inc., and Senior Citizens. There are many retired, competent, and caring people in every community in this country who have been "put out to pasture." A school could do itself a service plus fill a void in an elderly person's life by seeking them out and asking for that person's services.

Ms. Lillian Glickman, past Director of the Massachusetts Volunteer Commission has provided us with the following information.

> There are three major national advocacy groups for elders whose local chapters, if contacted, might be willing to provide volunteer services for schools. They are: The American Association of Retired Persons/National Retired Teachers Association (AARP), the National Council of Senior Citizens (NCSC), and the Gray Panthers. Beyond that, each state has a State Unit of Aging with regional area associations on aging and local councils on aging. These units can usually be a good source for information and referral in obtaining elders' voluntary help for schools. Perhaps the most direct route, however, is using federal volunteer programs for elders, headquartered in ACTION. Specifically, the Retired Senior Volunteer Program (RSVP) recruits and places elders in nonprofit organizations such as schools, libraries, and day care centers, and assists them with transportation to and from their place of assignment.

Also, the Foster Grandparents Program (FGP) provides an opportunity for low-income elders to serve children with special needs on a one-to-one basis. Foster Grandparents serve in residential institutions such as institutions for the mentally handicapped and homes for the physically handicapped and also in such nonresidential institutions as schools and day care centers. Foster Grandparents serve four hours a day, five days a week, and receive a modest stipend for their service.[2]

Since most community helpers possess similar degrees of unawareness of changes in schooling as parents, it would be wise to use the same criteria as mentioned with Parent Volunteers. In fact, it might be convenient for a school which is ambitious enough to run a parent volunteer and community helper program as a single program. There should be little difference in recruiting procedures and training.

SUMMARY AND CONCLUSION

In this chapter, we have identified some of the various groups that might be of extra help to school personnel. Procedures, recruitment, training, and the particular strengths and weaknesses of parent volunteers, university students (enrolled in regular classes and student teaching/interning), peer tutors, and community helpers have been discussed.

The degree of effectiveness of a school is strengthened by the consistency with which all persons within the school interact with children and each other. Those auxiliary persons who are at cross-purposes with the school staff do not help students to attain desired goals and objectives.

We have placed great emphasis on planning. Planning is essential to insure that auxiliary personnel have an understanding of school philosophy, practices, and procedures. It is with this understanding that they can make a free choice and commitment of function as cooperative and constructive participants. The changing school needs all the help it can muster. Nonprofessional aid may help the changing school reach its goals and supply the human resources needed to alter existing practices.

NOTES

1. Alan Gartner, et al., *Children Teach Children* (New York: Harper & Row, 1971).

2. Correspondence from Lillian Glickman, October, 1977. The information on federal programs comes from: ACTION, *Domestic Programs Fact Book* (Washington, D.C.: U.S. Government Printing Office, 1975).

SUGGESTIONS FOR FURTHER READING

Berclay, G. John, ed. *Parent Involvement in The Schools*. Washington, D.C.: National Education Association, 1977.

Brown, William Frank. *Student-to-Student Counseling: An Approach to Motivating Academic Achievement*. (Published for the Hogg Foundation for Mental Health) Austin, Texas: University of Texas Press, 1977.

Carter, Barbara, and Dapper, Gloria. *Organizing School Volunteer Programs*. New York: Citation Press, 1974.

DaSilva, Benjamin, and Lucas, Richard D. *Practical School Volunteer and Teacher-Aide Programs*. West Nyack, N.Y.: Parker, 1974.

Gartner, Alan; Kohler, Mary; and Reissman, Frank. *Children Teach Children*. New York: Harper & Row, 1971.

Hunter, Elizabeth, and Amidon, Edmund. *Student Teaching: Case and Comments*. New York: Holt, Rinehart and Winston, 1964.

Section Ten

Important External Considerations about the Changing School

21

Power Groups

The most well-planned change can go down the drain as a result of opposition from outside power groups. Students, professional and nonprofessional staff, and administration can be quite satisfied with the internal workings of their school only to see it all collapse due to external pressures. In our own experiences, we have seen such nonschool-affiliated persons occupying positions of power—city mayors, fire marshalls, and ministers—significantly affect an entire school system. Of course, the more common pressure groups of school board members, formal parent-teacher organizations, and informal parent groups have always been in our midst. It is safe to say that more people are getting "their fingers into the pie" than ever before. At times, it seems as though everyone is an expert on what is wrong with the local school.

We remember once driving around trying to find an elementary school in an urban area where we were to conduct a workshop. We pulled into a gas station and asked for directions. We were amazed when the service station attendant told us that "the school was clear on the other side of town" and that we need not bother with directions because "no one in their right mind would visit that place. The principal is a real weirdo. It is a zoo over there with children running wild and no discipline." We asked if he had ever visited the school. He said, "Nope, have not been in a school in thirty years; but the brother of one of my customers has a child who went there two years ago, and she heard the principal talk. . . ." We cut him short and told him that we would rather find out about the place for ourselves and if he could please give us the directions. Upon arriving at the school, we found it not at all like the attendant's description.

This story illustrates the phenomenon of working with the public. Lay people tend to believe what they hear, whether it is rooted in reality or not. One of our jobs as educators is to inform the public of what we are doing in ways that they can understand. Since most people do not get into our schools to see for themselves what is happening, they will form impressions of our school based on what they think of us. Therefore, we must be most sensitive to the image we project. It is with these concerns in mind, that three common guidelines are suggested.

Guideline 1

Let yourself and the staff be known personally as well as professionally. It is much more difficult to criticize a person with whom you are acquainted than with one whom you do not know. It is a mistake for a school leader and staff to be perceived as solely "educators" and not also as "just plain folk." Historically, there was a time when teachers and principals were put upon pedestals reserved for superior beings. The view held by the community was that educators led "proper" private lives. Educators did not smoke, were believed to be above drinking and dancing. Rather, their "leisure" was devoted to scholarly reading and contemplation. Today, it is our guess that if we interviewed the common man or women on the street, few would seriously hold those perceptions. Yet, many of us feel the need to continue to act a role that no longer has any credibility. Why must we remain distant and serious with the community? Both know better, yet the game continues.

"Not so!" some might say. We counter with this question. How many times has any incident like the following occurred? You are out dining with friends. After a few drinks, you feel relaxed, congenial, and somewhat boisterous. In the midst of this good time, you suddenly recognize a school parent or board member sitting across from you. After acknowledging each other's presence, your pleasant but rowdy behavior dissipates. You now feel on guard and defensive. In the same manner, why do we often feel the need to buy beer or liquor in a locality outside of our school district? For some reason, we do not want people to know that we are human, capable of being as serious or as silly as anyone else.

It is when we keep this distance and continue to live the "pedestal" myth that we invite others to shoot us down. Why not tell humorous stories about our personal inadequacies or let others know when we have really made some horrendous blunders? Why not share some of our misfortunes with others? By sharing with others, we convey feelings of mutual trust. If we divest some of our personal feelings to nonprofessional people, then the greater the likelihood that they will share with us, sealing a bond of admiration and friendship. With this bond, when there is criticism of what we do professionally, our friends will come to us first on a personal level to discuss the issue. This is obviously much better than an adversary relationship.

Guideline 2

Keep the appearances of the staff and the administration representative of community standards. At first glance this reads contrary to the first guideline. However, it would be foolish to accentuate the differences rather than the commonality between you and the public. Relaxing and being oneself is important. However, this can be taken to the extreme. We are not advocating shocking the community with behaviors or appearances that may be consistent with your lifestyle yet deviate from theirs. People will be comfortable with you when you are considerate of them and willing to admit to your humanness. A common link has then been established. Further comfort is provided if you also have a lifestyle and appearance similar to theirs. Too much deviance breeds contempt. To give a few extreme samples, it is not good political sense to been seen as someone who over imbibes alcohol in a predominately fundamentalist town. Likewise, it is not good to have the appearance of victorian frugality in a free-wheeling, liberal community.

Dress is an important indicator of congruence with the community. If one wears beads and blue jeans among conservatively dressed persons, then a message of separateness and detachment is perceived.

The type of clothing that one wears often waves a red flag in the eyes of others. Political connotations are readily attached to clothes; from blue jeans and "granny" dresses conveying radicalism, to slacks and open shirts conveying casual liberalness, to below-the-knee dresses and jackets and ties conveying conservatism. Although these stereotypes may be disappearing, one must remain sensitive to them. Many schools have been attacked by the public for inadequate or radical instructional programs, when in reality the attacks were aimed at the dress and the lifestyles of the educators who wore the clothes. (Some of the so-called textbook controversies are good examples.) Any appearances which convey a lifestyle incongruent with the majority in a community are perceived as threats to local morals and values. If you and your staff are truly committed to improve education, why fight a battle over length of hair and type of dress? You might win the legal and less significant battle of dressing as you please and lose the confidence of the public and thus the more significant war for instructional change.

Guideline 3

When addressing the public, frame the content of your talk around the community's educational expectations. Describe how the school is meeting their concerns before discussing innovation. Most persons, as Gallup Poll surveys have indicated, judge a school according to the criterion of firm discipline, stress on basic values, and the teaching of the three Rs. If you are an Alternative One school, compliance with such public expectations correspond nicely. However, if your school is representative of one of the two other models, you will need to make the case for how your school is meeting the public's expectations. For example, when speaking about your school, let's say it's an Alternative Three school, do not begin by emphasizing how the program encourages diversity and exploration. Rather, focus on what the school does to promote discipline, an understanding of values, and the learning of basic skills. Of course, the school's treatment of these concerns are weighted towards self-discipline and critical, individual decision making. However, this does not alter the fact that you and your staff are addressing the concerns of the public. In other words, you are a public school, responding to public expectations.

PRESSURE GROUPS

There is little chance that we can give you a fail-proof system for working with all people. There are simply too many diverse political, economic, cultural, and idiosyncratic points of view to find broad consensus. Anyone who would tell you that they have *the answer* to building unilateral support for your school is, in our opinion, selling a false bill of goods. Rather, we will attempt to look at some prominent power groups and suggest some useful approaches in working with them. We are not selling any absolutes nor do we think that the educational leader need "sell" their school. Instead we believe that effective support comes about through honest communication, combined with a sense of timing and tact. When communicating with others we need to know who they are, what they are about, and what ways we can help them to understand and empathize with us.

City or Town Officials

When we are referring to city or town officials, we are speaking about elected or appointed persons who serve in a capacity of legislating and/or executing community policy. This definition would include city council members, town selectmen, county supervisors, mayors, city managers, and county executives. These persons serve in a capacity one step above the school board. The school system is only one of several institutions that they influence.

In many cases, city or town officials have only one concern with schools. That concern is money. Many times they have campaigned on a platform of government efficiency and holding down taxes. The specific line items of a budget or the various ways in which appropriated money is to be spent is within a school board's jurisdiction. However, the total dollar figure to be allocated is legally and rightfully the responsibility of city or town officials. They must approve how much money will go to the schools, how much to highway maintenance, to police, to firefighters, etc.

Realistically, an individual school will not have a great impact on a council's annual decision concerning budget allocation for the school district. However, "every drop counts" and it makes sense to be on good terms with the political power of the community. Also, to help keep the political ax wielders away from your doors, it might help to keep some of the following advice in mind. (There appears to be a disturbing trend of public officials meddling in the inner workings of a school system. Much publicity is gained by attacking a school board and thus detracts attention from the official's own government operation.)

1. *If some candidates are running on an anti-school-spending platform invite all candidates to meet with you to discuss their concerns prior to the election.* This would probably need to be done with your superintendent's approval and perhaps presence. It is important to convey an atmosphere of willingness to listen to the candidates and to be open to working with whomever may be elected. By doing this prior to the election, you will have helped to establish a working relationship and defrayed some of the "attack" mentality of the candidates.

2. *Do not take a partisan position in political elections.* For example, supporting the Republican candidates only to have the Democrats win will leave you with some years of embarrassment to wait out. You will begin the new political era identified as the opposition. This will be a hard identity to diffuse and will be influential when decisions affecting your school come about.

3. *If you feel compelled to take a partisan position in political elections make sure you are on the winning side.* No explanation is necessary. If you have such a knack you might think of going into politics for yourself.

4. *When an official is elected, attend the inauguration or at least send a personal letter of congratulations.* If you have stayed out of the election, you will be off to a good start by letting the official know how pleased you are at the prospect of having him or her in office. Tell (or write) of your willingness to help the person during his or her incumbency.

If the educational leader can establish a nonpartisan relationship with the candidates, if he or she is willing to listen to their concerns, if the leader empathizes and gives support to their positions, then, after the elections, he or she will be on solid footing. These four steps are easy to follow, little of your own time is involved, and further contact with public officials after the election will be minimal.

School Board Members

It is a truism that board members seek election to make improvements in the schools. They usually run because of a perceived school problem that they think can be changed. Keeping the budget down is again the most prominent issue of today but they also feel a responsibility for the instructional program. They are concerned with student achievement, absenteeism, truancy, extracurricular activities, teacher competencies, etc. Their concern is with the visible outcomes of schooling. Members usually possess little knowledge of the internal processes of education. Most could not converse about different curriculum models in depth or on the advantages and disadvantages of specific programs. What they wish to know is the answer to this question—What are the taxpayers receiving for their money?

A wise superintendent will clearly delineate a board's responsibility in setting overall school district policy apart from the professional administration of individual schools.

1. *Follow the four steps for city or town officials when school board elections are taking place.* Do not take a partisan position, invite all candidates to talk with you and congratulate the winners. Unlike the degree of diminishing contact with elected city or town officials, the reverse holds true with school board candidates. After the election you might see them more often than your spouse. It is important to continue to cultivate their friendship.

2. *Have a get-acquainted meeting of all newly elected board members at your school.* Some superintendents plan a series of introductory meetings for each school. If this is not the case, you might take the initiative in having the superintendent and the new board convene one of their first meetings at your school. Ask for half an hour of their time to take all members on a tour of the facility and to present briefly a list of school strengths and weaknesses. Before discussing program strengths and weaknesses, members can feel more confident of their capacity to help the schools by first listening to physical building needs. (We all have had common experiences with leaking toilets and faulty boilers.) The new board will acquire a sense of being part of a larger team, where they are now expected to be knowledgeable of your school, and to use that knowledge when setting overall priorities.

3. *Keep board members informed of all happenings at the school.* A board member takes the position seriously. When asked questions by people in the community, he or she wishes to appear

informed. It is upsetting for a member to be confronted with a complaint by a community member when he or she has no knowledge of it. If anything happens in your school that has the slightest chance of being controversial or misunderstood, make a point of informing your superintendent and school board members immediately. It is better that they hear your side of the story before they hear it second hand. There are many ways to keep members informed. A quick but not so reliable way is to send out a periodic newsletter. These papers are often misplaced and not read. More reliable ways are to talk directly to members, either through periodic presentations scheduled into the board meeting agenda or informally before or after meetings.

4. *Attend all board meetings and make it a point to talk with each member.* Visibility and access are essential components of communication. Corner each member singly or in groups for a few moments and tell them what has been going on at your school. Ask them if they have any questions that you can answer. Even if such informal exchanges result in conversation no more profound than "Hello, how are you doing?" visibility will still have been realized. Try to milk these informal talks for all they're worth. You might receive some information about the "local scuttlebutt" circulating downtown that you were previously oblivious to. Many misunderstandings can be cleaned up in this informal manner.

5. *Invite members to all formal school functions.* Nothing strokes the ego of a person more than being introduced as a V.I.P. at official functions. Encourage board members to attend parent-teacher meetings, open houses, holiday celebrations, etc. Make a point to introduce them to the audience.

6. *When giving a formal presentation to the board, be concise, be businesslike, and "shoot the works."* School board members will form an initial impression of how you operate your school based on how you present yourself at meetings. A bumbling, rambling, disorganized presentation at a board meeting can create negative attitudes towards your administrative ability and the effectiveness of your school. On the other hand, you can create favorable attitudes by being organized. Stick to your time allotment. Give outlined handouts that contain your key points. Board members can then focus their attention fully on you. Provide background information to the board with sufficient lead time for reading. Use slides, transparencies, and illustrations to add detail and variety to your talk. In other words, impress them! (Junior military officers found this out a long time ago.)

7. *Credibility is enhanced by leveling with board members about the weaknesses of your school as well as the strengths.* One finds it difficult to believe a salesperson who is always talking about his or her new, advanced, superior product. Any leader who admits no

weaknesses will shortly wear thin any chance of credibility with board members. Board members can soon become suspicious of a "cover-up" if they never hear of anything short of perfection going on in your school. Be diplomatic, but be honest!

Parent Teacher Organizations

Few school people are thrilled when they must attend a P.T.O. meeting. At best, the meeting is alright, at worst it is unbearable. Overgeneralized? Of course, but we have attended too many of these meetings and heard too many teacher and administrator comments about them not to feel justified to make such generalizations. Why is it that the best of the meetings are those when the P.T.O. hands over a check to the school and adjournment is early? Why is it that the highlight of any particular session proves to be the homemade chocolate chip cookies?

The reason is simply because most P.T.O.'s, other than raising money and serving refreshments, have no purpose for their existence. If you, your staff, and parents are obliged to follow the ritual of sitting through five to six such meetings a year, why not make them worthwhile?

The critical element in a successful organization is involvement. The P.T.O. should have functions that are meaningful to the members as well as helpful to the school. Meetings should be balanced and consist of entertainment, information, and advisory input. The preliminary meeting to begin a year should be addressed to answering questions. Why have a P.T.O.? What kind of programs will be entertaining? What kinds of programs will be informative? What kinds of programs would give feedback to the school? A strong P.T.O. can be a tremendous support system for a school. Parents and teachers can continue to raise the expected funds but additionally they can bring in speakers to address controversial topics, organize volunteer programs, coordinate parent-training seminars, and serve as an open forum for parents, teachers, and administrators to discuss common concerns.

An ongoing, worthwhile P.T.O. is an invitation to parents to become a part of the school. It suggests to them that the school staff cares about them. A weak P.T.O. with sporadic meetings and poor attendance suggests the opposite. Parents learn that the school continues this ritualistic sham of a titled organization without purpose. The hidden message is that the staff does not really care about what parents can offer or what parental needs can be met.

Elements of a Strong P.T.O.

1. *Joint planning by parents, teachers, and administration.* At the beginning of the year, representatives from each group should

meet and discuss their thoughts for P.T.O. priorities. A consensus of priorities should be drawn up and programs developed accordingly.

2. *Ongoing monthly meetings.* One night each month should be set aside for the regular P.T.O. session.

3. *High teacher and principal attendance.* Teachers and administrators should attend these meetings. We would suggest that a teacher attend a minimum of three out of every four meetings so that at least seventy-five percent of staff are represented at all times. Parent attendance should also be high. We know that in some communities this is a problem. To get good initial parent attendance, it is best to have either children on the program (choir, concert, plays, etc.) or have teachers conduct classroom visits after the meeting. Parents have a greater tendency to be present if their own child is on the program or they will have the opportunity to hear about his or her classroom.

4. *Balanced meetings.* Each meeting should have a short business session followed by a main topic and then finally refreshments. The main topics should vary from entertainment (children's performance) to information (speakers on general topics such as drug abuse, effects of television viewing, the local school tax situation, and helping your child to learn) to advisory workshops (What does our school need to do better? Should the school teach sex education? What should realistic discipline procedures be?).

5. *The P.T.O. as a sponsor of other programs.* The P.T.O. should be involved in such efforts as coordinating parent-volunteer programs, determining possible courses for adults (in basic education, arts and crafts, effective parenting skills), fund raising and local support for the school, and other issues of parental concern.

6. *Both parent representation.* Most P.T.O.'s have traditionally catered to mothers. Such terms as "classroom or homeroom mothers" and "volunteer mothers" are indicative labels of discrimination. There is no reason why fathers need to be left out of the elementary school and its organizations. P.T.O. officials should be sensitive to this discrimination and encourage fathers to attend by tailoring meetings with topics and activities that have broad appeal.

7. *The function of the P.T.O. as advisory to the school should be made clear.* There is a point where welcomed advice can turn into troublesome demands. The school principal has to make clear, at the beginning of the year, the extent of influence that the P.T.O. will be given on school matters. This should be duly written in P.T.O. records. This understanding will help give the P.T.O. boundaries for deciding what their role will be. For example, perhaps they will be asked to determine policy on noninstructional issues (e.g., new playground equipment) but not on instructional issues (e.g., new

reading program). The boundaries will vary from school to school. An Alternative One school might keep the P.T.O. as advisory. An Alternative Two school might give the P.T.O. responsibilities for some decisions. An Alternative Three school might welcome full participation in all school issues. Regardless of the extent of influence given to the P.T.O., it must be clearly understood by all parties.

It is rather easy to list the elements of a strong P.T.O. It is another story to expect a dormant, apathetic organization to suddenly spring to life. To achieve all seven mentioned elements in one year is unlikely. One or two goals should be mutually sought. Perhaps the way to start is to get parents and teachers to attend meetings. If this is not already happening, then the initial thrust might be to schedule entertaining meetings with student performances. The following year, you might begin to expand the types of meetings, through joint planning. A third-year goal may be the P.T.O. sponsoring of parent courses, volunteer programs, and so on.

Enforcement Agencies: Fire Marshalls, Health Officials, and Police Chiefs

A special bias of ours is shown by including this heading in a chapter about power groups. One of us was once the principal of a school situated directly across from the city's fire station. As a result, we had an uneasy "glass house" experience of being in constant view of each other. If the fire trucks did not respond immediately to a call, we knew it. With one fire chief, the relationship was good; with another, it was not so good.

One day, one of the chiefs sprung a surprise tour of our building without checking in with the school office. He simply walked through the school, up the stairs, through the halls, and then exited. The principal was at home, sick with the flu. No fire inspection report was sent to the school. The principal learned of the inspection when awakened at home by a reporter calling for a comment on that afternoon's newspaper headlines. After informing the reporter of being unaware of the situation, the headlines were read to him over the phone. They read as follows: "Elementary School Declared a Fire Hazard."

For over a week, the school was in a turmoil. Calls were constantly coming in from parents concerned for the safety of their children. It was not until ten days had passed that the school received an official report from the fire department. Why would a fire chief release the report to a newspaper, make sensational headlines, and then wait ten days before notifying the school? Most of the cited deficiencies in the official report were minor and easily remedied. If the report had been simply sent to the school after the inspection, the corrections could have been made immediately. We suspect that the reason for the fire chief following such an unusual procedure had something to do with the upcoming election. Many persons had been criticizing the relative ineffectiveness of the incumbent chief. All at once, the chief was on the front page appearing as a bulldog guardian of the city's children.

The point might be made that the school was used for political purposes. There can be no argument that the inspection of schools is necessary. Health, safety, and fire reports are critical to the welfare of our children. What we are suggesting is that other factors are sometimes also at work. It is to a school's advantage to have these agencies working with you rather than against you.

Without dwelling on these matters we wish to mention some safeguards to avoid conflict.

1. Do your own periodic inspection of health, safety, and fire hazards. File an annual report to the superintendent and board. Keep copies for your own file.

2. Practice regular fire and emergency drills. Most states have minimum requirements. Surpass the minimum. Keep a report on each drill. Enter date, time, and observation in a log.

3. Send home a report to parents. Notify parents of what the school is doing to insure safety (include physical improvements, drills, and procedures). An annual report, in the fall, should be sufficient.

4. Invite health, safety, and fire officials to meet with your students. Either designate a particular grade (health–3rd grade, safety–4th grade, fire–5th grade), or have the entire student body listen to various speakers. Some agencies put together very entertaining and informative presentations.

5. If you do have a serious hazard, do something about it. Often, you do not need an official report on your school from an outside agency to be aware of a deficiency. You are ultimately responsible for your students, so take the initiative. If you need to, raise hell with the superintendent and school board. Do not let your students and staff work in a hazardous situation. Parents will support you and exert pressure for you in a cause that will alleviate imminent danger to their children.

CONCLUSION

Various power groups existing outside of the school organization can play a role in aiding or thwarting school change. A school leader cannot be content with a smooth relationship between students and staff. He or she must also focus on establishing working relationships with public officials, school board members, enforcement agencies, and Parent-Teacher Organizations. Some guidelines and considerations for working with particular groups have been suggested.

22

Meeting with Parents

A PRINCIPAL-INITIATED MEETING

Mrs. Freed has had a hellish week. Her child's principal called her on Monday to arrange a meeting with her and her husband. The principal assured her with these words, "Sam is in no trouble. He is a bright boy and a delight to be with. He is experiencing some learning difficulty that we thought best to discuss with you before setting up any special program. Will ten o'clock this Friday be all right?" Mrs. Freed acquiesced and the phone conversation ended.

Immediately Mrs. Freed thought to herself that something was wrong with Sam. Thoughts flittered through her head, "He must be a real problem. Perhaps he's emotionally disturbed. He was born ten days premature, maybe he's brain-damaged. Oh my God, what is wrong with my child?" After an hour of such thinking, she called her husband and told him of the principal's call. She filled in the details with her own interpretation. "Mr. Garvey, the principal, called to say that Sam is having real problems in school. He says that he's a good boy but he can't learn. Mr. Garvey wants to meet with us Friday." Mr. Freed listened to his wife's conversation but heard only that Sam "can't learn." He explodes with anger. "What does the principal mean that Sam can't learn. There's nothing wrong with our kid. He's smarter than all those ding-a-ling teachers at that school. If they could teach, he could learn! Wait until I see that principal, I'll tell him a thing or two."

So, as we can see, a rather innocuous phone call by the principal has set emotional wheels rolling. Mr. Garvey's explanation to Mrs. Freed was plain enough but she did not hear it. Mrs. Freed's explanation to her husband was clear enough but he did not hear it.

Why the lack of communication? First of all Mr. Garvey was talking about Mrs. Freed's child, the embodiment of herself, her flesh and blood. Secondly, Mrs. Freed was talking about Mr. Freed's child, his hopes and aspirations, his flesh and blood. The same child named Sam is quite different to each of his parents. When one speaks to another of their child, objectivity is lost. The parent is hearing a message about his or her subjective self.

Let's see how this emotionalism further clouds the communication process. At ten o'clock Friday morning, Mr. and Mrs. Freed check with the school secretary. She asks them to be seated in the principal's office while she goes to locate him in the building. While she is gone, an eerie metamorphosis takes place. Two adults waiting for the principal gradually lose the composure and outlook of maturity and regress back to their own youth as children sent to the principal's office.

Mr. Freed, who was known as cocky and belligerent child as an eleven-year-old, takes on that old defiant, unflinching look. Mrs. Freed who was a sensitive, well-mannered young girl draws back to the "good girl done wrong syndrome." She keeps her eyes down, fingers fidget, and she swallows hard.

Mr. Garvey finally walks in, extends a greeting and shakes hands. He is under the illusion that he is about to talk to two adults about a not too serious matter of helping their quite capable youngster. Instead, he is actually facing two eleven-year-old kids, one belligerent to the authority that he represents, the other one timid, and both feeling insecure about their own inadequacies.

It is no wonder that strange happenings occur when the principal meets with parents at school. Perhaps the portrait we have painted is extreme but when you mix together a school environment with all types of personal connotations (a traditional authority figure and discussion of a person's alter ego—his or her child) you have all the ingredients for unexpected occurrences.

Relieving Emotion and Clearing Expectations when Meeting with Parents

Keeping the above incident in mind, how can the school leader help to relieve parent anxiety and open up the channels for understanding? The principal needs to be cognizant of the fact that coming to his office is regarded by many parents as an uneasy chore. Really, no matter how clearly he has tried to explain the purpose of the meeting, on the phone without the face to face visual feedback, it is unlikely that the parent will have a full understanding. Coming to the principal's office as a child has always connoted serious problems, and now as a parent it is hard to think otherwise. Therefore, the principal must first attempt to lower the defensiveness and discomfort. He can do this in several ways. Beginning the meeting with idle, familiar chatter helps to break the ice. Even the best of friends, after an absence, greet each other with conventional topics such as their health, the weather, sports, and local goings on. The educational leader can establish a common, nonthreatening framework for later, more purposeful discussion by spending a few minutes in such talk.

Offering and sharing a cup of coffee or tea during the initial moments, also makes the atmosphere more homelike. (It is the authors' prerogative to point out that there is overt discrimination against tea drinkers in many of our public institutions; we refer to this as "coffee chauvinism" or "coffeeism." As tea drinkers ourselves, we wish to help raise the consciousness level of all school administrators to have *both* drinks available.) A final point about relaxing the atmosphere is to seat everyone comfortably. With various parents this might mean sitting around a coffee table in the office, or even moving to a lounge area. For most parents, it will be difficult to move out of the mentality of being a metamorphosized school child if the principal remains seated behind a large oak desk, while they squirm in high, hard-backed chairs. The physical situation will be too similar to the actual remembrances that they have of being set to the principal's office.

After the physical placement of parents has been arranged, drinks have been served, and off-target chatter has been concluded, it is time to address the purpose of the meeting. Before the leader puts forth a clarification, it is important to know first what needs to be clarified. This is done by asking the parent to describe his or her understanding of the meeting. The parent's response will give an indication of the degree of misinterpretation, and a corresponding index of emotional flooding which has colored the misinterpretation. One should look for the signs of hostility, defiance, and helplessness. Then, and only then, is the leader in a position to clarify the true purpose of the meeting and subsequently diffuse the emotions. In our incident with the Freeds, it behooves Mr. Garvey to ask Mr. and Mrs. Freed these two questions: (1) Did you understand why I asked to meet with you? and (2) Would you explain what you think is the purpose of this meeting? Now with the Freed's responses, Mr. Garvey can make a quick assessment of their understanding and emotional involvement. His reply would be to clarify and expand on their thinking. At least now all parties will have knowledge of what the real agenda is and the meeting can proceed.

The Meeting

We might discuss further the common-sense, human-relations strategy of discussing with parents the child's positive characteristics before zapping them with any negative concerns. This strategy has been discussed enough in other books and courses to be familiar to all and need only be mentioned here. After building on the strengths of the child, the principal needs to level with the parent about the real concerns. Sometimes this is difficult to do. We remember once meeting with an overanxious parent who had an adopted child who was having a problem in school. The parent was so worried that his child was not developing normally that he kept pressing the discussion with "But is my child normal?" Finally, in sympathy with the parent's troubled state of mind, we skipped any reference to our real concerns and instead made the session one of therapeutic assurance. The parent was told that he was indeed doing a good parenting job and the child was doing fine. In reflection, what we did was a disservice to the child and the parent. Instead of meeting the issue head on, we let it slide and left the parent with an unrealistic picture. There is little way that a parent can understand the school's concern with his or her child unless we tell them what is happening in school. Only then can we seek agreement to carry out a school and home program.

What we are saying is that during the heart of the meeting, we have to stand apart from feeding the parent's emotions and as Howard Cosell says, "Tell it like it is." In Mr. and Mrs. Freed's case, it is time to get on with Sam's disability. The disability needs to be described, evidence presented, and implications discussed for developing a special program.

The way that we have found to keep ourselves on track is to list the major points to be discussed, prior to the meeting. The list is then kept before us during the meeting and we can check off each point as it is made. This list serves as our guide and conscience. Looking at it, when the meeting has been concluded, makes it painfully clear to us whether or not we accomplished what we set out to do. We either went through the items or did not. This is much better than going into the meeting with a general idea of what we wish parents to hear and then not knowing if we really said what we needed to.

Let's return to Mr. and Mrs. Freed sitting with Mr. Garvey. Ready to plunge into the heart of the meeting, is Mr. Garvey better off with the general knowledge of Sam's problem in his head or the specific concerns written down in front of him? What follows is a list that he might use:

Items to Discuss with Sam Freed's Parents

- Sam's progress in reading and mathematics (show cumulative folder).
- Point out his decline in comprehension and corresponding difficulty as reported by the teacher in playing games with other children.

- The preliminary diagnosis is that Sam needs a special visual-and-motor program on a basic, primary level to help him screen visual stimulation and concentrate on tasks.
- Ask for his parent's agreement to have him further tested by a psychologist, and if tests concur, then initiate a school and home program

This list does not change appearance or waiver; a person might change. Therefore, while concluding the session, the principal can ask the parents to summarize the meeting and go down his list at the same time to see if there is concurrence. If there are gaps, then they need to be filled. Incidentally, this simple listing of key items to discuss is a valuable tool for teachers too, especially in parent-teacher student progress conferences.

A PARENT-INITIATED MEETING

Naturally the school leader cannot be as prepared for a parent-initiated meeting as for one that he or she initiates. Rarely does a parent seek to talk to the principal about a pleasant experience or about the wonderful job that everyone is doing for his or her child. Instead, if you receive a call or a parent simply walks into your office, you can expect that it is about some type of difficulty. How you approach such a meeting is quite different from the one that you initiate. You are now the receiver of the message. As such, you must first be sure that you receive and understand the full message.

When listening to a parent's complaint, do not jump in with an immediate answer, solution, or rebuttal. Be cool and be quiet! Allow the parent to go on (even if ranting and raving is involved) until the discourse is finished. Then ask questions about the situation. Only after you have listened and questioned, are you ready to reply.

Replying to an Irate Parent

To give a parent an answer when you really do not have one is leaving yourself vulnerable for further conflict. The reader might remember the case we described when one of us received a call from a parent complaining about her child being slapped by a teacher. Giving a denial of such an occurrence without proof was asking for trouble. Only if one knows the situation fully should one answer. It is the nature of the leadership position that one simply does not know all that is going on in the school. To try to keep up with every incident and be knowledgeable of all the dynamics between each individual child and teacher is impossible. Better to hear out the parent, admit one's lack of knowledge, and then get back to the parent once such knowledge is acquired.

Whether on the phone or in your office, set up a specific time (and date) to get back to the parent. In some situations, you might simply step out of your office, gather the information and return in a few minutes with a reply. On other occasions you may need a lengthy talk with a teacher, child, or other staff member before returning an answer. In such cases you might tell the parent on a Monday that you will get back to him or her (either by phone or meeting) at an agreed time on Wednesday. A waiting time, no matter how brief, also helps to cool a hot parent down. We remember how, on numerous occasions at the beginning of the school year, we would receive parent complaints about the classroom and/or teacher their child had been assigned to. We would listen to the parents reasoning and then explain that we needed to first talk to the teacher(s) and child before making any decision. We would have an answer for them in a day or two. Meanwhile, the child should continue to attend his or her assigned class. After talking with teacher and child, when we called back the parent with a decision, the parent would invariably say that he or she wished the child to remain where he was. The sole element of time away from the immediate situation helped in settling the conflict.

Although rather obvious, it needs to be said that a commitment to reply to a parent should always be honored. This is not a superficial technique for getting an irritating parent off one's back and leaving the situation hanging. Rather, it is a sincere attempt to gather the most information to make the most sound decision. A parent should know when the reply or decision is going to be made. If a parent is not satisfied with whatever conclusion is reached, then he or she should be advised of his or her right to pursue the issue through the proper channels.

CONCLUDING THOUGHTS

Before we leave this chapter on parent relations, we wish to mention a few more thoughts. Often a troublesome matter is brought by a parent to the principal when it really belongs with the teacher. If so, put the matter where it belongs. The principal then has the option of either being a participant with teacher and parent or he or she may wish instead to be the next contact for the parent if the matter is not resolved satisfactorily. Another factor to be considered is that sometimes a parent brings a complaint that is justified. The principal is morally bound to do what is best for children, not to defend the staff at all costs. Therefore, if a staff member does something improperly, the principal should use the parent's complaint to confront the teacher. Our last consideration (which we have expounded on fully in chapters 16 and 17 on "Schools within Schools") is that parents should, if at all possible, be given alternatives and not backed up against the wall. If a parent has a criticism, it is better not to give an answer such as "You are wrong" or "We are going to do this about the situation," but instead to offer some choices.

It might appear disconcerting to the reader that only one chapter in this book is devoted exclusively to parents. We do not wish the reader to interpret this as implying that the authors regard parents as unimportant. The reverse is true. Parents are critical and integral to the success of a changing school. This is why we have integrated discussions about parents throughout. It is this integrative function that we wish to stress. Parents are involved in many aspects of a changing school.

23

The Hidden Group

Rarely does one find included in books or courses for educational leaders any mention of the impact of noneducators on the school. Certainly secretaries, custodians, cafeteria workers, aides, and bus drivers are not visually hidden. We see them everyday. What is hidden, however, is the job that they can do outside of their prescribed role. A school can receive a favorable or unfavorable image based almost solely on the actions of these persons. They are a direct line to the community. They usually come from among the socioeconomic strata of people who have not in the past involved themselves directly with the school. The school information that many persons rely on is gathered from their friends who might be the custodian, aide, or cafeteria worker.

It must be remembered that these noneducators have not been trained to work with people. Their training has been task oriented. One need not possess great sensitivity to human needs in order to type a letter, empty a wastebasket, serve food, run-off papers, or drive a bus. Yet, when these tasks are done in a school setting among students and staff, then a human-relations dimension is added. For example, emptying a wastebasket during an important mathematics lesson does not particularly endear the custodian to the teacher (although the students might be happy about the disruption!). The secretary who continues typing an important letter while a first grader stands crying with blood on his hand will not be met with ecstasy by the parents of that child. In simple terms, there is an inescapable human dimension which exists within a school environment. Professionals may have been prepared for it, nonprofessionals may have not.

How do noneducators typically behave without proper training? First, some have an intuitive feel which keeps them in harmonious interaction with others. However, many attempt to create distance between themselves and the mainstream of students and teachers. They focus on getting their job done. Often they feel inferior to all the college-educated personnel around them. They sometimes displace this feeling of inferiority by becoming critical and arrogant. They often tell themselves that they can do a better job then the educators. The secretary says to herself, "I can reach those children who Mrs. Plider keeps sending to the office." The custodian says to himself, "If I had that class, I'd teach them to clean up their mess." The cafeteria worker says, "Why can't children stand quietly in line. They would not do that with me if I was their teacher." Finally, the aide might think, after working with remedial groups, "No wonder those children are behind, the teacher spends no time on sounding out the words. If I was her that is all I would do."

The responsibilities of the school leader with respect to non-professionals is multifaceted. The leader needs to make their job responsibilities clear. Secondly, he or she needs to engender mutual respect between them and others. Thirdly, he or she needs to work with them at their level of concern. Ultimately, the leader must insure that the noneducators are not, and do not become, roadblocks to change.

Oh yes, it is indeed a fact; they can be roadblocks to any school which is contemplating change or in the midst of it. The secretary is often the best known person in the community. He or she is the first person that a caller speaks to or a visitor meets. If the secretary has disregard for what is happening in the school, his or her feelings can spread rapidly throughout the town. Even the tone of voice or a roll of eyes can convey certain lasting impressions. The secretary, in our opinion, is the most important noneducator in the school. As such, we wish to pursue the nature of this position more closely in a later section of this chapter. For now, let it suffice to say that if he or she is against you, you can bet on trouble.

The custodian, although not as visible to the public as the secretary, can send reverberations throughout the school. The entire tone or climate of the school can be shattered by the large, booming voice of an irate male janitor in a female-dominated school. Students have been socialized to look up to the adult male. Often the custodian is one of the few male adults in the school. If he shows open anger, both students and teachers may cringe.

The cafeteria worker can set an equally unpleasant (or pleasant) tone during the lunch hour. A hostile attitude towards students and teachers can turn a lunch period into a stomach-churning, tension-ridden hour. A bus driver, like the cafeteria worker, has relatively little contact with the school. Both the bus driver and cafeteria worker see children during noninstructional times. Yet, their perception of the students at these times may influence their ideas of what happens during instructional time. Such preconceptions are easily bantered around the town after work hours.

The school aide has a closer connection with the classroom. He or she is often asked to work with individual students or groups. As a result, the aide has an intimate knowledge of what is transpiring within individual classrooms. Often teachers are reluctant to use aides who they suspect of being "gossip mongers." They are afraid of the "scuttlebutt" about themselves or their classes that might make the rounds.

In talking about the nonprofessionals, we have emphasized the negative impact that they can have upon school-community relationships. Of course, the reverse can be true and such persons can be among a school's strongest assets. We simply wish to make the case that this is a powerful group that must be reckoned with. A leader of a school in the process of change must be aware of the potential impact of such personnel and insure that they are working with and not against school goals.

RESPONSIBILITIES OF THE EDUCATIONAL LEADER

The first responsibility is to make each noneducator's position clear. They should be aware of their job descriptions. What are the specific tasks that they are responsible for? This is rather straightforward, but the more vexing problem is delineating those behaviors expected when dealing with children and teachers. What are their responsibilities in regard to student behavior? Do they criticize and correct students? What is their procedure for registering a complaint about a teacher or a student? Whom do they take directions from, teachers or the principal? These guidelines need to be tightly fit into the overall direction of the school. A school that values a warm and permissive atmosphere certainly does not wish a noneducator verbally bombasting children in the hall. The principal needs to meet with all nonprofessional personnel at the onset of the year and go over guidelines. As we amplified in chapter 21, we advise putting all guidelines in writing, explaining each item, asking for feedback, and then having each person sign a copy that indicates their understanding. Of course, the professional staff also needs to be versed in that information.

The school leader also has the assignment of engendering mutual respect between professionals and nonprofessionals. This is difficult due to the reasons of inherent differences in status. Nonprofessionals feel inferior, professionals feel superior. To attempt to break down those walls, the leader can begin by demonstrating respect for all people. If he or she shows respect towards nonprofessionals, the staff will be more likely to follow. The leader can do this by keeping his or her office door open to all. He or she need not treat nonprofessionals as mere positions in a bureaucracy, but rather as living, breathing human beings who have ideas, questions, and concerns that are worthy of attention. When the leader makes the usual morning rounds of classrooms and teachers, he or she should also greet and talk to each secretary, custodian, and aide. Normal staff meetings should be open to *all* personnel within the school. Noneducators should be specifically asked to attend meetings that will have agenda items directly affecting them. This is a healthy situation for everyone. Many times teachers will gripe about the poor custodial care of their classrooms. At the same time, the custodian will often complain about the messiness of students and teachers. Instead of the principal being the sounding board and mediator between teachers and custodian, why not bring them together to work out their mutual problems?

Another consideration in working with nonprofessionals is recognition. Since everyone has a sense of greater self-esteem when he or she knows that others care about and value what one is doing, it behooves the principal to mobilize the staff toward that effort. Nonprofessionals can be shown appreciation by being invited to general staff socials or to a special occasions in their honor. A must for any school leader is to mail holiday cards and present seasonal and end of the year gifts on behalf of the school. We can remember the delight on the faces of the cafeteria women on the day that a teacher pinned pink carnations on their aprons and the custodian's embarrassed grin when he was given a fifth of scotch on St. Patrick's day. One might view such actions as superficial and small if professionals on a daily basis treated their nonprofessionals poorly. The point is well taken; such a school would probably not take any of the time to be so hospitable. "The proof is in the pudding." The principal and staff who care will show it in many ways and develop a kinship among all its members.

Noneducators have job concerns that are different from educators'. The principal needs to be cognizant of this and deal at that level of concern. Often an issue will arise that is outside of the educational arena but particularly important to the noneducator's task. Children arriving at the cafeteria line a few minutes late can disrupt the food service operations of clearing the tables and getting ready for the next shift of students. Children not picking up papers on the floor at the end of the day can create enough extra work for a custodian so that he is unable to get into every classroom. These matters may appear to be trivial, but they are of great importance to the person trying to do the job. The school staff needs to be reminded of these matters so that they can be considerate.

When the school and classrooms are undergoing educational changes which will affect the noneducator's job, the principal needs to take particular care to keep all parties informed. A lack of such information can be the source of much hostility and conflict between the two groups. For example, implementing an individualized instructional program that will involve adding room dividers and irregularly shaped furniture will change the working conditions of the custodian. Now he will have more difficulty in vacuuming the floor, he will need to move furniture and go around more objects. It is only natural that he comes to resent the "newfangled education." The custodian should be informed of the educational need for such a change and also tactfully told that schools are for the education of children and not for making less work for adults. The principal should discuss and entertain suggestions whereby students and teachers might be able to help alleviate some of the extra work (i.e., perhaps each class will clean their own room once a week and thus lighten the custodian's load).

The school leader must insure that the noneducators do not become a roadblock to the changing school. We have already mentioned such concerns as delineating job responsibilities, fostering respect, providing recognition, and communicating on the level of concern. Let us add a few more. Included in a clear definition of job responsibilities should be an allegiance of confidentiality of information. All staff in a school have much access to information about students and each other. This information needs to be respected and any criticism that a person has of others (or of the school) should be vented through in-school channels. These channels should be made apparent.

Besides merely informing workers of changes in school and classrooms, they might be included in the change process. If so, it is more likely that they will be supporters and defenders rather than adversaries. Some ways that we have seen schools do this is by:

- Having the secretary teach children how to type and how to use the phone.
- Having the custodian take on students as helpers during his rounds
- Having him or her instruct students in the school's heating and plumbing system
- Having him or her teach children carpentry skills
- Having the cafeteria workers discuss nutrition
- Having the children work in the cafeteria line
- Having them discuss the entire system of food service
- Having the bus driver explain pick up routes on a map

- Having him or her give safety hints
- Having him or her tell children how a bus works
- Having the school aide take small groups of children on various outings in the community
- Having him or her show students how to work the duplicating machines
- Having the aide help students prepare materials to be used for younger children

A great deal of attention in educational publications has been focused on the use of community resources. Perhaps before we begin to tap such outside resources, we should first tap the resources in our midst.

FACING IRRECONCILABLE SITUATIONS

After expounding on a principal's responsibilities, we get to, as they say in Washington, the "bottom line." There will be situations, due to temperaments of individuals or basic differences in opinions, which will be unsolvable. When such a situation develops between professional and nonprofessional staff members, the school leader cannot hide and hope that the issue will resolve itself. If the differences are real, if the positions are entrenched, and if the situation is having adverse effects on the children, then decisive action is necessary. Let us give some examples of what might be intolerable situations for some schools.

- A custodian who constantly looses his temper with children and verbally berates teachers in front of students.
- A secretary who is caustic or flippant in talking on the phone with parents.
- A cafeteria worker who refuses to serve food to particular children.
- A bus driver who uses obscene language or tells "dirty jokes" to students.
- A school aide who spreads gossip around town about individual teachers.

If such incidents are intolerable, then the principal needs to act. A meeting with the offender should be held. A description of the alleged improprieties should be given with an opportunity for rebuttal. Finally, the desired behavior should be described and the offender given a probationary period of time to comply. In keeping within legal guidelines, the principal should keep records of all meetings, including all allegations and observations. During the probationary period, the leader should document all evidence available (personal notes, as well as feedback from teachers, students, and parents). If data have been recorded and the nonprofessionals have not made sufficient improvements, dismissal proceedings should begin. Many times, the district business manager might arrange for the person to be transferred to another school where the same concerns would not exist. If this is unlikely, and the person must be dismissed, then the principal can be clear (although feelings of empathy may linger on) that he has done what was right. The school leader has to be guided by the larger concern of what is the optimal educational environment for students. Although it is not pleasant to tell someone that he or she is no longer needed, such a responsibility comes with being a leader.

(We are well aware of some of the political nepotism which may exist. If the dismissal of a person will bring the wrath of a school board member down on the principal or staff, then obviously discretion is advised. There may be times when the educational leader may have to put up with an incompetent worker because of more detrimental ramifications caused by initiating dismissal procedures. Hopefully, such cases are rare.)

SECRETARIES

We cannot leave this chapter without a specific section on that "person of persons" who is all things to all people in a school setting, the school secretary. What is a school secretary? Here are some of her functions. The reader can add more.

- She is the school receptionist.
- She is the principal's consultant.
- She is the principal's clerk, treasurer, and typist.
- She is the teacher's confidant.
- She is the teacher's clerk, treasurer, and typist.
- She is the liaison between school, home, and the central office.
- She is the ad hoc school nurse.
- She is the student's contact with the office.
- She is the school's number one public relations person.

The school secretary is a unique creature. When a school has a personable, outgoing competent person, then school operations proceed smoothly. If the secretary is an irritable, disagreeable, and inefficient person, he or she can bring the entire operation to a halt almost singlehandedly. That the secretary is important is an understatement. That the secretary is underpaid and undertrained for the role is also an understatement.

A school leader in a changing school *has to have a good, supportive person in this position.* Any less of a person will be a constant source of disruption and despair. If there are a number of incompetent nonprofessionals in the school and the principal does not have the heart or energy to seek them all out at once, then the one to begin with is the secretary. This position is the base for much of the later efficiency of the school.

The secretary is trained for work of limited scope. Nowhere is there a professional secretarial school, to our knowledge, that specializes in training public school secretaries. As a result, the beginner is not prepared for the amount and complexity of tasks which engulf him or her. The principal can help make the job more manageable by providing some definition and limitations.

To begin with, *the secretary is not the assistant principal* and he or she should not function as such. Decisions to be made in the principal's absence should be delegated to a professional staff member. One might appoint a particular teacher or rotate the job. It is a sad commentary for a school if the secretary does function as the substitute principal. It does not say much for the qualifications of a principal, if he or she can be so readily replaced by an unprepared person.

Do not overload the secretary with every new task that comes along. To expect him or her to do the normal receptionist, clerical, and typist work and then to suddenly add on additional chores (e.g., monitor the lunchroom) is a bit unrealistic. Some secretaries are too ready to please others and will accept additional burdens with a smile. This sounds chauvinistic and (with a gulp) we are of the opinion that many good secretaries need to be protected from the extra work that everyone in the school is wishing to pile on. The only way that the secretary can be protected is for the leader to make clear what the actual responsibilities are and what they are not. The staff needs to know how the secretary can, and cannot, be used.

The secretary should be listened to, perhaps more attentively than anyone else. Often teachers who are feeling intimidated by the principal will use the secretary as a sounding board for their complaints. They expect that the principal will get the message through him or her. The secretary is in constant contact with parents and will possess knowledge of the talk around town. If he or she lives in the community and has worked in the school for a number of years, he or she could be a most vital link between the school leader and community.

Finally, cherish and adore your secretary. If the principal is male and the secretary female (or vice versa), we are not advocating a romantic affair. What we are saying is that we often take for granted those who are doing an excellent job. The secretary lives a hectic life and needs all the recognition and support that one can provide.

CONCLUSION

In concluding this chapter, we have hoped that the reader realizes the great significance of nonprofessional persons in the school. They can be an important asset or detriment. The school leader needs to approach them in ways that will facilitate productivity and morale. If particular individuals do not act in a manner consistent with the school's overall philosophy, then they must be replaced. Lastly, we have stressed the importance of a competent, pleasant, and supportive secretary as an individual who is a vital link between community and school.

Epilogue

Now that we have made our points and have put down our last thoughts, we have to think of what we have said and what we have accomplished. On the first page we began by describing a harried principal who, returning home from a fruitless day in school, asked, "What have I done? What is my school accomplishing? What can I do to come home with a sense of satisfaction?" We made a promise to help that principal or any other person who was committed to improving education for children. We want the reader to hold us to that pledge and make us answer this two-pronged question: What have we done for the school leader, who is contemplating or in the midst of change, to achieve satisfaction, and for ourselves, to be equally satisfied?

Let's begin with ourselves. As the saying goes, "we have been around." We are not that old, but we have experienced and seen a lot. We have seen and worked in some wonderful schools for children and, candidly, in some horrendous ones. Yet, whether the schools were horrid, mediocre, or terrific, the teachers and administrators cared for children. They wanted the best for their kids, and those from the schools that were less than great knew that they were not delivering. We knew this by the frustration in their voices, their sighs, and their dejection. It appeared that no matter how hard they tried to teach, the children never succeeded. Some who had encountered enough frustration finally quit trying and began looking for others to blame, whether child, parent, principal, or community.

Those who kept on trying looked to the university for expert consultation or they read the books that told of how things should be. But this search was usually of little value. No book or expert is going to make a school more effective. Meaningful and lasting change must come from within.

Since we know that public school people care, we do not join the ranks of academic critics who throw stones, present a single utopian vision, and somehow expect for school people to miraculously follow that scholarly light. Let us repeat, it is only the people in the schools who can bring about change. We conceptualized our task as one of offering the leader and his or her staff some alternative view of schooling and considerations which we believe to be "practically" important. A true professional educator is one who knows what choices are available and what the consequences of each choice will be. Only then can the educator bring all of his or her intelligence and sensitivity to bear in selecting the most appropriate paths of action. We feel personally satisfied in being able to provide some general knowledge which might serve as a small aspect of the decision-making base.

How does the principal achieve satisfaction as a result of this book? Let us try to state it simply. The principal achieves satisfaction when he or she and the staff have a purpose for what they do. Satisfaction increases as practicing dimensions of schooling begin to fall into place with one's philosophical and educational intentions for children. And at least, when a school does have purpose and demonstrates practices consistent with that purpose, the bothersome details of school operation become more tolerable. The principal will still face situations that are unpleasant, but in perspective, will know that he or she is part of a powerful organization of individuals working cooperatively to maximize student growth and facilitate the process of children becoming all that they are capable of being. In conclusion, we would like to include a story that a friend of ours tells.[1] He asked a four-year-old girl to tell him what the world is like. She looked up at him, thought hard, and said, "The world is green in summer and white in winter and has trees and stuff." She then looked down, concentrated hard, and said "I might have left out one or two things."

We have described three alternative models of schooling, a procedure for the assessment of beliefs and practice, and other considerations we believe are important to a school in the midst of change. We, as the little girl, might have also left out one or two things.

NOTES

1.   Charles Wolfgang, *Helping Aggressive and Passive Preschoolers through Play* (Columbus, Ohio: Charles A. Merril, 1977).

Appendixes

A

What Is Your EP?*

INSTRUCTIONS

Please check the answer under each item that best reflects your thinking. You may also want to check more than one answer for any one of the questions.

1. What is the essence of education?
   A. The essence of education is *reason* and *intuition.*
   B. The essence of education is *growth.*
   C. The essence of education is *knowledge* and *skills.*
   D. The essence of education is *choice.*

2. What is the nature of the learner?
   A. The learner is an experiencing organism.
   B. The learner is a unique, free choosing, and responsible creature made up of intellect and emotion.
   C. The learner is a rational and intuitive being.
   D. The learner is a storehouse for knowledge and skills, which, once acquired, can later be applied and used.

3. How should education provide for the needs of man?
   A. The students need a passionate encounter with the perennial problems of life; the agony and joy of love,

*"What is Your EP: A Test which Identifies Your Educational Philosophy" by Patricia D. Jersin appears in *Clearing House* Vol. 46, January 1972, pp. 274-278. (The reader may note that Jersin has identified four philosophies. Since we are of the mind that educational *practice* is reflected in three, we would subsume her philosophies in this way—Perennialism (belief in changeless knowledge) grouped with Essentialism, Progressivism as Experimentalism, and Existentialism as itself.)

reality of choice, anguish of freedom, consequences of actions and the inevitability of death.

B. Education allows for the needs of man when it inculcates the child with certain essential skills and knowledge which all men should possess.

C. The one distinguishing characteristic of man is intelligence. Education should concentrate on developing the intellectual needs of students.

D. Since the needs of man are variable, education should concentrate on developing the individual differences in students.

4. What should be the environment of education?

A. Education should possess an environment where the student adjusts to the material and social world as it really exists.

B. The environment of education should be life itself, where students can experience living—not prepare for it.

C. The environment of education should be one that encourages the growth of free, creative individuality, not adjustment to group thinking nor the public norms.

D. Education is not a true replica of life, rather, it is an artifical environment where the child should be developing his intellectual potentialities and preparing for the future.

5. What should be the goal of education?

A. Growth, through the reconstruction of experience, is the nature, and should be the open-ended goal, of education.

B. The only type of goal to which education should lead is to the goal of truth, which is absolute, universal, and unchanging.

C. The primary concern of education should be with the development of the uniqueness of individual students.

D. The goal of education should be to provide a framework of knowledge for the student against which new truths can be gathered and assimilated.

6. What should be the concern of the school?

A. The school should concern itself with man's distinguishing characteristic, his mind, and concentrate on developing rationality.

B The school should provide an education for the "whole child," centering its attention on all the needs and interests of the child.

C. The school should educate the child to attain the basic knowledge necessary to understand the real world outside.

D. The school should provide each student with assistance in his journey toward self-realization.

7. What should be the atmosphere of the school?

A. The school should provide for group thinking in a democratic atmosphere that fosters cooperation rather than competition.

B. The atmosphere of the school should be one of authentic freedom where a student is allowed to find his own truth and ultimate fulfillment through nonconforming choice making.

C. The school should surround its students with "Great Books" and foster individuality in an atmosphere of intellectualism and creative thinking.

D. The school should retain an atmosphere of mental discipline, yet incorporate innovative techniques which would introduce the student to a perceptual examination of the realities about him.

8. How should appropriate learning occur?

A. Appropriate learning occurs as the student freely engages in choosing among alternatives while weighing personal responsibilities and the possible consequences of his actions.

B. Appropriate learning takes place through the experience of problem-solving projects by which the child is led from practical issues to theoretical principles (concrete-to-abstract).

C. Appropriate learning takes place as certain basic readings acquaint students with the world's permanencies, inculcating them in theoretical principles that they will later apply in life (abstract-to-concrete).

D. Appropriate learning occurs when hard effort has been extended to absorb and master the prescribed subject matter.

9. What should be the role of the teacher?

A. The teacher should discipline pupils intellectually through a study of the great works in literature where the universal concerns of man have best been expressed.

B. The teacher should present principles and values and the reasons for them, encouraging students to examine them in order to choose for themselves whether or not to accept them.

C. The teacher should guide and advise students, since the children's own interests should determine what they learn, not authority nor the subject matter of the textbooks.

D. The teacher, the responsible authority, should mediate between the adult world and the world of the child since immature students cannot comprehend the nature and demands of adulthood by themselves.

10. What should the curriculum include?

A. The curriculum should include only that which has survived the test of time and combines the symbols and ideas of literature, history, and mathematics with the sciences of the physical world.

B. The curriculum should concentrate on teaching students how to manage change through problem-solving activities in the social studies . . . empirical sciences and vocational technology.

C. The curriculum should concentrate on intellectual subject matter and include English, languages, history, mathematics, natural sciences, the fine arts, and also philosophy.

D. The curriculum should concentrate on the humanities; history, literature, philosophy, and art—where greater depth into the nature of man and his conflict with the world are revealed.

11. What should be the preferred teaching method?

A. *Projects* should be the preferred method whereby the students can be guided through problem-solving experiences.

B. *Lectures, readings,* and *discussions* should be the preferred methods for training the intellect.

C. *Demonstrations* should be the preferred method for teaching knowledge and skills.

D. *Socratic dialogue* (drawing responses from a questioning conversation) should be the preferred method for finding the self.

SCORING THE TEST

This test is self-scoring. Circle the answer you selected for each of the questions checked on the test. Total the number of circles below each column.

What Is Your EP?

	Progressivism	Perennialism	Essentialism	Existentialism
1	B	A	C	D
2	A	C	D	B
3	D	C	B	A
4	B	D	A	C
5	A	B	D	C
6	B	A	C	D
7	A	C	D	B
8	B	C	D	A
9	C	A	D	B
10	B	C	A	D
11	A	B	C	D

IMPLICATIONS

The four answers selected for each of the questions in this multiple-choice test represent positions on educational issues being taken by hypothetical spokesmen from the major educational philosophies heading each column—Progressivism, Perennialism, Essentialism, and Existentialism. If, in scoring your test, you find that a majority of your choices, no matter how much doubling up of answers, falls in a single column, you are selecting a dominant educational philosophy from among the four. For example, if you find your totals: Progressivism (9), Perennialism (1), Essentialism (3), and Existentialism (2); your dominant educational philosophy as determined by this test would be *Progressivism* (9 out of 15 choices being a majority). If you discover yourself spread rather evenly among several, or even all four, this scattering of answers demonstrates an eclectic set of educational values. Indecisiveness in selecting from the four positions could indicate other values and beliefs not contained within one of these major educational systems.

In all formal systems of philosophy, an important measure of the system's validity is its consistency. Your consistency in taking this test can be measured by comparing the answer you selected for item #1 that identifies *essences* with your other answers. The more of the remaining 10 responses you find in the same column where you circled item #1, the more consistent you should be in your educational philosophy. The fewer of the other 10 responses in the same column as item #1, the more you should find your responses contradicting one another—a problem inherent in eclecticism. Again, keep in mind, lack of consistency may also be due to valuing another set of educational beliefs, consistent in themselves, but not included as one of the possible systems selected for representation here.

B

Philosophical Concepts—Assumptions Checklist*

Metaphysics

Basic Reality (BR)

The Orderly, Knowable, Sensible World
Creative, Purposeful, Spiritual Energy
Experience of Individuals-in-Society
Experience of the Solitary Individual
Human Nature (HN)

*"Philosophical Concepts—Assumptions Checklist" by Charles Dennis Marler *Philosophy and Schooling.* (Boston: Allyn and Bacon, 1975), pp. 319-322 and 371-382. This checklist concerns itself with the major components of a philosophy—What is real? (Metaphysics) What is knowledge? (Epistemology) and What is good? (Axiology)— and basic assumptions related to each component. Each staff member would check those assumptions that he/she must strongly concur with. Those checked assumptions can then be matched against the common assumptions indicative of Idealism, Realism, Pragmatism, and Existentialism. Idealism and Realism are reflected in the educational philosophy of Essentialism, Pragmatism of Experimentalism, and Existentialism of itself.

Inherently Evil

Inherently Good

Inherently Superior or Inferior

Constructed and Evaluated Transactionally

Constructed and Evaluated Individualistically

Free Will and Determinism (FW&D)

The Free Self

Basic Determinism

God and Faith (G&F)

The Orthodox God

The Humanistic God

The Denial of God

Epistemology

Mind (M)

Mind or Soul as an Immaterial Entity

Function of Bodily Processes

Purposeful, Problem-Solving Behavior

Ideas (I)

Archetypes of Existents

Reflections of a Natural, External Reality

Man-Created Plans of Action

Experience (EXP)

Contact with a Given Reality

Transactional Doing and Undergoing

Being on the World

Objectivity (OBJ)

Alignment with a Given Reality

Intersubjectivity

Intrasubjectivity

Frame of Reference (FoR)

Limitation-to-Be-Transcended

Self-in-Becoming

Knowledge and Truth (K&T)

Consistency Theory

Correspondence Theory

Transactional Theory

Appropriational Theory

Axiology

Value: Its Nature and Locus (V/N&L)

Property of Objective Reality

Creation of Subjective Choice

Product of Contextual Inquiry

Value Judgments: Validation (VJ/V)

Through Traditional Modes of Knowing

Through Authentic Choice

Through Experimentation

Values: Classifying and Ordering (V/C&O)

The Hierarchy of the Given

The Hierarchy of Individual Decision

The Hierarchy of the Situation

Morality (MOR)

The Morality of Seeking and Conforming to Objective Good

The Morality of Autheticity

The Morality of Critical Inquiry

Obligation and Conscience (OBL&C)

Obligation to Follow Conscience toward the Good

Obligation of Free Commitment

Obligation to Be Intelligent

Ends, Means, and Progress (E-M-P)

Growth toward an Ultimate Goal

Growth in Self-Direction

Growth as Its Own End

Social Philosophy

The State and the General Welfare (S&GW)

The Limited State

The Active State

Individual and Society (I&S)

The Individual within Tradition

The Interdependent Society

Freedom (F)

Freedom without License

Freedom as Power

Justice and Equality (J&E)

Just Rewards

Egalitarianism

Community (C)

Voluntary Association

Dynamic Association

Social Progress (SP)

Through "Competitive Individualism"

Through "Cooperative Individualism"

COMMON ASSUMPTIONS OF
PHILOSOPHIES

Idealism: Common Assumptions

A. Metaphysics
  BR: Creative, Purposeful, Spiritual Energy
  HN: Inherently Evil
  HN: Inherently Good
  HN: Inherently Superior or Inferior
  FW&D: The Free Self
  G&F: The Orthodox God
B. Epistemology
  M: Mind-Soul as an Immaterial Entity
  I: Archetypes of Existents
  EXP: Contact with a Given Reality
  OBJ: Alignment with a Given Reality
  FoR: Limitation-to-Be Transcended
  K&T: Consistency Theory

Realism: Common Assumptions

A. Metaphysics
  BR: The Orderly, Knowable, Sensible World
  HN: Inherently Evil
  HN: Inherently Good
  HN: Inherently Superior or Inferior
  FW&D: The Free Self
  FW&D: Basic Determinism
  G&F: The Orthodox God
  G&F: The Humanistic God
  G&F: The Denial of God
B. Epistemology
  M: Function of Bodily Processes
  I: Natural Reflections of an External Reality
  EXP: Contact with a Given Reality
  OBJ: Alignment with a Given Reality
  FoR: Limitation-to-Be-Transcended

      K&T: Correspondence Theory

C. Axiology

Realists hold the widest variety of axiological assumptions

Pragmatism: Common Assumptions

A. Metaphysics
- BR: Experience of Individuals-in-Society
- HN: Constructed and Evaluated Transactionally
- FW&D: Basic Determinism
- G&F: The Humanistic God

B. Epistemology
- M: Purposeful, Problem-Solving Behavior
- I: Man-Created Plans of Action `
- EXP: Transactional Doing and Undergoing
- OBJ: Intersubjectivity
- FoR: Self-in-Becoming
- K&T: Transactional Theory

C. Axiology
- V/N&L: Product of Contextual Inquiry
- VJ/V: Experimentation
- V/C&O: Hierarchy of the Situation
- MOR: Morality of Critical Inquiry
- OBL&C: Obligation to Be Intelligent
- E-M-P: Growth as Its Own End

Existentialism: Common Assumptions

A. Metaphysics
- BR: Experience of the Solitary Individual
- HN: Constructed and Evaluated Individualistically
- FW&D: The Free Self
- G&F: The Orthodox God
- G&F: The Denial of God

B. Epistemology
- EXP: Being in the World
- OBJ: Intrasubjectivity
- FoR: Self-in-Becoming
- K&T: Appropriational Theory

C. Axiology
- V/N&L: Creation of Subjective Choice
- VJ/V: Authentic Choice
- V/C&O: Hierarchy of Individual Decision
- MOR: Morality of Authenticity
- OBL&C: Obligation of Free Commitment
- E-M-P: Growth in Self-Direction

C

Dimension Tally Sheets

CURRICULUM DIMENSION TALLY SHEET

Questions	Responses		
	1	2	3
Subassesment A			
A			
B			
C			
D			
E			
F			
G			
H			
I			
J			
K			
L			
M			
N			
O			
P			
Subassesment B			
A			
B			
C			
D			
E			
F			
G			
H			
I			
J			
K			
L			
M			
N			
O			
Total			
Percentage			

STUDENT MANAGEMENT DIMENSION TALLY SHEET

Questions	Responses		
	1	2	3
Subassesment A			
A			
B			
C			
D			
E			
F			
G			
H			
Subassesment B			
A			
B			
C			
D			
E			
F			
G			
Subassesment C			
A			
B			
C			
D			
E			
F			
G			
H			
Total			
Percentage			

SUPERVISION DIMENSION TALLY SHEET

Questions	Responses		
	1	2	3
Subassesment A			
A			
B			
C			
D			
E			
F			
G			
H			
I			
J			
K			
L			
M			
N			
O			
P			
Q			
R			
Subassesment B			
A			
B			
C			
D			
E			
F			
G			
H			
I			
J			
K			
L			
Total			
Percentage			

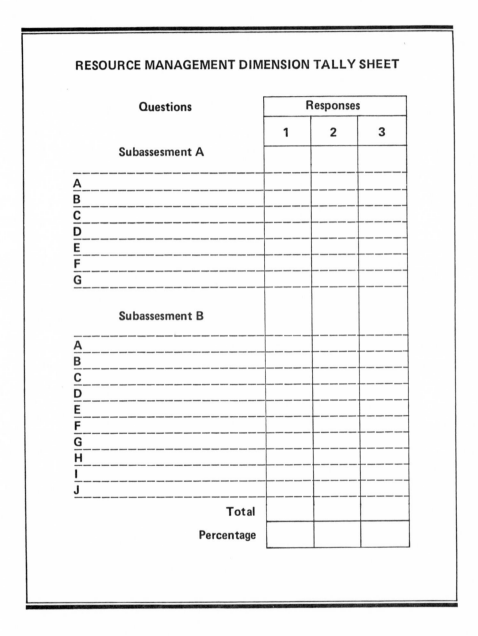

RESOURCE MANAGEMENT DIMENSION TALLY SHEET

Questions	Responses		
	1	2	3
Subassesment A			
A			
B			
C			
D			
E			
F			
G			
Subassesment B			
A			
B			
C			
D			
E			
F			
G			
H			
I			
J			
Total			
Percentage			

Author Index

Subject Index